Garden Foliage
for
Flower Arrangement

Close-up Section of Foliage Border in the Author's Garden, showing *Phormium tenax, Philadelphus coronarius* 'Variegatus', *Cotinus coggygria* 'Foliis Purpureis', *Bergenia cordifolia, Salvia officinalis* 'Purpurascens', *Lonicera nitida* 'Baggesen's Gold', *Berberis thunbergii* 'Atropurpurea', *Thuja occidentalis* 'Rheingold', *Santolina chamaecyparissus, Hebe armstrongii*

Garden Foliage
for
Flower Arrangement

by

SYBIL C. EMBERTON

FABER AND FABER

London

First published in 1968
by Faber and Faber Limited
24 Russell Square London WC1
Reprinted 1970
Printed in Great Britain by
Latimer Trend & Co Ltd Plymouth

ISBN 0 571 08512 1

Acknowledgements

I should like to express my sincere gratitude to the following:

Miss Elsa M. Megson, whose professional skill has produced such fine illustrations, often in most difficult circumstances, which she tackled with unfailing resource, cheerfulness and enthusiasm.

Dr. William T. Stearn, Sc.D., V.M.H., not only for the kind permission to draw upon his recent work, *Botanical Latin*, for the abridged vocabulary included in Chapter X of this book, but also for his generous and immensely welcome offer to look over the draft for that chapter and for putting me right where I went astray.

The Earl of Morton, M.A., F.L.S., V.M.H., in whose garden full of connoisseur's plants we found some fine subjects for illustration (Nos. 9, 10, 11, 13 and 19). Other less tangible benefits also resulted from many casual conversations with so experienced a plantsman, each recent visit teaching me something of interest or of practical value about unusual foliage plants.

The many good friends and colleagues who encouraged this endeavour and helped to fill the gaps in my experience regarding the behaviour of unfamiliar leaves as cut material.

And, finally, Mr. Richard de la Mare who, though probably unaware of my special addiction to leaves, could not have suggested a more congenial subject for this book; and his staff, whose friendly touch makes the writing of books enjoyable rather than intimidating to the amateur.

Contents

9

Illustrations

11

Illustrations

CHAPTER 1

Introduction

Before beginning to explore the intriguing miscellany of leaves which may be grown out of doors for floral decoration perhaps we should first take a look at the constantly changing field of flower arrangement in order to decide for what kind of operator this book is intended: for I am well aware that some will have little use for what is to others, as to me, an endless source of delight.

Wishing to understand, and so more fully to appreciate the highly disciplined beauty of Japanese flower arrangement, I once took some elementary lessons in Ikebana, for which I would painstakingly select choice bits of garden material, spending much time in the contemplation of line and branch before cutting and aiming always at some subtle colour combination of leaf and bloom—only to resort after all to the beech or oak or some such commonplace woodland foliage from the free-for-all in the teacher's sink. Not only was this on the whole much more readily adaptable to the clear-cut basic lines required for the set piece of the day, but—and this is what chiefly sticks in my un-oriental gullet—there was in fact very little scope for subtle blending of colour in an assemblage of two or three bare twigs, or branches pruned of most of their foliage, supplemented by three flowers or less, with the possible addition of a few short-stemmed leaves to screen the pin-holder. Now I admit that these are only the most rudimentary principles of Moribana, but I can quote the unassailable authority of Stella Coe that to the Japanese flower arranger 'colour is of the smallest importance', whereas in traditional or mass arrangements in the western style it is usually of first consideration and, in my own case at least, the colour of a leaf is no less beguiling than that of a flower.

13

Introduction

Such is the economy of plant material in the popular Sogetsu school of Japanese flower arrangement that, pushed to the limit in the *avant-garde* style illustrated by Mrs. Coe in *The Art of Japanese Flower Arrangement* (1964), we get the grouped pieces of white rock on a black lacquer base recommended as an 'excellent table arrangement', with or *without* the three roses included in an alternative version illustrated on the same page.

And the most modern trends in Great Britain are scarcely less stark in their use of natural plant material. I hope I am not doing our own floral artists an injustice when I say that in their concept of the abstract the sheer natural beauty of a flower or a leaf often seems largely irrelevant. When either is used in an arrangement its function is usually a subsidiary one, complementing some dramatic design of bare branch, looped cane, knotted liana, bent reeds or metal tubing; and indeed foliage may even be clipped into unnatural shapes or otherwise distorted or transformed. In other words plant forms are required to serve as a medium only, to be moulded or manipulated to express a meaning or mood, convey a message or conform to an abstract pattern of three-dimensional shapes and voids, much as stone, wood, metal and clay serve as the raw materials of the sculptor's art.

It is certainly not my intention to jeer at the very latest trends either in Ikebana or in the western styles, any more than I would be brash enough to write off the most modern music, poetry, painting or sculpture because these are beyond my own uneducated aesthetic understanding. But I fervently believe that flowers, or fruits, or foliage, or any combination of these forms of plant life, should *predominate* in examples of the art or craft to which we have given the name of flower arrangement. And for this reason it seems to me that the time has come to draw a distinction between 'floral art' and 'flower arrangement', leaving exponents of the former to draw their inspiration from *avant-garde* art forms and to pursue their abstract intellectual exercises whither their fancy may lead them, while the rest of us, with our more traditional regard for the natural habit of growth of flowers and foliage, get on with exploiting the wealth of natural beauty, culled largely from our own gardens, for the decoration of our less modern private houses, stately homes, cathedrals, churches, historic buildings and public institutions.

Each has its place in the movement, but I doubt whether there is room for both under the same umbrella-term today. If I must, I am willing to concede that ours is a craft and theirs an art. Unprogressive we may be; but to a great many of us this is what flower arrangement is all about. And so, in writing about garden leaves for floral decoration, I shall, within the terms of my own definition, have the 'flower arranger', or traditional craftsman, chiefly in mind, rather than the modern 'floral artist'.

I should like to add here that I hope the male practitioner will forgive me if I refer to the flower arranger as female throughout, in order to circumvent the clumsy complication of 'his' and 'hers'. I am none the less aware that although women so far predominate numerically in the flower arrangement movement, a steadily increasing proportion of its truly great experts are men.

CHAPTER II

History of an Addiction

I have elected to write about hardy foliage plants for floral decoration for the simple reason that, both as a gardener and as a flower arranger, I love leaves. In the latter role I could more readily dispense with flowers than with the infinite variety of colour, texture, form and habit of foliage plants; and in the garden a suitable proportion of fine foliage is just as necessary to me as the more eye-catching flowering plants for the year-round beauty of the whole. Although I have not confined myself to foliage arrangements in my demonstrations to Flower Clubs unless specially invited to do so, I regularly include one or two by way of encouraging an interest in as many unfamiliar leaves as possible and I also use a great deal of interesting home-grown foliage as a foil to flowers, fruits and seedheads.

Enthusiasms, I know, have a way of 'busting out all over'. Nevertheless I was not aware that my addiction to leaves was so conspicuous until I was told, a short time ago, by the members of a Dorset Flower Club, that they always think of me as 'the Foliage Lady'. With this book in mind, but as yet unwritten, I was indeed grateful for such a timely piece of type-casting! But I think I was originally type-cast many years earlier—and for this some of the responsibility lay with an unwitting Constance Spry. Having assembled my very first competitive exhibit, a modest little foliage arrangement in an old wooden chalice, as competently as my shaking fingers would allow, I had my head turned in no uncertain manner at my first taste of beginner's luck. 'I really envy you this enchanting arrangement,' wrote that legendary figure—and I was launched on air. Mrs. Spry was of course the most generous of commentators, whose kindly encouragement has probably transformed many another goose

16

into a temporary swan and had I been less green I would, I like to think, have taken this compliment with a grain of salt. But what novice could command a becoming modesty in the circumstances? Certainly not I! And rather too soon afterwards a run of prize-winning luck in foliage classes at national level helped to establish my image and swell my head still further.

If you sense that this threatens to become the autobiography of a pot-hunter, please now take heart. Modesty tends to increase rather than to diminish with experience and no flower arranger can get very far without a capacity for ruthless self-criticism. Once having made this salutary discovery I soon became aware that, as Sir Winston Churchill once remarked of a colleague commended to him for his modesty, I too 'had a lot to be modest about'.

This, then, was how my foliage addiction began. And because I found some early success with my leaves my interest grew and I began to seek out the less familiar foliage plants for the garden. The more I grew the more I came to love the quiet beauty of their colour range, their infinitely varied shapes and sizes and the contrast of their surfaces, whether glossy, egg-shell or matt; woolly, satiny or velvety; ribbed, pleated or crumpled. And so the thing snowballed. I had not lost my love for flower colours and shapes meanwhile, but no matter how I might yearn to pick up the subtle colour harmonies of some ancestral drawing-room, or those of the ancient murals or mosaics of an historic cathedral, with magnolias, camellias, azaleas, soft-hued tree peonies and other flowering shrubs from my garden, inevitably I found myself selected for the large foliage arrangements which always find a place in the decoration of stately homes, historic monuments and exhibition halls. Nowadays when helping to plan undertakings of this kind I have only to remark, in all innocence, 'That would be rather fun to do,' to find that I have type-cast myself all over again, with some vast arrangement of foliage, or of foliage and fruits, echoing the colours of an ancestral portrait or an ancient painted tomb. Whether I like it or not, the image of 'the Foliage Lady' has evidently come to stay. Certainly I am happy with it today.

CHAPTER III

Grow It or Go Without

It goes almost without saying that the flower arranger with a penchant for foliage must also be a gardener, since the loveliest of leaves cannot be bought at will.

How odd it is that while containers, gadgets and aids to floral decoration proliferate and even the plant breeders devise new and intriguing off-beat flower hues with the whims of the flower arranger in mind, it is still impossible to buy any but the most limited and unenterprising assortment of foliage in the average florist's shop. No slur is intended on the florists for, as a rule, they cannot help it. The kind of foliage they would no doubt stock if they were able to is just not available to the trade and there are not many fortunate enough to have a lien on a private source of supply for the more unusual leaves. Generally speaking it is not possible to buy even the very ordinary but indispensable bergenias or hostas, though surely many a gardener would be glad to make a little pocket-money by helping to fill this gap in the florist's repertoire. The latter is usually delighted to take what one can spare in the way of interesting and long-lasting foliage, if not regularly, at least for special customers or special occasions.

But as things are, the flower arranger without a garden may have to make do with the inevitable pittosporum, the gruesomely stiff and spiny "Butcher's Broom", dyed grevillea and cycas, or Victoriana such as smilax and asparagus fern. Neither the smilax nor the "Butcher's Broom" (*Ruscus aculeatus*) should however be confused with *Danae racemosa* (alias *Ruscus racemosus*), notwithstanding some mix-up over the names in the trade. The danae is in fact a delightful exception amid the dull assortment of commercial foliage, with immensely graceful, long, arching sprays of slender, shining, dark green leaves; but although this is a hardy evergreen it unfortunately does not appear to be on sale all the year round. Alas that there should also be a close season in the trade for the lovely imported eucalyptus, which so frustratingly seems to disappear from the market whenever it is most needed for an occasion of major importance!

Discounting greenhouse and house plants, which are outside my terms of reference, it would seem that town-dwellers and flat-dwellers are mostly dependent for their foliage on spasmodic trips into the country to collect what they can from woodland, waterside, meadow and hedgerow, or to beg from rustic friends. On the other hand we, the rustics, with gardens of our own, should make the most of our good fortune by growing some of the most beautiful of the leaves we cannot buy.

As a gardener my inclination is to avoid *overloading* my one-third of an acre with foliage plants to the exclusion of much-loved flowering shrubs and trees. But if, as a serious flower arranger, I had an even more limited space at my disposal, I would fill it with foliage without hesitation, since one can at least buy flowers of some sort at any time of year—even if they be more commonplace than those we might choose to grow for ourselves. It so happens that there are a large number of plants, and of shrubs in particular, in which beauty of bloom and of leaf are happily married, so the alternatives for the pocket-handkerchief garden are not as uncompromising as might at first appear (see pages 206–210).

19

CHAPTER IV

Some Necessary Explanations

I have been somewhat puzzled as to the proper definition of a foliage plant in the present context.

For horticultural purposes we might say that it is one whose leaves are either more decorative, or no less decorative, than the flowers or fruits; for although there are many trees and shrubs, in particular, in which the honours are fairly evenly divided between the flowers and/or fruits and the foliage, there are very few plants indeed which have no flowers whatever, though the latter may be so insignificant as to escape detection by the unbotanical. Where no mention is made of the flowers in the plant descriptions it may be taken to mean that they are of no special interest.

If a number of experienced flower arrangers were to compile their own lists of favourite leaves I feel sure these would include some that I, foliage addict though I am, have never even thought of trying. The 'eye of the beholder' is unpredictable in its assessments and the flower arranger's garden has a way of surprising more orthodox gardeners. She may well grow colchicums, hemerocallis, *Escallonia x iveyi*, or even peonies for the sake of their foliage rather than for their flowers and she may rate the leaves of agapanthus, aquilegias, macleaya or primroses, for instance, on a par with their blooms, though others would probably deem such plants unworthy of garden room if their leaves were their only asset.

Subjects of this kind will certainly get a mention here. But I propose to leave the controversial topic of 'leaf-like' bracts well alone, although these may be classified as foliage for judging purposes within the terms of the current Schedule Definitions of

20

Some Necessary Explanations

the National Association of Flower Arrangement Societies. And autumn colour is another aspect of the foliage question which I propose to by-pass for the moment. Lovely though they may be for a brief period indoors, autumn leaves are even more ephemeral as cut material than as a garden spectacle. For this reason I see little point in growing them purely for cutting purposes, nor do I find it necessary to plant specifically for autumn colour in this acid-soiled garden, where so many fine ericaceous flowering shrubs in particular provide an incidental bonus of yellow, flame, copper, scarlet, crimson and purple leaf colour in the autumn, offset by evergreens of glaucous and silver hues. However, for those interested in the subject of autumn foliage I have included a list at the end of the book (Appendix A) of some which may be expected to hold their leaves for a day or two in water.

The subject of indoor plants, which has already been fully taken care of by well-known professional growers and other experts, is none of my business, having neither greenhouse nor garden frame, nor even adequate house room for plants in pots. And in the confines of this small garden there is even a limit to the number of hardy foliage plants which can be accommodated without detracting too much from the gaiety of the spectacle as a whole. Some readers of my earlier book, *Shrub Gardening for Flower Arrangement*, seem to have been left with the impression that my garden is immense, though I took great pains to stress that it is not. So I repeat, the total area, including lawns, paths and kitchen garden, remains at barely one-third of an acre. And a further limitation—that of garden climate—largely dictates what may or may not be attempted on this north-east slope, 900 feet up, which uncompromisingly turns its back on what scant sunshine comes our way during the average British summer.

However, if I cannot write of every plant I mention from first-hand horticultural experience, I do grow, or have grown, the majority of them myself. And as for the rest, at least I shall have borrowed most of them for floral decoration at some time or other and shall therefore be familiar with their behaviour as cut

21

material in most cases and where possible I shall have sought advice from those with the experience I may lack in individual instances.

As I have already said, if we want these leaves for floral decoration we shall be obliged to grow them for ourselves and it is therefore important to be aware of their cultural requirements. So I have done my best to keep you informed about the degree of hardiness of each; its preferences regarding soils and situations; when and how to prune, if at all; and, of course, to make recommendations as to the most suitable type of conditioning after cutting.

Having explained the various methods of conditioning flowers and foliage at some length in *Shrub Gardening for Flower Arrangement* I do not propose to cover the same ground in detail here. I would however remind the inexperienced of the following points:

1. Woody stems should be split or crushed for a couple of inches and the bark removed from this portion.

2. Stems containing milky juices (and certain others) should be singed by holding the cut end over a flame.

3. Boiling consists of holding the stem-end in a pan of continuously boiling water for thirty seconds or more according to the solidity of the stem, keeping the business end away from the steam in the process.

4. Soaking involves total immersion of the leaf or branch in cold or tepid water, usually overnight, or at least for several hours, except in isolated instances which will be mentioned.

5. Stem-tipping means removing a short piece from the tip of the stem *under water*. This is not the impossible feat I once believed it to be, for it does not involve fumbling one's way through chicken wire or moisture-retaining substances with the scissors to get at the stem-end inside the container. It should be done at the start of the soaking process and does not need to be repeated if the stem is re-cut later. In the case of leaves requiring no preliminary soaking a separate basin of water should be kept at hand at the time of arranging, for the underwater removal of the stem-tip. Stem-tipping often

works where other methods have failed and is particularly useful for stalks containing a central thread (e.g. primrose or tellima leaves).

6. Material which requires no special pre-treatment does nevertheless need to be put into water directly it is cut (i.e. straight into a bucket of water taken with you as you pick) and given a long, deep, cold or, preferably, tepid drink in a cool place before arranging.

7. Flagging material may often be revived by boiling and re-soaking or by standing the stems in very hot water, which may need renewing once or twice as it cools.

8. All but the most dependable subjects will last better in water if not allowed to become parched during the growing period (i.e. at least a week) prior to cutting.

9. Most silver foliages, and certain others, wilt rapidly in moisture-retaining substances such as Oasis, Florapak, Stemfix, Mossette, etc.

10. An almost clinical cleanliness is recommended for flower buckets, containers, etc.

Where no special conditioning instructions are given for individual plants they should be treated as in 6 above. Subjects described as 'Untried' are those on which I have no information regarding their lasting qualities when cut, but there are very few leaves which cannot be induced to last satisfactorily in water by one method or another.

We are now almost ready for the plant-by-plant descriptions, which follow in alphabetical sequence for ease of reference, irrespective of whether they happen to be trees, shrubs, herbaceous perennials, bulbs, annuals or whatever. This miscellany is sorted into horticultural categories in the index, in order that the reader may pick out at a glance the kinds of plant she is concerned with. A further re-classification according to foliage colours will be found in Appendix B.

An asterisk after a plant name denotes a lime-hating subject and should be treated with respect.

Some Necessary Explanations

AWARDS
The various awards made by the Royal Horticultural Society are given, when these are known to me, in brackets after the botanical Latin plant name, with the date of the award:

A.M.   = Award of Merit
A.G.M. = Award of Garden Merit
F.C.C. = First Class Certificate

COLOUR DESCRIPTIONS
The Horticultural Colour Chart which I explained in detail in *Shrub Gardening for Flower Arrangement* has since been superseded by the R.H.S. Colour Chart in which individual colour names have been discarded for a system of numbers and letters within the comprehensive colour groups of Yellow, Yellow-Orange, Orange, Orange-Red, Red and so on through the spectrum to Yellow-Green, with an added section of Greyed Colours and Brown, Grey, Black and White groups. While lamenting the loss of evocative names such as Egyptian Buff, Mandarin Red, Bishop's Violet or Carnation Green, which are so much more easily memorized than mere numbers in a large colour group, I find the colour quality of the new chart far superior to the other. Nevertheless it is not always easy to match off-beat foliage hues even in the wider range covered by the new chart, but where I have been able to do so the colour group will appear with initial capitals, followed by the hue number and the letter A, B, C or D, denoting one of the four tints of that hue. For example, the olive-khaki of *Hebe armstrongii* is most nearly matched against the darkest sample of 152 in the Yellow-Green Group, but for the sake of brevity the word 'Group' will be omitted throughout, making the Colour Chart reference in this instance: Yellow-Green 152A.

Double quotation marks have been used throughout to indicate common names and nicknames (that is, names of no botanical standing) in order to distinguish them from botanical cultivar names, which are enclosed in single quotation marks in accordance with the recommendations of the International

Code of Nomenclature for Cultivated Plants (see Chapter X, p. 235).

As regards the use of the terms 'gold' and 'silver', I can think of no foliage plant with true gold leaf colour and have therefore discarded 'gold' in favour of 'yellow' throughout. I have used 'silver' to describe only grey foliages and not as pseudonym for white, as so often applied to white variegation, for instance.

CHAPTER V

What to Grow, and How

ACANTHUS—"Architect's Plant", "Bear's Breeches"
Hardy perennial

Renowned throughout the centuries for its boldly ornamental design, the acanthus leaf is nevertheless a somewhat disappointing one with which to lead off here, being of questionable reliability as cut material. In spite of its more formidable prickles I think the foliage of *Acanthus spinosus* is superior to that of *A. mollis latifolius*, for our purposes, on two counts. The shiny, very dark green foliage of *A. spinosus*, which is as much as 2 ft. long by 1 ft. wide, deeply divided and tapering to a point, not only has a more ornate pattern but also has more body than the rather floppy, less deeply lobed, spineless leaf of *A. mollis latifolius*, which is broader in relation to its length (see illustration facing p. 64). Neither is fussy as to soil or position, though full sun encourages flowering and, I suspect, may help to toughen up the leaves and so make them more reliable in water. Plants spread rapidly and seed themselves freely. The bold, fiercely spined mauvish flower spikes, which are similar in each case, dry well when fully mature.

As for conditioning, I find that some leaves in a batch picked simultaneously will respond to boiling or singeing, stem-tipping and soaking while others will not. Pricking or slitting along the main vein before soaking seems to assist the intake of water, thus helping the leaf to remain turgid; but for the best results I recommend soaking in a starch solution (follow the directions on a packet of Instant Starch) after lightly slitting the main vein along the back of the leaf. Foliage so treated holds its poise well

26

for several *months,* in water, but not in moisture-retaining substances.

ACER—"Maple"

Acer japonicum 'Aureum'* (F.C.C. 1884)—Form of "Japanese Maple"
Tree or shrub; deciduous

Certain maples also have a bad reputation as foliage for cutting, but this one is as well-behaved as it is beautiful. The leaves are much lobed and toothed at the edges and are held rather horizontally—a habit which suits us well for flower arrangement purposes. When the shrimp-pink casing which enfolds the leaf-buds first parts to reveal the tightly pleated fans in spring these are an intense lime-yellow (Yellow-Green 151B)—the perfect colour complement to the sheath—gradually changing to a softer, true yellow with maturity. If this maple has a fault it is that it is woefully slow-growing. It will ultimately make a bushy small tree of 15 ft. or so, but although quite a young plant will provide a pool of sunshine in the garden scene the flower arranger will have to wait awhile before she dare remove anything more than an occasional modest snippet.

This is not generally listed as a lime-hater, but I would say that it needs a slightly acid, or at least a neutral, soil if it is to prosper rather than struggle for existence. Shelter from spring winds in particular and adequate moisture at the roots are essentials and in my experience partial shade produces more attractive colour and prevents the leaf scorch which disfigures so many yellow foliages growing in full sun.

Boil and soak for a brief period only. As with many maples, cutting the foliage in the half-unfurled stage and allowing it to open indoors in the arrangement is particularly successful.

A. negundo 'Variegatum'—"Box Elder" of U.S.A.
Tree; deciduous

This maple makes a much larger tree and does so much more quickly than the last-mentioned. The loose framework of cool green and white variegation provides a charming background for a dark-hued clematis trained through its branches and does not, to my mind, look incongruous in the shrub borders, as some of the bolder variegations tend to do. For the flower arranger the leaf pattern is perhaps rather too haphazard for anything of less than pedestal proportions; but once the tree is able to spare some fair-sized branches these make an attractive outline for large arrangements for weddings and such-like.

Culturally it is one of the easiest of maples, with no special soil fads and more tolerant of wind and drought than its Japanese relations. If plain green shoots develop these should be cut out right back to the point of origin.

It can only be lack of proper conditioning which has gained it a reputation in some quarters as unreliable cutting material. After being boiled, soaked and stem-tipped, branches from this garden once travelled from Hindhead to Hayling Island by car and thence next day to Yorkshire and were reported to have been as good as new at the close of the exhibition after several days in a hot hall.

A. palmatum 'Atropurpureum'*—Form of "Japanese Maple"
Tree; deciduous

Shaped like a miniature outspread hand, as the name suggests, the dainty leaf pattern of *A. palmatum* 'Atropurpureum' is made to look comparatively clumsy alongside the still more finely cut foliage of the variety known as 'Dissectum Atropurpureum'. But the former has the advantage of much more rapid growth, fairly quickly becoming a graceful, smallish tree when conditions are to its liking, whereas the other takes many years to make a low, dense and rather humped umbrella which, to me, has a somewhat unnatural, Bonsai-like appearance among the usual run of trees and shrubs, but looks delightful when grown as a single specimen in a carefully chosen setting. What is loosely termed purple in leaf colour is, in the case of these maples, an attractive copperish-bronze, pinker in spring, more bronze-crimson at maturity and reddening in the autumn.

What to Grow, and How

Both cultural requirements and conditioning are the same as for *A. japonicum* 'Aureum'. The foliage seems to stand better in water when young and no amount of careful preparation will ensure that mature foliage will not curl up from sheer desiccation (unless repeatedly sprayed with tepid water) in an excessively hot atmosphere such as that of the glass-roofed R.H.S. Halls when packed with humanity on a summer's day. On the other hand it is unlikely to let one down in the less trying conditions of a living-room.

A. pseudo-platanus 'Brilliantissimum' (A.M. 1925)—Form of "Sycamore"
Tree; deciduous

This makes a more solid, larger-leaved tree than those already described. In spring its brilliant apricot-pink, pleated young leaf-growth is an enchanting spectacle, later fading gradually through paler apricot in early summer to become an unremarkable light green at full maturity. If I were starting again I would find room for this if I could, but I cannot squeeze one into my tight-packed shrub garden at this stage nor am I now patient enough to wait for cutting material from this slow-growing beauty, which will eventually reach no more than 15 ft. or thereabouts.

It is said to put up with exposed situations and any kind of soil.

I am assured on good authority that it needs no special conditioning, though I would have expected the immature foliage to need the boiling, stem-tipping and soaking which I find essential for the lovely mahogany-tinted young leaf-shoots of the closely related common sycamore of our native countryside. (Untried.)

ACORUS calamus 'Variegatus'—Form of "Sweet Flag", "Sweet Sedge"
Hardy perennial

The "Sweet Flag" of our native streams and waterside is so named because of the sweet scent of the leaves when crushed—

to me a nostalgic, summery smell, recalling days on the river at Oxford and, more practically, one which commended it in earlier times as a floor covering. The foliage is very iris-like, but longer (often 3 ft.) and narrower than that of most irises, and in the case of 'Variegatus' it has a cream or white stripe running the length of one edge of the blade only, with a pinkish tinge at the base. Although usually seen with its feet well into the water it will also grow in marshy positions, in sun or shade, though rather less vigorously. (Untried.)

ACTINIDIA kolomikta (A.M. 1931)
Climber; deciduous

The actinidias are commonly described as vigorous and easy to grow, but I think this rather depends on one's garden climate. At least for *A. kolomikta* I feel sure that a certain amount of warmth is necessary to promote strong growth and colourful results. The whole virtue of this climber, or twiner, which averages about 10 ft. in both directions, lies in the curious variegation of the elegantly shaped leaves. These are of an elongated heart-shape, about 6 in. long, and the majority are adorned at the terminal end with large splashes of pink and white in the earlier part of the season, this effect being much more marked when the plant is grown against a sunny wall (i.e. south or west aspect). Indeed in my own cold hillside garden, which leans away from the sun towards the north and east, it could only be attempted in a sunny wall position; and even then belated spring frosts so repeatedly ruined the newly unfurled leaves, just as the intriguing vestiges of pink and white were beginning to appear, that I finally tired of recurrent heartbreak and brought myself to grub it out. Do not be discouraged if the variegation fails to appear in the first few years after planting, for the tricolour effect is not usually evident until the wood matures.

I have seen the foliage used for cutting and do not believe it to be difficult. (Untried.)

AGAPANTHUS—"African Lily", "Lily of the Nile"
Hardy perennial

Agapanthus campanulatus (*umbellatus mooreanus*), (A.G.M. 1928), is not perhaps usually regarded as a foliage plant, nor would I claim that it has any merit as a garden decorator by virtue of its leaves alone. But much though I admire the hyacinth-blue flower umbels in late summer and the spidery seed-heads afterwards, my plants often fail to flower in this cold garden climate, even though this is an entirely hardy species and is grown here at the foot of a south wall. They do however regularly put forth a clump of long, broadly strap-shaped, blunt-nosed leaves which take on slight curves of special value to the flower arranger and are also very well-behaved in water. This agapanthus exists in a white-flowered form bearing the cultivar name of 'Albus' (A.M. 1960), which is generally considered less effective for garden purposes but is a lovely flower for cutting.

As far as flowers are concerned, the finest of any of the out-door kinds are those of the Headbourne Hybrids, but they are perhaps not quite as tough as the species. In the garden of their origin on a cold, north-east slope in Hampshire they are helped through the winter with a little mulch.

All agapanthus appreciate a rich diet and plenty of sunshine.

AJUGA reptans—Form of "Bugle"
Hardy perennial; ground cover; evergreen

There are several interesting forms of the creeping *Ajuga reptans*, of which I think the two best are 'Multicolor' (or 'Rainbow,) and 'Variegata'. The one has copper-brown leaves splashed with lighter tints from cream to apricot in a mixture which seems to me almost unique and the other is a pretty combination of green and white with an occasional tinge of pink. The leaves are obovate, glossy and deeply veined, mostly about 2 in. long by less than 1 in. wide, and the habit is ground-hugging. The pity of it is that these attractive carpeters cannot be used as freely as one might wish since they are too invasive to be trusted alongside dwarf plants of less aggressive character; but one of their virtues is that they will rapidly cover the ground in the most awkward spots which suit little else, being perfectly happy in poor soil, dry shade and other discouraging conditions. Both yield relatively small sprays for cutting (averaging about 9 in.) and although there are plenty of satisfying alternatives for the green and white 'Variegata' I know of nothing quite like the glistening mahogany of 'Multicolor' splashed with lighter tints.

ALCHEMILLA mollis (A.M. 1958, A.G.M. 1965)—"Lady's Mantle"
Hardy perennial; ground cover

Few flower arrangers will agree with the statement of a well-known horticultural writer that *Alchemilla mollis* is grown almost entirely for its handsome kidney-shaped leaves and that the flowers are of no importance—and I imagine that it was as a flowering hardy perennial that this plant earned its awards. Indeed I would say that most of us tend to overlook the beauty of the leaves in our besotted enthusiasm for that flowery froth of lime-yellow which associates so happily with every other hue. Nevertheless the slightly lobed and pleated, somewhat pelargonium-like leaves with a diameter of up to 6 in. on single 6- to 8-in. stems, are lovely in their own right, making a dense, ground covering hummock of silver-green plush occasionally tinged with light apricot as the leaves pass the prime of youth.

This is one of the easiest of plants, seeding itself in the most inhospitable places with almost weed-like determination. The flowers can be dried by hanging upside down and the leaves may be preserved by glycerining. (See Chapter IX.)

AMELANCHIER canadensis—"June Berry", "Snowy Mespilus"
Tree; deciduous

Humdrum enough for much of the year, *Amelanchier*

canadensis is nevertheless a garden ornament on several counts, providing a springtime spectacle of airy white blossom—tits, sparrows and bullfinches permitting—offset, or else closely followed, by the tender pinkish-copper of the newly unfurled leaves which are about 2 in. long, roughly oval, slightly downy and gracefully disposed on slender branches. While this is not in the top rank of fine foliage for the flower arranger it provides two separate seasons of attractive leaf colour and the small tree will stand any amount of lopping about, so that large sprays can be cut for indoor use. As a rule its autumn colour is particularly vivid; but if your garden is plagued, as mine is, by rumbustious winds at all seasons you may find the brilliant autumn mantle of scarlet, flame and apricot not very enduring.

The Snowy Mespilus will grow just about anywhere and scatters seedlings far beyond the confines of the garden in districts where the flower buds are not stripped by the birds long before they have a chance to bear fruit.

ANAPHALIS triplinervis (A.M. 1961) and A. yedoensis

Hardy perennials

The species most often seen is *A. triplinervis*, with pearly clusters of little "everlasting" daisies rising above a low clump of semi-evergreen, ribbed, oval, grey-green leaves backed with white suède. But despite the pleasing leaf pattern and colour the best of the foliage is too ground-hugging and the rest too sparsely spaced on the curving, semi-prostrate, white-furred, reddish stems to be really effective as foliage for cutting. In the erect-habited *A. yedoensis*, however, the woolly white stems are much more closely furnished with narrower, neatly tapered grey leaves backed with white, with the characteristic longitudinal veining, providing upstanding foliage shoots 2 ft. long with some resemblance to an entire-margined type of artemisia. Both species like full sun and good drainage.

Stand in hot water.

ANGELICA archangelica
Hardy biennial

My own immense enthusiasm for this massive, architectural umbellifer is chiefly centred on the great spherical green flower-heads, but the ornate foliage is an additional asset for flower arrangement, whether used in the pale green stage or when fading to a soft pale yellow. Every part of the plant has the deliciously cool, clean smell we associate with it in its crystallized state. No matter where it grows it multiplies exceedingly and the forests of seedlings become something of a nuisance, but resist the temptation to uproot the lot in desperation, or you will destroy the essential biennial sequence of seedlings one year and flowers the next.

If it is possible to immerse the large, branching, juicy foliage completely in a starch solution for some hours it is thoroughly reliable, but it does not always respond well to boiling, singeing, soaking, stem-tipping and so on (though pricking the veins before soaking seems to help). Even though the whole leaf may possibly flag fairly quickly indoors unless starched, the branching segments are still big enough to be useful and these will stand well in water if detached and used separately after a preliminary soaking.

AQUILEGIA—"Columbine"
Hardy perennial

I am old-fashioned enough to prefer the fusty old double "Granny's Bonnets" to the gaily coloured modern millinery of the newer long-spurred hybrids for floral decoration. But whichever way one's taste lies the leaf design is always delightful (combining something of the maidenhair fern and of *Thalictrum glaucum* in its make-up) and the foliage colour often unusual. Evidently I am in a minority, for the "Bonnets" have now almost entirely disappeared from the catalogues. But if it is still to be found, a white form—at one time stocked by the Sunningdale

34

Nurseries but dropped from more recent lists—called *Aquilegia vulgaris nivea*, or "Munstead White Columbine", is said to have the greyest leaf colour of any. It is however still possible to obtain the pretty dwarf species, *A. alpina*, which combines comparatively large blue and white flowers on 12-in. stems with lovely, and also large, though short-stalked, blue-grey-green leaves sometimes tinged with pink and which obligingly seeds itself in unlikely spots in this garden.

All types seem well able to put up with a fair amount of shade, but will also thrive in sunshine in a leafy and preferably moist, but well-drained, soil.

ARAUCARIA araucana (*imbricata*)—"Chile Pine", "Monkey Puzzle"
Tree; evergreen

Although so popular in the last century this unusual-looking conifer is not to everybody's taste today. No doubt it fell into disfavour because it was so often unsuitably sited against an ugly background of Victorian red brick, though if this was done by way of protection it was quite unnecessary, for it will stand any amount of wind and makes an imposing specimen in an open setting where its silhouette may be viewed against the sky. Araucarias are not often planted today, but sausage-shaped lengths of their scaly dark green branches are much sought after by modern floral artists in particular. Such portions are most easily come by in a desiccated state, since the lower branches turn brown and fall to the ground as they die, whereas the live green ones are usually far beyond our reach. (See Chapter IX.)

ARBUTUS unedo (F.C.C. 1933)—"Strawberry Tree"
Tree or shrub; evergreen

This is usually seen as a small tree of 10 to 15 ft., but it can also be grown in bush form, though in this case the beauty of the low-forking red-brown trunk is lost. The dark evergreen foliage is tough, slightly glossy and shaped like a bay leaf, but with a neatly toothed margin. It is from the round, reddish-orange and yellow fruits which accompany the pitcher-shaped little cream-white flowers in late autumn that the common name derives. The fruits are edible, but only just.

This beautiful plant is quite hardy and is surprisingly accommodating in one or two other ways. Though it requires some shelter from the wind in infancy, even coastal gales rarely harm a mature specimen; and, above all, it is one of the very few members of the *Ericaceae* which will tolerate a limy soil.

There is also an attractive pink-flowered cultivar called 'Rubra', which gained an A.M. in 1925.

ARTEMISIA—"Wormwood"

Word pictures are so unhelpful in identifying the numerous and often somewhat similar herbaceous artemisias that the wisest course is to make one's selection from live samples if possible. The following brief notes include some of those most useful for cutting.

Hardy perennials:

A. absinthium 'Lambrook Silver'—makes a beautiful clump of delicately cut, silky, silver-green foliage topped by tall flower spikes (3 ft.).

A. pontica—"Old Lady"—which is comparatively dwarf, has little grey-green leaves designed on the same pattern in miniature and is feathery to the point of fluffiness. It is more willing than most to tolerate wet feet in winter (1½ ft.).

A. gnaphalodes; A. ludoviciana (A.G.M. 1935)—"White Sage", "Cudweed"; and *A. purshiana* are all much alike, with more willow-like leaves, silvery in the case of *ludoviciana* (3 to 4 ft.) and whiter in the case of the other two (both about 3 ft.).

Like so many other grey-leaved plants the silvery artemisias appreciate hot, dry situations with good drainage, but they will put up with almost anything except waterlogging, although the colour will suffer in shady positions. For those varieties which tend to straggle it is advisable to pinch out the tips of the shoots periodically if a neater and more compact shape is desired. (See also Chapter IX.)

Artemisia arborescens
Shrub; deciduous or semi-evergreen

I would infinitely rather possess this beautiful small shrub than any of the herbaceous varieties just listed, for *Artemisia arborescens* is an outstanding ornament in any garden sufficiently warm and well drained to offer it a comfortable home. It makes a 3- to 4-ft. mound of silver filigree with silky wisps of foliage which glint as though polished and the effect is one of ineffable delicacy, grace and gaiety. But after one short-lived attempt in this thoroughly unsuitable garden climate I shall not try it again. For those possessing sufficiently favourable garden conditions for this rather tender shrubby artemisia it will still be important to prevent water collecting round the base of the main stem, since this is more damaging than quite sharp frost, provided that the latter is of comparatively brief duration.

Mrs. Desmond Underwood, who is not only a specialist grower of silver foliage plants but is also experienced in flower arrangement, tells us that grey foliage must never be immersed. I confess that I often soak some of the more difficult ones and have not thought that their appearance suffered, after drying out; but I feel I must bow to her wide experience in this field and shall not therefore recommend soaking to you, even though I may continue the practice on my own with some of the more unreliable leaves. Boiling or singeing, followed by a long drink in cold or tepid water should suit all kinds of artemisia. Most artemisias are unsafe in moisture-retaining substances.

ARUM italicum 'Pictum'—Form of "Cuckoo Pint", "Lords and Ladies", "Soldiers and Sailors"
Hardy perennial

The greenish arum-flowers in summer are not specially good of their kind and although the fat, shining orange-berried spikes which follow are fine for autumn arrangements it is above all for the beauty of the foliage that we prize this obliging plant (see illustration facing p. 49). The glossy, arrow-headed leaves, shaped like those of the wild arum, are adorned with conspicuous light veining on a rich green ground, providing first-class foliage for the flower arranger at a time when this is hard to find. The leaf clump surprisingly begins to push through the soil in early autumn, growing to a height of about 18 in. throughout the winter and persisting into early summer or even midsummer, slugs permitting. The tender, juicy look of this arum leaf is rare indeed among winter foliages, but it survives all kinds of seasonal hazards to emerge as fresh and fair as ever once it has thawed out after a prostrating spell of refrigeration.

It will prosper in sun or shade and is sometimes recommended for growing beneath trees and shrubs, but I think flower arrangers would be well advised to give it a fairly sunny position, in order to enhance the white veining. On the other hand a moist soil (not always compatible with sunshine) yields larger leaves; but this can also be achieved by regular feeding during the growing period or by providing rich soil conditions. My own finest leaves come on 18-in. stems, with the sides of the arrowhead measuring up to 15 in. on a 9-in. basal diameter—and here I would stress the importance of the regular application of slug bait if the leaves are to be of any use for cutting. The berries produce seedlings if allowed to ripen.

Although the varietal names 'Pictum' and 'Marmoratum' are both widely applied to *A. italicum*, neither has any botanical validity. In some forms the foliage is however so much better marked than in others that I have retained the name 'Pictum' because the plant described above is more usually listed as such.

The foliage is very well behaved in water, if previously soaked. To prevent the awkward stem-curl resulting from immersion I pack as many stems as will fit fairly tightly into a narrow tube such as a plastic toothbrush-holder during the soaking period, from which they emerge as nearly straight as one could wish. This does not preclude the subsequent stroking of the stems into gentle curves if necessary.

ARUNCUS sylvester (*Spiraea aruncus*)—"Goat's Beard", and ASTILBES
Hardy perennials

Aruncus sylvester has handsome bipinnate leaves modelled on those of the astilbes (among which it used to be included) but many times magnified. Some measure as much as 2½ ft. from stem-junction to leaf-tip, by 2 ft. wide, with large, finely serrated leaflets. In the case of the astilbes a number of varieties have attractively bronzed foliage, often also with red stalks. These are both subjects which I would not feel inclined to grow for their leaves alone, but the combination of good foliage and fine flower makes them useful dual-purpose plants. The aruncus has large and immensely tall cream plumes and the much shorter astilbes range in flower colour from cream, through various pinks to crimson. The latter are moisture-lovers, but the aruncus is a rumbustious perennial which thrives in any conditions.

Put into warm water.

ASPIDISTRA elatior—"Cast-iron Plant", "Parlour Palm"
Ground cover; evergreen

It is perhaps scarcely ethical to admit the aspidistra to the company of the hardy plants within our terms of reference. But it is said to be possible to overwinter it in the open in this country and so to use it as ground cover beneath trees in really mild localities. Such is my affection for this bold, shapely, almost everlasting leaf for cutting purposes that I would stoop to something of a quibble to get it included here; but although I have read that plants have come through the winter success-fully in the open in this country my own experiment was a not unexpected failure and it would only be fair to admit that in most parts of the British Isles the role of Parlour Palm evidently suits it best.

Indoors *Aspidistra elatior* (often wrongly named *A. lurida*) is of course one of the easiest of plants and yet it is often seen in pretty

39

poor shape. When well grown the smooth, arching blades may be as much as 16 in. long by 4 or 5 in. wide, of a rich deep green and firm of texture; but they are frequently undersized, sparse, rather papery and browning at the tips from sheer neglect. They thrive in cool, dry shade, preferring a north or north-east window indoors. John Innes No. 1 or No. 2 compost is recommended and plants should be re-potted in March if necessary, shaking off some of the old soil and replanting more or less on the surface, much as for iris rhizomes. Pieces of root with a leaf attached may be potted on separately to become strong new plants within two months or so. The plain green type appreciates regular feeding, but care should be taken not to apply the fertilizer to the soil when it is dry and not to let it come in contact with the leaf surfaces. Superannuated leaves should be removed to encourage new ones and if this is done before they become too dilapidated they may be dried or glycerined. The foliage is so long-lived on the plant that the dust must be washed off periodically and I find that an occasional sponging with Bio Leafshine improves the gloss without overdoing it.

The variegated form, *A. elatior* 'Variegata' is if anything even more desirable than the plain green one, having cream, ivory, or white longitudinal stripes or wider bands on a green ground. Plants usually produce a number of leaves almost or entirely devoid of variegation, particularly when grown in the shade. I have read that this is also caused by too much nitrogenous fertilizer and certainly the striation on my own plants has become more pronounced since I stopped regular feeding.

Both forms last interminably in water (I bring mine back from demonstrations and use them over and over again) and both are particularly good subjects for glycerining. (See Chapter IX.)

ASTRANTIA major 'Sunningdale Variegated'—Form of "Masterwort"
Hardy perennial

A happy accident has prompted some mention of *Astrantia major*, which we all prize so highly for its curious greenish-white flowers. The well-shaped, deep green leaves last well in water and they turn to a fine bright yellow in the autumn, but although I often make use of them others do not seem greatly to value them, so I had been in some doubt about their inclusion here. However, I have just discovered a self-sown seedling in my garden with a distinct, neat margin of clear yellow to the bright green leaves and at the same time have come across a form in commerce with a differently variegated leaf, which has bold splashes of cream and yellow on a green ground. Where the plain green foliage fails to excite interest the best of these variegated forms can hardly fail to do so. The leaf shape is the same as in the type plant—more or less circular, with five markedly serrated lobes cutting almost to the stem junction, and each leaf is borne on a single stem.

ATRIPLEX

A. halimus—"Sea Purslane, "Tree Purslane"
Shrub; evergreen or semi-evergreen

This hardy, slender-branched shrub has smallish, rather diamond-shaped leaves which are more dull grey than silver. It rapidly reaches 6 ft., retains its foliage in winter in all but the coldest districts, makes do with the poorest of sandy soils, revels in salt sea winds and stands any amount of cutting. It is indeed widely recommended for this purpose; but my own feelings towards it are lukewarm, chiefly I think because as a garden plant I find it untidy rather than graceful, though it is often so described. However, its loose habit yields long, graceful sprays for flower arrangement. Further pruning to improve its shape and to keep it within bounds may be done in the spring. (For glycerining see Chapter IX.)

Condition cut sprays in very hot water.

A. hortensis—"Mountain Spinach", "Orach"
Hardy annual

A. hortensis 'Rubra' is the form most commonly grown. Every part of the plant is colourful, from the beetroot arrow-head leaves on purple stems to the beetroot flowers and disc-shaped seeds, which dry to a pleasant light biscuit. The main stem will grow to a lanky 6 or 7 ft. on its own, if this is what you prefer for cutting, but a better-looking, bushier plant will result from frequent pinching out of the growing tips. It seeds itself with abandon; but if you should need to sow it it is as well to bear in mind that it dislikes being moved.

Such seedsmen's catalogues as list the Mountain Spinach are rather confusing, one, for instance, mentioning two forms of *A. hortensis* 'Cupreata' (one having red leaves on violet stems and the other with yellow leaves, but both sharing the same name) and also listing an "Orach, Giant Red", all three of which I have just received for trial—and for disentanglement if possible.

A rich, moist soil and sunshine produce the best results and the original sowing of any of these should be made where a permanent colony may be allowed to establish itself. 'Giant Red' is guaranteed edible (possibly others, too), the colour being said to disappear in the cooking; so perhaps one should eat up surplus supplies rather than give them away, in view of their objection to transplanting. Nevertheless I believe that most of us get going with seedlings transplanted from other people's gardens.

Boil.

AUCUBA japonica 'Variegata' ('Maculata')—"Spotted Laurel"
Shrub; evergreen

The aucubas are not related to the laurels, though of somewhat similar general appearance. *Aucuba japonica* 'Variegata' had a tough time of it in the last century in the darkest, dankest parts of Victorian "shrubberies" where little else would grow; but flower arrangers have raised its status today and because lime-yellow foliage is now so popular with most of us this aucuba is often accorded a place of honour in the sun, which enhances the yellow colour of the heavily splashed and spotted leaves. Being evergreen these are particularly valuable for winter decoration, when this gay foliage colour is scarce.

A. japonica 'Goldenheart'
Shrub; evergreen

There are several different variegated forms of aucuba and I have recently acquired a new one called 'Goldenheart' in which the whole of the leaf centre is yellow, with a speckled margin. This seems to me much superior to the rather muddled spotting of the common Spotted Laurel; but it may be slightly more difficult, since it is said to need shelter and shade. (See also Chapter IX.)

AZALEA*

Although it is technically more correct to include the azaleas in the genus *Rhododendron*, for the sake of clarity I propose to deal with them here, under their own separate head.

Deciduous Azaleas
Shrubs; deciduous

These are not commonly regarded as foliage plants except for ephemeral autumn colour, but there are a fair number of Ghents and other more modern hybrids with attractively coloured leaves throughout the summer. To get the best of both worlds one should visit growers when the plants are in bloom, to select varieties combining beauty of flower with interesting leaf colour. Unnamed seedlings are much cheaper than named varieties and the best of them are often just as good. In my own garden the best for summer foliage is a nameless seedling of the Farall strain, with lovely light vermilion flowers set among leaves of a warm copper hue; and another I like for its cut foliage is the yellow-flowered Ghent, 'Nancy Waterer', whose leaves are tinged with a curious, *subfusc* kind of gunmetal overtone.

Dwarf Evergreen Azaleas
Shrubs; evergreen

A number of these with the most vivid foliage hues are too

compact and dwarf-habited to spare much for cutting, at least in their earlier years, but meanwhile they are superlative garden decorators as winter foliage plants, quite apart from the prodigious quantities of flowers they provide in spring and early summer. The crimson-flowered 'Hinodegiri' is one of the most outstanding for its brilliant scarlet flush on the winter foliage, but it will only yield short pieces for cutting. More generous in this respect is 'Addy Wery', whose mature foliage is attractively copper-tinted. But perhaps the best of the lot, in the present context, is *Rhododendron amoenum*, or its cv. 'Coccineum', sometimes listed as 'Tyrian Rose'. The foliage is identical in either case, but the vivid magenta flower colour of the species is less generally popular than the crimson of 'Coccineum'. The leaf colour is in fact more subdued than any—an unusually dark olive green (a darker shade of Green 137A) throughout the summer and only faintly tinged with maroon in exposed situations in winter—but it has most attractively tiered, horizontally fanning branches adorned with innumerable tiny, shining, oval leaves, growing fairly quickly to 4 ft. or more.

All evergreen azaleas enjoy part-shade and since they will grow faster, taller and more lax-habited in such positions this suits both them and us. In my garden ten-year-old plants of all the above, except 'Hinodegiri', are now long-limbed enough to spare quite large branches of interesting shapes for floral decoration. Given an acid soil they are very undemanding, requiring little or no attention unless they become stricken with Azalea Gall (*Exobasidium vaccinii*). This is a fungus disease which shows as grotesque swellings and distortions on the new leaf shoots in spring and early summer and since these are usually concealed among the lower branches or beneath other growth at the start the disease is likely to get a firm grip on a plant before it is discovered unless one is constantly on the look-out for it during the danger period. Where its presence is not suspected it is often first betrayed by the exaggerated pendulum or bouncing action of a twig, which is set in motion at the slightest touch, owing to the unnatural weight of the elephantiastic swelling on the affected part. It is when these obscene-looking growths become coated with a whitish powder that the disease is most malignant and a bad attack may reduce flowering or even prove fatal if the affected shoots are not picked off and burned. It is a waste of time to pick off a single swollen leaf in the hope of saving the shoot, which is bound to succumb in the end. Timely spraying with a zineb fungicide such as Dithane just before the new leaves open up in spring is the likeliest means of preventing an outbreak. If it fails to do so spraying should be continued periodically throughout the summer and diseased parts removed by hand as already described.

I have dealt with this problem in some detail because I find that so few amateur gardeners are even aware of the enemy in their midst, and so lose valuable plants without knowing why, when prompt action would have saved them. Indeed a specimen which is badly infested one season may be entirely free the next if it has been carefully picked over during the attack.

BALLOTA pseudo-dictamnus
Shrub; evergreen or semi-evergreen

This plant is wrapped in thick silvery down in every part— stems, pale silver-green leaves and attractive matching whorls from which the tiny lilac flowers rather tiresomely emerge. The small, broadly heart-shaped, 1-in.-wide leaves bear a close resemblance to those of the less woolly and much more tender *Helichrysum petiolatum*. (See illustration facing p. 64.) The ballota is fortunately a lot hardier than it looks, requiring only a sunny, well-drained site to succeed. It makes a dwarf, rather sprawling shrub of about 2 ft., which can be kept to a more compact and tidier shape if the flowered shoots are trimmed in autumn and the whole pruned back to 6 in., or less, in spring. In any case it will usually receive a good deal of incidental pruning, for flower arrangers are much addicted to the graceful sprays of furry foliage interspersed with the spherical clumps of whorled bracts which encircle the main stems. The bracts dry well, if picked before they become over-mature and stripped of their leaves. No judge who knows her N.A.F.A.S. Schedule

45

Definitions would disqualify an entry in a Foliage Class in which these bracts were present, but she might well do so if she spotted any of the little flowers among them. Since the almost undetectable tiny greenish-mauve flower buds are apt to open quickly in a warm room it is safer to pluck out the (admissible) unopened buds as well, when the material is to be used in competitive exhibits.

As for conditioning, often only a long, tepid drink is necessary, but I prefer to boil because the soft tips of young shoots are otherwise inclined to droop.

BERBERIS—"Barberry"
Shrub; deciduous

Berberis thunbergii 'Atropurpurea' (A.M. 1926, A.G.M. 1932)

This makes a ferociously spiny 6-ft. shrub composed of gracefully arching sprays of tiny obovate leaves of that useful foliage colour described as purple but in truth a rather indeterminate mahogany-bronze with occasional purplish overtones. The barberries comprise some of the most lethally prickly subjects in cultivation and although this is one of the worst, depositing the tips of its needle-sharp armature to fester in fingers and thumbs, for me its colour and habit make it indispensable as cutting material, with the aid of a stripping tool. It is very easy to please, but the leaf colour will be no more than a murky greenish-bronze if grown in the shade.

B. thunbergii 'Atropurpurea Superba'

The addition of 'Superba' to the rest of the name might be taken to indicate that anything the other can do this can do better. It is indeed more vigorous and upright in habit, with larger leaves of a more intense purplish-mahogany; but to be bigger is not necessarily to be better and in this case I should be glad to find room for both if I could.

B. thunbergii 'Atropurpurea Rose Glow'

A most attractive recent introduction, this is dwarfer than the type, growing to about 4 ft. on its own but requiring to be cut back annually in order to obtain the delightfully coloured, tender, pink new growth with paler variegation. If left unpruned, and at maturity, the leaf colour is much more akin to that of the ordinary *B. thunbergii* 'Atropurpurea'. Furthermore it needs plenty of light to achieve this lovely colouring. As cut material it stands well in water if properly conditioned, as directed below.

Boiling and soaking is essential for all three in the early part of the season and often necessary for most of the summer.

BERGENIA (*Megasea*)—"Elephant's Ear Saxifrage", "Pig Squeak"
Hardy perennial; ground cover; evergreen

The bergenias are one of the indispensable 'props' of flower arrangement. Among their many virtues they thrive in any soil, being particularly good on lime or chalk, they are with us all the year round, their leaves are of a fine, solid shape and texture, and range in colour from a good medium green to maroon, crimson, scarlet, flame, liver or amber according to seasons, soils and situations, and to some extent dependent on varieties. Nor should one overlook the value of the sturdy pink, magenta or white flower clusters which mostly bloom in earliest spring. It must however be remembered that all are not equally hardy.

B. cordifolia

The two species most often grown, no doubt for the reason that they are among the hardiest, are *cordifolia* and *crassifolia*. *B. cordifolia* is the one with the almost circular, heart-shaped leaves with maximum dimensions of about 8 in. each way. They are more matt-surfaced and leathery than those of *crassifolia*, with a wavy outline, some being a medium green, some liver-tinged and others colouring brightly and variously in winter. The foliage lasts almost interminably in water without any special conditioning at maturity, though soaking is advisable early in the season. (For glycerining see Chapter IX.)

B. crassifolia

In this case the shiny, obovate or spoon-shaped leaves measure up to 10 in. long by 7 in., but, as in the case of all the larger-leaved forms, sizes vary widely on a single plant. The foliage colours well in exposed situations but remains more or less consistently green, or sometimes pale yellow—in my garden anyway—in the shade. It lasts well in water if stem-tipped during the preliminary soaking, but I find it less foolproof and long-lived when cut than that of *cordifolia*.

B. 'Sunningdale' (A.M. 1963)

Before leaving the large-leaved types mention should be made of the welcome new-comer, 'Sunningdale', which has handsome red-bronze winter foliage colour and is reputed to be of a sturdy constitution. (Untried.)

B. purpurascens

Of the more miniature species *B. purpurascens* is among the most vividly coloured foliages, with rather narrow, upright, paddle-shaped leaves not usually exceeding 6 in. in length. Though hardy, this one is not very vigorous and is apparently hard to come by. The *B. cordifolia* 'Purpurescens' or 'Purpurea' of nurserymen's lists is not the same plant.

Soak.

BUDDLEIA—"Butterfly Bush"
Shrub; deciduous

Buddleia foliage is fairly uninteresting as a rule, but two variegated forms have recently appeared which are anything but dull. Both derive from the vivid purple-flowered *B. davidii* 'Royal Red': 'Royal Red Variegated' being margined and mottled with cream and 'Harlequin' more heavily marked with cream and white. Though the only commercial information so far avai labl

1. Ornamental Cabbage, cream and white variegated form

2. The marbled arrow-heads of *Arum italicum* 'Pictum'

about them is conflicting in the extreme, especially as regards their comparative vigour and ultimate height, most growers are agreed that 'Harlequin' is the better plant, both because of its more spectacular variegation and also because it is less liable to revert. Both are less vigorous than the parent. (Untried.)

BUXUS sempervirens—"Common Box", "Tree Box"
Shrub; evergreen

Being a very accommodating plant as regards soils and situations, Box is especially valuable in limy districts, where the choice of evergreens is more limited than on acid soils. The flower arranger may not perhaps have a high regard for it in its plain green garb, but there are one or two most colourful yellow-leaved forms which are immensely useful for cutting, in winter in particular. Probably the most effective are 'Aurea Maculata', in which the leaves are streaked and blotched with yellow, and 'Aurea Marginata' which is yellow-edged; or, if a much dwarfer habit is preferred, 'Latifolia Maculata' ('Japonica Aurea') makes a compact shrub of 3 ft. or so of vivid yellow colouring. I find those with white variegation rather lack-lustre by comparison with the foregoing varieties, but for those who may disagree with me *B. s.* 'Elegantissima' is a neat-habited dwarf of 3 to 4 ft. with white-margined grey-green leaves which are said to keep their colour even in sunless positions.

All are very long-lasting in water and the green *B. sempervirens* glycerines beautifully. (See Chapter IX.)

CABBAGE and KALE, Ornamental
Hardy annuals

The main difference between ornamental cabbage and kale is the same as in the more utilitarian forms of these vegetables, the one making a spherical cluster of crimped foliage at ground level and the other bearing a number of separate, stalked leaves on a woody main stem crowned with a small leafy head. The colour in either case varies from purple, mauve and cyclamen to palest pink; or a mixture of green and cream or white. In the

D

cabbage the cream predominates in the rather open heart, with just enough of the green parsley-curled trimming to emphasize the intricately frilled edging to the leaf, as may be seen in the illustration facing p. 48. I believe that particularly beautiful named varieties of ornamental cabbage are now on the market but I have been unable to trace a source of supply. To my eye, however, even those flower-like shapes and colours raised from a packet of mixed seed are far lovelier than the ornamental kales, and if the cabbages are less commonly grown for flower arrangement it can only be that they are less widely known—though admittedly those large, dense, peony-like heads need more skilful handling.

Strictly speaking both the cabbage and the kale are annuals, but the latter can become perennial if cut back and prevented from flowering. Like all the cabbage tribe these prefer a rich, limy soil and need to be grown in full sun for the sake of compactness and fine foliage colour. In the purple mixtures the colour reaches its maximum intensity in late winter.

Soaking is advisable in the case of individual kale leaves and charcoal tablets help to defeat the cabbagey smell if added to the water in the container.

CALLUNA vulgaris*—"Heather", "Ling"
Shrub; ground cover; evergreen

New foliage cultivars of heaths and heathers tumble off the production lines almost faster than even the specialist growers can keep pace with them at the present time, but I have done my best to make an up-to-date selection of those most likely to be of use to the flower arranger (ignoring the dwarfer varieties in favour of those averaging 1½ ft. or more), after studying the appearance of as many new ones as possible both in specialist nurseries and in the heather garden at Wisley.

'Blazeaway' and 'Robert Chapman' (A.M. 1962)

These two seem fairly similar, with most spectacular bright

red winter foliage fading to attractive apricot and flame at other seasons.

'Beoley Gold' (A.M. 1968) and 'Golden Feather' (A.M. 1965, F.C.C. 1967)

The white-flowered 'Beoley Gold' and 'Golden Feather' (unflowered at the time of writing) have lime-yellow foliage in early summer, deepening later to soft orange. Both have well-furnished sprigs, but the latter is a particularly fine foliage plant with truly feathered shoots which show a pinkish flush up the centre as they begin to burnish. This should be one of the best for cutting if not kept too severely clipped.

'Gold Haze' (A.M. 1961, F.C.C. 1963)

It is worth while having a look at 'Gold Haze' in early summer and again in autumn in the R.H.S. Garden at Wisley, where a bold drift is to be seen among other heaths and heathers at the wild garden end of Seven Acres. Early in the season the foliage is a vibrant lime-yellow and later it is a lovely sight in bloom, when the white flowers mingle with the brighter yellow leaves of late summer to give an effect of soft cream-yellow in the mass.

'Joy Vanstone'

This is one of the newer varieties, in which the yellow summer foliage turns in autumn and winter to an excellent light apricot-orange, with which the pinkish-mauve flowers in autumn blend more happily than most.

'Serlei Aurea' (A.M. 1961)

Looking, from a distance, across the nursery beds with their blocks of widely assorted foliage hues, it struck me that our old friend 'Serlei Aurea' still stands out as vividly yellow as any of the new-comers and its sturdy, upright growth particularly recommends it for cutting. Personally I prefer white flowers, as this one has, to complement yellow, orange or red foliage.

'Silver Queen' and 'Hirsuta Typica' (A.M. 1962, F.C.C. 1964)

'Silver Queen' is scarce as yet, but 'Hirsuta Typica' may be easier to get and it has the same long foliage shoots of a woolly, almost powdery-looking deep grey rather than silver. This undoubtedly provides an intriguing colour contrast among the yellows, oranges, reds and bronzes of other foliage cultivars, but I personally do not much covet this foliage for cutting. The flowers are mauve—this time a happy colour harmony of leaf and bloom.

Growing as they were in full exposure these heathers had developed the utmost intensity of colour in their foliage and many were truly spectacular. Indeed the heather garden at Wisley is an infinitely brighter spectacle than it used to be, with the inclusion of broad sweeps of many of the newer vivid and varied foliage hues. But it is a waste of time to attempt to grow coloured foliage varieties of heath and heather except in full sun, for even a little shade for a part of the day seems to dim their brilliance. While I do not pretend that these are of inestimable benefit to the flower arranger, many do appreciate the wide assortment of vivid leaf colour for use in small arrangements and it is, I think, beyond dispute that any flower arranger's mixed foliage border will be very much the gayer for their inclusion in sunny positions among the front-row verge plants, provided the soil is lime-free. (See also Erica.)

CAMELLIA japonica*
Shrub; evergreen

Amongst the finest of all evergreen flowering shrubs, *Camellia japonica* and its countless varieties are nowadays recognized to be entirely hardy, requiring only such protection as will prevent frosting of the opening flowers: that is to say, a position where the sun cannot reach these until they have had time to thaw after a night frost. The foliage does not differ very widely among *C. japonica* cvs.—strong-textured, glossy, oval dark green leaves between 3 and 4 in. long by 2 in. wide, faintly toothed and tapering sharply to a slender point. I know of one form, 'Imbricata Rubra'—and there may be others—in which a natural variegation sometimes occurs, but as a general rule yellow-blotched foliage is either a sign of disease or of chlorosis due to the presence of lime in the soil. Such flower arranger-gardeners as are apt to hail this leaf coloration with delight ought rather to view it with misgiving.

Choice of flower depends on your personal preference for single, formal double, or a number of shapes in between, as well as for colour ranging through carmine and pink to white, or flecked and striped combinations of these. But if you are able to choose from a wide selection of plants in bloom, remember that habit and ultimate height vary considerably and that those of specially slow or compact growth should be avoided if you want foliage for cutting later on.

Beds at the foot of north or west walls suit them well and they are the worthiest of subjects for such important positions. But wherever they are sited a moist, acid soil is essential and plenty of water is particularly necessary in July when next year's flower buds are forming. In limy districts they may, of course, be grown in tubs filled with suitable soil, so long as the roots are not frozen solid during the winter. In any circumstances I find they benefit from a mulch of well-rotted manure in late July.

The leaves last for months in water and may be preserved by glycerining. (See Chapter IX.)

CASSINIA fulvida (*Diplopappus chrysophyllus*)—"Golden Heather"
Shrub; evergreen

The term "gold" or "golden" as applied to leaf colour is, to my eye, hardly ever justifiable and although *Cassinia fulvida* is invariably so described in trade catalogues (as well as in its doubly misleading common name) I detect more olive-yellow than gold in its unusual make-up. Viewed from above the longish, slender leaf shoots are a dark olive green, whereas the stems and the underside of the leaves are an intensely acid lime-yellow (Yellow-Green 153B), combining to most telling effect in the winter garden landscape and providing attractive and long-lasting slender foliage sprays, particularly when used back to front, for indoor decoration. The minute leaves are certainly somewhat heather-like, but this plant is of course no relation of the callunas and is perfectly happy in a limy soil, though its English pseudonym sometimes misleads would-be growers on this point.

It makes a 3- to 4-ft. shrub which thrives in seaside conditions and does well enough in much harsher surroundings, though I would not expect it to succeed in cold gardens in the shade, as it is said to do in coastal areas. It becomes rather lanky and ragged-looking if not fairly hard pruned in spring and trimmed again in late summer, but will stand a good deal of hacking about at any time of year.

CEDRUS atlantica 'Glauca'—"Blue Cedar"
Tree; evergreen

The lovely glaucous-leaved cedar is a tremendous garden ornament where the surroundings are to scale, but if we contemplate planting a tree of such grandeur we should bear in mind that it grows upwards and outwards surprisingly quickly, spreading its branches over a wide area down to ground level. I now realize that it was a mistake to plant one in this small garden, particularly in a bed of mixed shrubs—but then I had no room to plant it in isolation, which is the way to see it at its best—and after eighteen years' growth it would now smother everything within a 20-ft. radius if I had not somewhat mutilated it by lopping off much of the lower growth. The weight of snow in our bleak winters is also liable to tear off large branches from time to time.

It lasts wonderfully when cut, provided the room atmosphere is not so dry as to make the needles drop prematurely. But it is exceptionally heavy material of markedly drooping habit as a rule, so that it is almost impossible to obtain an upright line, although some individual trees tend to produce more rigid-tipped branches than others.

CENTAUREA gymnocarpa
Shrub; evergreen

Like so many silver-leaved plants *Centaurea gymnocarpa* has beautifully cut foliage and is tantalizingly undependable in cold districts. The long, much divided, velvety silver-grey leaves are about 1 ft. long by 3 in. wide at maturity and are plentifully borne on a dense, mounded bush of about 2 ft.; but for me the drooping carriage of the foliage somewhat detracts from its beauty as a garden plant, though individual leaves are very ornamental for cutting.

Boil or put into hot water.

CHAMAECYPARIS—"False Cypress"
Shrub; evergreen

The tall, pyramidal conifers provide an excellent contrast of form among other trees and shrubs of more loosely branched habit and their evergreen character is especially valuable to the flower arranger at Christmas time, for swags, plaques, wreaths and other garlands appropriate to the season which are largely made up of short pieces of long-lasting foliage. The widest variety of colour, size and leaf design is to be found among the *Chamaecyparis* genus, of which almost 100 species and cultivars are stocked by Messrs. Hillier, who probably offer the largest assortment of conifers of all kinds of any grower in this country. Here again it pays to study the many different forms of chamaecyparis in specialist nurseries, botanical gardens and elsewhere before making one's selection rather than settle for the commonest with which one happens to be familiar. The foliage comes in blue-greens, yellows, silver-greys, bronzes, bright greens and variegations. It can be cut several weeks in advance, when preparing for Christmas, for instance, and left lying on the damp ground in a shady spot out of doors until required. Some recommend covering the cut pieces with damp sacking, but I have found them to last indefinitely in winter-time without any covering so long as they are in contact with the moist earth, or grass, or leaf mulch, in a sheltered corner beneath trees or bushes. When made up into swags, etc., damp moss helps to keep the foliage fresh, but in a cool atmosphere it will last in good condition for about a fortnight without any kind of moisture.

CHARD, Ruby (Rhubarb Beet)
Hardy annual

The leaves of Ruby Chard are shaped rather like those of beetroot or spinach, but heavily waved and crinkled. They have a deep bronze sheen and ribbed, rhubarb-like, glistening ruby stems, with midrib and veining of the same vivid hue. This is irresistible material for cutting and is easily grown from seed sown in the open in a good, rich soil. The chief difficulty is to keep these large and immensely handsome leaves free of slug holes.

Soak.

CHOISYA ternata (F.C.C. 1880)—"Mexican Orange Blossom"
Shrub; evergreen

Though no doubt chiefly prized by gardeners for its sweetly scented white blossom in early summer, *Choisya ternata* is even more likely to be grown by the flower arranger for its glossy, fingered evergreen leaves. (See illustration facing p. 80.) One is often advised to grow it in the shade, since the leaves become a much yellower green in a sunny position and maybe this hue is not quite so attractive as the bright, rich green attained in shady conditions; but it is not an absolutely hardy subject and in less favourable garden climates, where survival is the first consideration, it would be wiser to give it a sheltered position in the sun. Elsewhere a bed at the foot of a north wall suits it well. The scent of the attractive, waxy, orange-blossom flowers, in addition to the decorative value of this sleek, neatly mounded evergreen bush, makes it an ideal subject for patios, terraces and other sitting-out places.

The famous gardener, William Robinson, writing in *The*

56

English Flower Garden in 1883, makes the remarkable claim that 'a spray cut in the autumn will have retained its original freshness even in April or May'. Having lost my own specimen in a cold winter I have had no opportunity to make so prolonged a test, but I am assured that it is not exaggerated. The important point is, I think, that the foliage would only be so long-lasting when fully mature. If very soft young growth is present on the cut sprays it can easily be pinched out to prevent wilting. Choisya is an excellent subject for glycerining. (See Chapter IX.)

COLCHICUM autumnale—"Meadow Saffron", "Naked Ladies"
Corm

In a recent gardening article I found colchicum foliage described as 'frankly rather gross', which is, I feel, frankly unjustifiable. In fact I have no great affection for the flowers of the mauve form which I grow exclusively for its splendid leaves, though admittedly the much more expensive white *C. autumnale* 'Album' has a beautiful flower. These colchicums are very easy to please in any well-drained soil, multiplying steadily and even thrusting through a much-trodden path in this garden. The green snub-noses pierce the ground shortly before Christmas and then bide their time, to expand in earliest spring into units of three broad, recurved, glistening, rich green blades fanning out in a triangle on a solid 6-in. stem. The clump shown in the illustration facing p. 80 was photographed in April. From the time they first show above the ground until they begin to yellow at the tips and so lose their looks in late spring or early summer they need constant protection from slugs.

Soak for a brief period.

CONVOLVULUS cneorum
Shrub; evergreen

I find it more than tantalizing to see this lovely Spanish shrublet thriving in the warm seaside gardens of a number of my friends, knowing that it is useless to attempt it in my much harsher garden climate. The narrow, gleaming silver leaves are covered with silky hairs and the flowers, of typical "Bindweed" shape, are white with a pink tinge. I note that its height assessment varies from 1 to 3 ft. in growers' catalogues, but I have never seen a plant more than 1½ ft. high. Though it is said to require superb drainage it grows happily in a heavy clay soil near the Sussex coast. In borderline areas it may get cut to ground level during a bad winter but may possibly break again from the base. In conditions of this kind a poor soil will prevent lush growth and make for greater hardiness. The spent flowers should be removed so that the plant's vigour is not wasted in setting seed.

Boil.

CORNUS —"Cornel", "Dogwood"

C. alba sibirica 'Variegata' ('Elegantissima') and C. alba 'Spaethii' (F.C.C. 1889)
Shrubs; deciduous

The more spectacular members of the *Cornus* genus, with their pink or white flower-like bracts in early summer, are not specially remarkable for their foliage except in the autumn; but a number of others are essentially foliage plants and foremost among these are *Cornus alba sibirica* 'Variegata' ('Elegantissima') and *C. alba* 'Spaethii'. Both are deciduous shrubs of medium size (size rather governed by the type of pruning) with red-barked stems which are particularly ornamental in their naked state in winter.

The former has cool-looking pale greyish-green leaves broadly edged and streaked with cream-white, slightly pink-tinged in autumn, and 'Spaethii' has similarly shaped, elegantly tapered green leaves variegated with bright yellow, generously applied. One of the most colourful of variegated shrubs, it is not however to everyone's taste (my own plant was a throw-out from a friend who thought it hideous). Whereas the leaf colour is perhaps too strong to associate amicably with some flowering shrubs it will make a valuable contribution in a grouping of mixed foliage colours and the combination of exceptionally vivid yellow on green provides a striking acid lime-yellow effect for floral decoration purposes.

Both the winter colour in the stems and the quality of the foliage in each case are improved by pruning hard back in March ever other year or so. Rather than cut the whole plant drastically back at one time I prefer to cut out alternate stems one year, leaving the rest (or those of them which have not been taken for indoor use) to be pruned hard the following year, always with an eye to the shape of the bush. Both do well in semi-shade, but are not averse to sunshine, and both are excellent shrubs for waterside planting, where the bare red winter stems contrast delightfully with yellow-stemmed willows or dogwoods; but a moist situation is not essential. In short these are easy plants to please in all respects.

Put into hot water.

C. mas 'Elegantissima' ('Tricolor') (F.C.C. 1872) and C. mas 'Variegata'—Forms of "Cornelian Cherry"
Trees or shrubs; deciduous

If you want flowers as well as foliage interest you may care to try one of the variegated forms of *C. mas*, which has such charming little yellow flower clusters along the naked branches in earliest spring. Its variegated forms are of course quite distinct from those of the *C. alba* species just described, in spite of the similarity of the cv. names in both species. I have not seen *C. mas* 'Elegantissima' ('Tricolor'), which sounds the more attractive, with pink and yellow variegation on green, whereas *C. mas* 'Variegata' has smallish, narrow leaves of light green and white of a somewhat muddled appearance. Neither is as vigorous or as free-flowering as the type. (Untried.)

COTINUS (ex Rhus)—"Smoke-bush"
Shrub; deciduous

Although the cotinuses are now botanically separated from rhus nurserymen almost invariably continue to list them under the latter head. The green-leaved cotinuses are, I suppose, chiefly renowned for their spectacular autumn colour rather than for their summer greenery, but the pattern of the rounded leaves grouped in whorls and more densely concentrated at the tips of the shoots is in itself excellent for flower arrangement, as are also the curious, fuzzy inflorescences from which its common name derives. The best of the green-leaved forms are the tall *C. americanus* (*Rhus cotinoides*), which has the largest leaves, blue-green in summer and brilliant flame and scarlet in autumn, and *C. coggygria* (*Rhus cotinus*), or "Venetian Sumach", which is less tall and more spreading, with smaller leaves of 2 to 3 in. in diameter turning vivid yellow and apricot in autumn. Its pinkish-grey flower-fuzz is more interesting in the garden landscape than the inconspicuous greenish inflorescences of *C. americanus*, but the latter is the better foliage plant, provided it is not overfed. *C. coggygria* is the one most properly described as the "Smoke-bush" or "Smoke Plant".

Amongst the so-called purple-leaved varieties my own favourite is *C. coggygria* 'Foliis Purpureis'—not to be confused with 'Atropurpureus', which is named for its purplish-pink floral smoke-cloud and not for its foliage colour, which is in fact green. The leaf colour in 'Foliis Purpureis' is less intense than in some of the more vaunted cultivars such as 'Kromhout', 'Notcutt's Variety' (A.G.M. 1930), or 'Royal Purple', which are too nearly akin to beetroot for my taste. Showy though these may be, the quieter purplish-bronze of 'Foliis Purpureis' is to my mind a better mixer, whether indoors or out. (See illustration facing p. 65.)

These do best in hungry soils and the purple ones develop a more intense colour when grown in full sun. They put forth their leaves rather belatedly, in early summer.

In all cases the cut foliage needs boiling and soaking early in the season, but when fully mature it usually requires only a long, cool drink. It objects to moisture-retaining substances.

COTONEASTER horizontalis (F.C.C. 1897, A.G.M. 1925)—
"Herring-bone Cotoneaster"
Shrub; deciduous

This most accommodating shrub will spread its fishbone fans flat on the ground, or upwards or downwards over banks, against walls and rock-faces, thriving in most umpromising soils and situations. I like the pattern of tiny, glossy, dark green leaf and neatly regimented branch best when it is uninterrupted by the little pink flowers or scarlet berries, and even when the branches are bare the skeleton still retains its eye-appeal. The branches are in fact never naked for long, for the leaves begin to appear as early as February and cling on almost until Christmas. It does however seem to me wasteful of the valuable space provided by house or garden walls to plant so tough a shrub in such positions, nor does it usually look its best when flattened against a wall, rarely rising to more than 4 or 5 ft. and leaving the upper wall surface bare. Both in green leaf and in bare branch it provides interesting cutting material, but I value it most of all when preserved to a rich dark brown by glycerining. (See Chapter IX.)

C. horizontalis 'Variegatus'

A charming dwarf form, with tiny grey-green leaves edged with white and flushed deep pink in autumn, *C. horizontalis* 'Variegatus' is similar in habit to that of the type, but the plant is so slow-growing and so much more miniature (rarely more than 2 ft.) that it would not, I think, be of much use to the flower arranger.

CRAMBE maritima—Wild "Seakale"
Hardy perennial

Although *Crambe maritima* grows in the wild in sheer sand and shingle on our native seashores, in cultivation it makes a much handsomer plant when grown in a rich soil, preferably alkaline. In such conditions the large kale-leaves are a beautiful, bloomy grey-blue-green, crinkled and scalloped at the edges and attractively folded along the midrib, so that they are completely reversible as cut material. The utmost vigilance is required to protect this singularly tempting fare from slugs and snails and, having defeated these, one may well find that caterpillars lurking on the undersides of the large leaves will wreak no less havoc in late summer almost before their presence is detected.

I believe that the flowers of the large green-leaved *C. cordifolia* are considered more decorative than the stout, 2½-ft. stems of cream-white bloom of *C. maritima*. Certainly *C. cordifolia* is much more commonly listed; but as foliage for flower arrangement that of the glaucous wild seakale is much the finer of the two. My own feeling is that this is a plant for the cutting border only, having something of a kitchen garden look about it, especially when not in flower, however well it may be grown.

CRYPTOMERIA japonica 'Elegans'*—Form of "Japanese Cedar"
Shrub; deciduous

In adolescence and middle age this is one of the loveliest of conifers, and in particular when its feathery purplish-green summer foliage turns to its winter garb of russet-red. It is fairly fast-growing, making a tall, bushy, broad-based pyramid, and should be planted as a really small specimen owing to its tendency to become top-heavy with age. Careful staking at the time of planting and shelter from the wind should help the roots to gain a firmer anchorage and some clipping and shaping as growth develops may aid stability and neatness. However, it objects to severe pruning and the fact remains that old plants are usually both insecure and untidy. It requires moist, acid soil conditions.

CUPRESSUS macrocarpa 'Lutea'—Form of "Monterey Cypress"
Shrub; evergreen

As in the case of the chamaecyparis, there are so many good species and varieties of cupressus that selection must be governed by personal preference. But the easy, fast-growing, tall, soft yellow pyramid of *C. macrocarpa* 'Lutea' is one of the most effective in the garden landscape, particularly in winter, and it also provides plenty of long-lasting evergreen foliage for cutting. Though this genus is not of cast-iron hardiness I have had no trouble with this variety here and most of them should succeed in all but the very coldest areas. The practice of selling some of these conifers by the foot in certain nurseries may tempt one to extravagance for quick results, but parsimony in this case will usually prove to be true economy, since the root anchorage is much more likely to be effective if one starts with a small, pot-grown infant rather than a large, top-heavy and expensive specimen.

CURTONUS paniculatus (*Antholyza paniculata*) (A.G.M. 1947, A.M. 1956)—"Aunt Eliza", "Giant Montbretia"
Corm

Curtonus paniculatus is still more commonly listed under the now obsolete name of *Antholyza paniculata* and it is also more likely to be classified as a hardy border plant than among bulbous subjects, though it grows from a corm. A small clump quickly multiplies in any conditions. I find this one of the most indispensable of all my non-shrubby plants for cutting. Curving sprays of mahogany-orange florets of giant montbretia design fan out above rigid 4-ft. stems in late summer and are succeeded by seedheads on the same graceful pattern. But it is the leaves which I chiefly prize. The pleated blades come four or five to the stem, rising almost to the height of the flowers, and are about 2 in. wide, tapering to a pointed tip. The colour is a fresh green for most of the season, turning buff and russet from the tip downwards in autumn. In their fresh state they stand exceptionally well in water and they keep much of their autumn colour when dried, but glycerining produces a richer hue and better texture. (See Chapter IX.) The seedheads dry particularly well.

CYCLAMEN—"Sowbread"
Corm

The hardy cyclamen are dwarf species with comparatively small leaves (mostly about 2½ in. in diameter) on somewhat sprawling stems, but some of them are beautifully marked and are useful for small arrangements. Among those with the most interesting leaves are the pink-flowered *C. neapolitanum* (A.M. 1955, A.G.M. 1961, F.C.C. 1967) and its white form, *C. neapolitanum* 'Album' (A.M. 1937, F.C.C. 1959), in which the dark green, heart-shaped leaf is beautifully and very variously marbled with silver and lighter grey-green backed with dull crimson. The foliage appears after the autumn flowering and persists throughout the winter. Of the two, 'Album' possibly has the more decorative leaves.

The early spring-flowering crimson *C. repandum* (A.M. 1952) comes into leaf and flower simultaneously, with dark green, silver-mottled foliage which varies considerably in outline.

All of these are easy, enjoying cool shade and a soil rich in humus, preferably limy, and when conditions are to their liking they will become naturalized under deciduous trees, etc. Dry corms rarely succeed and it is therefore safer to start either from seed or from pot-grown plants. Though more expensive a very few of the latter planted no more than 1 in. deep in spring will rapidly multiply in suitable conditions if allowed to set seed; but it is as well to cover the tiny self-sown seedlings with light

3. *Acanthus spinosus* (left) and *Macleaya microcarpa* 'Kelway's Coral Plume' (right)

4. *Ballota pseudo-dictamnus*

5. *Cotinus coggygria* 'Foliis Purpureis'

twigs or wire-netting to prevent the birds scratching them up before their roots get a grip on the soil.

CYNARA

Hardy or Half-hardy perennial

Cynara cardunculus (A.M. 1957), more familiar to flower arrangers as the "Cardoon", is closely related to the "Globe Artichoke" (*C. scolymus*) and differs from it in appearance only in the more intense silvery-grey-green of the huge, deeply divided leaves and in the prickliness of its large purple thistle-heads. *C. scolymus* is at its best as a foliage plant in the form known as 'Glauca' which, as the name suggests, has more blue-green in the leaf colour than the type. In both species the leaf design is reminiscent of *Acanthus spinosus*, but of a stouter, rougher texture and more gracefully recurved and inclined to fold along the stout midrib. The young foliage, which appears very early in the year, is quite short and compact when it first becomes usable for cutting, but it rapidly reaches several feet in length at maturity.

Both need a well-drained, sunny spot and in particular resent excessive winter damp. They have occasionally survived some less severe winters in this cold garden and are more likely to do so if they are cut down in autumn, surrounded with weathered ashes and mulched with some sort of litter before prolonged frost is likely to set in. In a more average garden climate they seem hardy enough without special protection.

Though one is advised never to soak grey foliage I personally would not trust mature cardoon or artichoke leaves to stand well in water without first boiling and soaking and have never thought that they looked any the worse for it. Certainly they are a sorry sight if they have not been adequately conditioned after cutting, though, somewhat surprisingly, the younger the leaves the more dependable they are as cut material. It pays to bind the stem-ends before using in an arrangement to prevent splitting.

CYTISUS—"Broom"
Shrub; deciduous

Foliage sprays of *Cytisus scoparius*,* the "Common Yellow Broom", are widely used for flower arrangement and a number of garden species and varieties provide a similar framework of tiny leaf and graceful dark green twiggery, but with more sophisticated flowers. Not being much addicted to bicolours, my own favourites are *C.* 'Cornish Cream' (A.M. 1923) and *C. scoparius* 'Sulphureus'* (*pallidus*), the "Moonlight Broom", both of which are self-descriptive large-flowered types, and the earlier *C. x praecox* (A.G.M. 1933), with smaller cream-coloured flowers. But one of the most interesting from a foliage point of view is *C. battandieri*, which is a remarkably untypical broom, both as regards the corn-cob-shaped, pineapple-scented yellow blooms and the rather laburnum-like trefoil leaves of a beautiful silky, silvery-green. This makes a fine, tall wall shrub if trained out fanwise, but without such shelter it is not universally hardy. In a favourable climate it makes long, leafy shoots, covered all over with the same silky hairs, which can well be spared for cutting since some pruning is advisable after flowering.

The *scoparius* varieties are allergic to lime but the rest thrive on any light, dry soil, so long as they are kept regularly cut back to prevent gaunt, top-heavy growth.

Only the soft young foliage shoots of *C. battandieri* need boiling when cut. The slender, twiggy branches of the other species with their tiny leaves can be bound into curves and sinuous shapes and left to soak before using in a fresh condition or being hung up to dry. (See Chapter IX.)

DANAE racemosa (*Ruscus racemosus*) (A.M. 1933)—"Alexandrian Laurel", "Victory Laurel"
Shrub; evergreen

The exceptionally graceful, leafy sprays of *Danae racemosa* are one of the very few attractive foliages to be had from the better kinds of florist and, even then, only during the winter months as a rule, so that it pays to grow one's own, for a year-round supply of this highly desirable evergreen. The slender, arching branches are several feet long, furnished at intervals with side-shoots of 6 in. or so at the lower end, which decrease in length towards the tip of the main branch, producing an airily tapered effect. The leaves are a glossy, darkish green and most elegantly shaped, about 2 in. long and narrowly elliptical, tapering to a slender point. Although this shrub was a great favourite with Gertrude Jekyll and, I believe, with William Robinson, more than half a century ago, it is only now coming into its own again at the hands of the flower arranger after a long period of eclipse. If it is not more commonly grown for cutting today it can only be that it is not widely known to be a hardy garden plant, or possibly because its obsolete generic name of *Ruscus* is mistaken for that of the unlovely *Ruscus aculeatus*, or "Butcher's Broom", which is so forbiddingly stiff and prickly and, even worse, is often dyed in lurid and unnatural colours. The infinitely more charming *Danae racemosa* is one of those semi-rarities for which we flower arrangers should create a demand before it disappears altogether from the nurserymen's catalogues.

It is a shade-loving plant, lifting its graceful wands upwards and outwards from ground level. It will put up with drips beneath trees so long as the soil is moist and preferably peaty, though not necessarily acid. Some sort of pest nibbles disfiguring holes in my young plants, but I have not yet discovered what is to blame for the damage.

The cut sprays last for weeks in water and are beautiful when glycerined. (See Chapter IX.)

DAPHNE odora 'Aureo-marginata'
Shrub; evergreen

It is unusual that a variegated form should be so much hardier and altogether easier than the plain green species from which it derives, but this is fortunately so in the case of *Daphne odora*

'Aureo-marginata', which has glossy, oval, narrowly tapered, 4-in. leaves of a brighter green at the tip end (Green 143A), only very thinly edged with light yellow. The shrub is low-growing and spreading rather than upright, making a broad evergreen mound 3 or 4 ft. high, in which the delicate touches of yellow give an effect not so much of variegation as of a lighter, more cheerful green. It is indifferent as to soil, requiring only to be sheltered from the north and east and a sunny spot, for preference. The fragrant, red-purple flowers sometimes appear before the end of the year, and persist into late spring. (Untried.)

ELAEAGNUS
Shrub; evergreen

E. macrophylla

The genus includes several fair-sized evergreen shrubs of inestimable value for flower arrangement, of which *E. macrophylla* (A.M. 1932) is one of the best, though not to my mind of outstanding garden merit. In full exposure its growth is too dense to yield the long, sinuous sprays we like so much for cutting and the effect is rather a stodgy mass. And when grown in the shade the result is too tentacle-like for beauty, but these lengths are ideal stuff for large flower arrangements, often with a graceful downward sweep ending in a tapering upward flourish. The plant grows fairly fast to 10 ft. or so in such a position, but more slowly in full exposure. The rather orange-buff shoots and leaf-stems provide an effective contrast to the hoary undersides and the greener-grey upper surfaces of the broadly spoon-shaped leaves, which are about 4 in. long, with a wavy margin. Do not be fobbed off with *E. x ebbingei* as your nurseryman's 'nearest'. Some consider it a better garden plant, and admittedly it is hardier; but for flower decoration the leaf shape and habit are nothing like so ornamental as in *macrophylla*.

E. pungens 'Maculata' ('Aureo-variegata') (F.C.C. 1891)

This is even more of a favourite among flower arrangers, as among gardeners, though if I had to choose between this and *macrophylla* for cutting purposes I would probably settle for the latter, for which I can think of no comparable substitute among evergreen foliages of similar colour, size and habit. The shoots of 'Maculata' are more angular than graceful, but the more narrowly oval leaves are edged with two shades of rich green and most strikingly splashed with bright yellow (approximately Yellow 137A) above, with a scaly silver reverse.

E. pungens 'Variegata' and E. pungens 'Dicksonii' ('Dicksonii Aurea')

My impression is that because the alternative name of 'Aureo-variegata' for the foregoing tends to be confused with that of *E. pungens* 'Variegata' the latter form has found its way into a number of gardens more by accident than by design—for a small garden cannot easily accommodate both and the cream-yellow marginal variegation on a rather dull green is much less effective, whether indoors or out, than the broad, vivid yellow streaks and splashes of 'Maculata'. It may be, of course, that 'Variegata' is sometimes intentionally planted in preference to 'Maculata' because of the latter's tendency to revert. But any plain green shoot is so conspicuous among the brilliant variegation that it is a simple matter to cut it out as soon as it is detected. One rarely sees *E. pungens* 'Dicksonii', which bears a closer resemblance to 'Maculata', but with a much lighter green in combination with abundant deep yellow variegation. I find this much more effective than *E. pungens* 'Variegata', but the overall hue lacks the richness of 'Maculata'. All these variegated forms are slower-growing, at any rate to start with, and eventually make smaller shrubs than *macrophylla*.

All are fairly indifferent to soils and situations though, being very slightly tender, they may need some protection in their early years from frost, but not from wind. In all cases any plain green shoots should immediately be cut out. People are sometimes misled by the unusually dull, light brown colour of the new shoots into the belief that their plant is dying. This hue is particularly noticeable in the tips of the young shoots of *E. macrophylla* in spring and should cause no alarm.

All are very long-lasting in water and such varieties as I have tried give interesting results when glycerined. (See Chapter IX.)

ELYMUS arenarius—"Lyme Grass"
Grass

The name *Elymus arenarius* is, I believe, more up-to-date than *Elymus glaucus*, which was easier to remember because of the fine blue-green colour of this tall-growing ornamental grass. Its "grasses", which are glaucous when fresh and dry to a light straw colour, are usually well over 1 ft. long in the head, rising on erect 3-ft. stems adorned with arching ½-in.-wide blue-green ribbons of foliage. It does not often appear in nursery catalogues, though growers who do not specialize in ornamental grasses occasionally list it among their hardy herbaceous plants. But any gardener who grows one of these ornamental clumps will almost certainly be glad to spare a chunk, for they are inclined to be invasive. This grass can also be found in the wild on sand-hills on the seashore in certain parts of Britain.

The leafy shoots need boiling and soaking.

EOMECON chionantha—"Chinese Poppy", "Cyclamen Poppy", "Dawn Poppy"
Hardy perennial; ground cover

Beautiful alike in flower and in leaf, *Eomecon chionantha* has branching spikes of poppy-like white flowers over a long period and long-stalked, large-lobed, heart-shaped, smooth, pale blue-grey-green leaves. In a moist, shady position it has slightly invasive tendencies, though rarely becoming a nuisance. It perhaps looks most appropriate in a woodland setting, but will also grow in full sun in leafy soil.

I have not been able to try the cut foliage in water, but it is so much beloved of flower arrangers that it cannot be difficult. (Untried.)

EPIMEDIUM—"Barrenwort", "Bishop's Hat"
Ground cover; evergreen or semi-evergreen

The epimediums all have beautifully precise, strong-textured, heart-shaped leaves which are tinged with light copper in spring and with darker copper-bronze in autumn, usually persisting thus throughout the winter. The foliage is gracefully disposed on wiry stems, forming dense, low clumps which spread slowly by underground rootstocks, revelling in cool, shady places beneath trees and shrubs. I am not familiar with all the species and varieties available, but my own favourites as foliage plants are the crimson-flowered *Epimedium x rubrum*, with an average height of about 9 in., which develops particularly good autumn and winter leaf colour, and the rather larger *E. x versicolor* 'Sulphureum', of 15 to 18 in., with beautifully tinted young spring foliage. The little pale yellow flower sprays of the latter are much more to my taste than those of *E. x rubrum*.

Although they are all particularly happy in the shade they grow perfectly well in full sun, which tends to enhance the copper foliage colour. I find I was mistaken in describing the epimediums as calcifuge in my earlier book, *Shrub Gardening for Flower Arrangement*, for they are reputed to be unfastidious about soil, as I might perhaps have expected of relatives of the mahonias. It is advisable to remove the old leaf stems in March, both to reveal the pretty little flowers and the newly unfurling foliage in the beauty of youth.

Young foliage needs singeing and soaking and is even then unreliable if too immature when cut, but older leaves need no special treatment. It is also said to glycerine well. (See Chapter IX.)

ERICA—"Heath"
Shrub; mostly ground cover; evergreen

E. arborea alpina* (A.G.M. 1933, A.M. 1962)

Not only one of the hardiest but also one of the most decorative of Tree Heaths, *Erica arborea alpina* forms a fairly compact evergreen pyramid of about 7 ft. in most circumstances, made up of long feathery plumes of foliage of an unusually brilliant green, each topped in spring with large spikes of fragrant ash-white heath-bells. The intense viridic hue of the foliage is most striking in the garden and is a valuable asset to the flower arranger, who can cut plenty in late spring and early summer with a clear conscience, since fairly hard pruning is advisable at that time to aid compactness. It does no harm to cut the flower spikes either, as they should in any case be removed in the pruning process once the blooms are spent. The shrub is far handsomer when grown in full sun, becoming taller and more gangling in shady positions. Though strictly speaking a plant for acid or neutral soils, I have known it to do well enough in only slightly limy conditions. I would not agree that it is of cast-iron hardiness, as is sometimes claimed, but it has survived all but the severest winters here with little damage, and even though it was split to matchwood and down to ground level by the cruel *verglas* of the 1962–3 winter it broke afresh from the base and eventually built up a new framework of dense green plumage.

E. cinerea*

Although the low-growing types of heath are not on the whole as useful to the flower arranger as the heathers (callunas), with their stouter, stronger foliage growth, there are several excellent garden decorators, with attractive year-round leaf colour which is often intensified in winter. The summer-flowering *E. cinerea* species includes 'Ann Berry' (1 ft.) which is highly recommended for its bright yellow leaf colour (of which I have only seen one tiny plant); 'Golden Drop', with prostrate but dense copper-bronze summer leaves intensifying to cinnamon-red in winter; and 'Golden Hue', which is more erect (1½ ft.) and is yellower in summer and red-tinged in winter. The last two I do grow and to my mind their reluctance to produce their mauve-pink flowers is a further recommendation, since these spoil rather than enhance the foliage effect.

What to Grow, and How

Like the heathers, all types of heath with colourful foliage need full sun to do themselves justice. The *E. cinerea* and other summer-flowering varieties also appreciate an annual clipping over in spring, just before the new growth starts.

ERYNGIUM
Hardy perennial

Many of the eryngiums are valued for their precisely chiselled steel-blue "flowers", but there are some whose leaves are also sufficiently ornamental to be of interest to the flower arranger.

E. bourgatii

The comparatively dwarf *E. bourgatii* is one of the most silvery in all its parts, with small flower cones surrounded by a fierce but ornate dog-collar of long, sharply-toothed involucral bracts, on 18-in. stems, above a clump of leaves of such complicated design that they might have been fashioned from wire-netting, if not from crumpled barbed wire. The spiny tangle which makes up a leaf is roughly triangular, about 3 in. long with a base about 2½ in. wide, and these too are silver-green, with white veining in all directions.

E. variifolium

The most striking eryngium foliage I know is that of *E. variifolium* and it is perhaps significant that the specific name refers to the leaves rather than to the flowers. Not that the flowers are unworthy of attention. These sit in a large ruff of delicately fashioned, spiky bracts on 2-ft. stems above the broad, basal clumps of glossy dark green leaves strikingly veined with white, rather on the lines of *Silybum marianum* in this respect. But in this case the strong-textured foliage is of an elongated heart-shape, with a scalloped border.

These are not fussy as to soil, but dislike parched conditions.

ERYTHRONIUM
Bulb

To most gardeners the nodding, starry flowers of the erythroniums are their objective, the beauty of their leaves being only incidental; but almost all have handsomely mottled foliage which is a separate delight. The commonest of all, *E. dens-canis* ("Dog's Tooth Violet"), which comes in a variety of flower colours, is as good as any in this respect. The leaves are bronze mottled with vivid jade green and overlaid with an almost metallic sheen, broadly lanceolate, upwards of 6 in. long by 2½ in. wide, borne singly on short stems. The slightly taller *E. revolutum* (*californicum*) 'White Beauty' provides a different colour combination with foliage of light green spotted with cream, to which is added the most exquisite cream-white flower with a yellow centre in April or May—slightly later, that is, than the "Dog's Tooth Violet". The leaf is less spectacular than the other, but the flower makes the combination irresistible.

For plants with such an air of superiority the erythroniums are unexpectedly easy to grow and will readily become naturalized in suitable conditions. All appreciate a moist, but well-drained, peaty or woodland type of soil and partial shade. They are usually grown from tubers planted in September and are easily increased from seed.

The leaves are long-lasting in water.

ESCALLONIA x iveyi (A.M. 1926)
Shrub; evergreen

Even if one were to discount its fine, fragrant white flower panicles in late summer *Escallonia x iveyi* would, I think, deserve a place as a foliage plant in its own right. It makes an upright-habited evergreen shrub of 8 ft. or more, with very dark green, glossy leaves considerably larger and broader than is usual for the genus (often 2 in. long by 1 in. or more wide). These look something like wavy camellia leaves in miniature and grow on long shoots. I do not deny its slightly tender constitution, but my seven-year-old plant has made rapid growth and has come more or less unscathed through some pretty severe winters here without protection other than that afforded by neighbouring shrubs. Nevertheless a wall position may be necessary in the coldest areas and some shelter is advisable in almost any circumstances.

The cut foliage is very long-lasting and also glycerines well. (See Chapter IX.)

EUCALYPTUS
Tree or Shrub; evergreen

There are about half a dozen species of eucalyptus which are said to be hardy in most parts of Britain and several others which might well succeed in the milder areas, but my own experience is limited to *E. gunnii* (A.M. 1950), known in Australia as the "Cider Gum", and *E. perriniana*, both of which are hardy species providing some of the most beautiful of all garden foliage for flower arrangement, provided that a well coloured specimen is selected in the first instance. In the case of *gunnii* the juvenile leaves are small and roundish and of an intensely silver-blue tinged with pink (amounting to near-lilac in effect) and the larger, adult leaves are more elongated, narrowly ovate or slightly sickle-shaped and of a duller but still highly attractive blue-grey-green. *E. perriniana* has even more fascinating juvenile foliage, of fairly similar colouring to that of *gunnii*, but considerably larger and consisting of disc-shapes encircling the shoots at intervals and graduated in size like a string of beads. The adult leaves are longer, more pendulous and of a bluer-green than those of *gunnii* and are often purple-tinged. Both produce a fuzz of cream flowers in July or August.

As regards cultivation there is so much to be said that I propose to mention only some of the most essential points and to refer you for further information to the expert and detailed article entitled *An Introduction to Some Garden Eucalypts* by Mr. R. C. Barnard—a former specialist grower and authority on the subject—published in the *R.H.S. Journal* in 1966 (Vol. XCI, parts 5, 6 and 7) or to the second edition of the Supplement to the *R.H.S. Dictionary of Gardening*. Other helpful literature on the cultivation of hardy species, including an informative *List of Eucalypts for Planting in the British Isles* and a leaflet of detailed planting instructions, is issued free of charge by Mr. A. J. T. Bayles, who bought the Grey Timbers Nursery from Mr. Barnard in 1967. Both growers stress that since eucalypts occur in nature over such a wide range of altitude and climate, only plants grown from seed obtained from high altitudes subject to frosts can be expected to succeed in British gardens, even among those regarded as hardy species.

Other important points to bear in mind about cultivation are that really young plants grow on much faster than large ones; that they should be planted out in early summer, with the top of the root-ball 2 in. below ground level and must not be allowed to dry out during their earliest years; that firm staking of these fast-growing subjects is important to prevent wind-rocking; that manuring and other forms of feeding are a mistake because they make the top growth outstrip the root anchorage; that some protection from frost and freezing winds is advisable in a cold district during a plant's first winter; and that they are unhappy in wet soils and shady sites. This brings me to the question of acid or alkaline conditions, which appears to be debatable. Whereas Messrs. Hillier state that they have found almost all species to be calcifuge, Mr. Barnard says that they will grow in acid or alkaline soil conditions. I can only add that one of the most prosperous young specimens of *E. gunnii* that I know grows in a very slightly limy garden swept by salt sea winds.

As cut material only the soft young shoots need boiling and soaking. The mature foliage may also be air-dried or glycerined. (See Chapter IX.)

EUONYMUS

Some of the deciduous members of the genus are noted for their autumn colour, but those that concern us here are the evergreen species, which are of more permanently ornamental foliage value.

E. fortunei 'Gracilis' (*radicans* 'Variegatus')
Shrub or Climber; evergreen

This makes a dense 2-ft. bush when grown in the open but performs a surprising conjuring trick when grown against a wall or solid fence, climbing quite quickly to 10 ft. or more and clothing a large area, to which it clings by aerial roots, like ivy, requiring little support. It has small, oval evergreen leaves which are of a rather bright green, broadly margined or streaked with cream in spring and fading later to a greyer green and white, often becoming attractively flushed with pink or purple in winter. It is indifferent as to soil or aspect, but I am of the opinion that the winter flush is more pronounced in a dry, exposed position. The rather similar *E. fortunei* 'Silver Queen' is a beautiful form with bigger leaves, but it is slightly tender by comparison with 'Gracilis'.

No special conditioning is usually required, but if cut sprays show an inclination to wilt, boil and soak.

E. japonicus
Shrub; evergreen

The taller *Euonymus japonicus* so often used for seaside plantings has a number of effective variegated forms. Among the most vivid yellows are 'Aureo-pictus', which has an unfortunate tendency to revert to plain green, and 'Ovatus Aureus' ('Aureovariegatus') which is only seen at its colourful best in a sunny position. Those with cream or white markings, such as 'Albomarginatus' or 'Macrophyllus Albus' ('Latifolius Variegatus') are particularly elegant but seem to be less hardy than the rest. What a pity it is that so little imagination has gone to the naming of these varieties which all sound so confusingly similar! The variegated forms are less tall-growing than the type, averaging around 5 ft.

EUPHORBIA—"Spurge"

Though it may be argued that 'leaf-like bracts' are classified as foliage, for schedule definition purposes, by the National Association of Flower Arrangement Societies, I prefer to limit my own terms of reference to foliage proper, not only for considerations of space, but also to steer clear of the highly controversial question as to what constitutes a 'leaf-like bract'; for I cannot willingly subscribe to the inclusion of poinsettia (*Euphorbia pulcherrima*), for instance, in a 'foliage arrangement', though the scarlet bracts which encircle the tiny flowers in a petal-like manner are officially considered to be 'leaf-like' and thus admissible in a Foliage Class. Nevertheless the garden euphorbias have so much to commend them as foliage plants for flower arrangement in the strictest sense that I find myself describing as many as eight in the present context, even though the majority of these are grown primarily for their decorative bracts, which we loosely refer to as "flowers".

E. characias, E. sibthorpii and E. veneta (*wulfenii*) (A.M. 1905)
Hardy perennials; evergreen

The reason for my dealing with these three together is not only that their tall, handsome foliage shoots are almost identical, but also that there is considerable difficulty in distinguishing between these species, as far as the make-up of the "flower" is concerned. The general opinion seems to be that *veneta* is most nearly all lime-yellow and that *characias* is maroon-eyed, but some of the experts are unwilling to give so definite a ruling. On visiting the University Botanical Gardens at Oxford, where I had hoped to sort out the confusion, I was assured that things are not as simple as this, contradictory traits often being combined in a single plant, thus making hard and fast definitions impossible. I was however able to ascertain that *veneta* is usually the most massive, its variety *sibthorpii* a close second and *characias* slightly shorter and more compact than the other two. To add still further to the confusion it seems that we must now learn to use the specific name *veneta* for what we have hitherto known as *E. wulfenii*. And here I must stress that the pundits at the Botanical Gardens were somewhat shocked that I should be recommending any of these for cutting purposes, since they tell me that the juice is a deadly poison and may also cause blindness. My own feeling is that having given this solemn warning it is wiser to include these euphorbias than to omit them, since flower arrangers are unlikely to renounce such splendid material and at least they will now be aware of the risk involved. We all delight to use the flowers, but the massive bottle-brush leaf-stems finished with an irregular terminal rosette make an unusually handsome contrast of form in a winter foliage arrangement.

I believe the two kinds I grow to be *veneta* and *characias*, or hybrids between the two, and neither appears to be 100 per cent hardy in my cold garden, thriving best in a sunny bed at the foot of a house-wall in this district. They seed themselves freely and hybridize among themselves, which adds still further to the confusion as well as to the interest attaching to these large-headed types. The progeny should be transplanted when very small, because bigger plants are reluctant movers.

Singe and soak.

E. lathyris or lathyrus—"Caper Spurge", "Mole Plant"
Hardy biennial

There is some question as to whether the accepted specific name, *lathyrus*, which is Greek for vetch and arose from a slip of the pen, should be discarded for *lathyris*, which does mean euphorbia; but meanwhile I gather that we are at liberty to do as we please about it. This is a biennial spurge with narrow, rather glaucous green leaves about 4 in. long with a conspicuous grey-white midrib, which stand out horizontally and are spaced with geometrical precision all the way up the erect 3-ft. stems.

The latter finally branch out at the top into sprays of greener arrow-head bracts, which are also particularly useful for cutting.

Once established *E. lathyris* will continue to seed itself with abandon for ever after and will succeed anywhere. The growth is however much more luxuriant in a rich soil, where it takes on the appearance of a tree in miniature. This, too, is better transplanted when quite small, if transplanting is necessary. I cannot personally vouch for its reputation as a mole deterrent, but I understand that it is not without foundation.

Singe and soak.

E. marginata—"Ghost Weed", "Snow-on-the-Mountain"
Half-hardy annual

This attractive little variegated spurge needs a warmer garden climate than mine to succeed. In favourable circumstances it should become a bushy 2 ft. or so, forming neat rosettes of pale green leaves veined and edged with white and further adorned with petal-like bracts in late summer.

Singe.

E. myrsinites (A.M. 1965)
Hardy perennial; ground cover; evergreen

Though frequently described as grey, the curious, scale-like, fleshy foliage of *E. myrsinites* is in fact of an intensely glaucous hue, contrasting delightfully with the acid lime-yellow of the flat, bracted flower heads borne at the end of trailing shoots in spring. If you are unfamiliar with this intriguing plant picture a globe artichoke in which the calyx composed of overlapping scales is elongated to a trailing, blue-green sausage-form of about 2½ in. in diameter, like a fleshy segment of "Monkey Puzzle". (See illustrating facing p. 81.) It might well be mistaken for a hothouse succulent plant, but it is by no means difficult. The foliage shoots of one season produce the flower heads of the following year and die off after flowering.

6. The spring foliage of *Colchicum autumnale*

7. *Choisya ternata*

8. *Euphorbia myrsinites*

It needs a position in full sun and its creeping habit makes it particularly suitable for crevices in dry walls and rock faces.
Singe.

E. robbiae (A.M. 1968)
Hardy perennial, ground cover; evergreen

Similar to, but handsomer than the wild spurge, *E. robbiae* is a great favourite of mine, not only for its spires of yellow-green bracts on 12- to 18-in. stems in spring, but equally for the neatly constructed, flower-like rosettes of narrow, very dark green leaves on 9-in. stems which precede them and from which the flowers spring. They somewhat resemble those of *Pachysandra terminalis*, but are more compact and of a darker green and more leathery texture, providing first-class evergreen ground cover in sun or shade. This spurge spreads slowly by underground stems and will grow almost anywhere, but the more humus there is in the soil the handsomer the results.
Singe.

E. sikkimensis (A.M. 1930)
Hardy perennial

E. sikkimensis has flat heads of acid yellow bracts throughout the summer which I esteem most highly for cutting, but long before this the emerging shoots in early spring delight us with their short, glistening, light scarlet pokers which Mr. Will Ingwersen has aptly compared to ruby glass. The colour suffuses the main stem and leaves for a time as the shoots unfurl, but the translucent ruby hue gradually fades to red-bronze in the stem and to green with pink or red veining in the leaf as this matures. When the colour is at its best the young shoots are not more than about 8 in. long, but the ultimate height is about 4 ft., with a further bonus of good foliage colour in the autumn. I find sunshine and a rich, moist soil make for better flowering than shady spots.

The tender-looking young shoots are remarkably well-behaved in water after singeing.

F
81

Finally, let me remind you that all trace of the clinging, sticky juice of the euphorbias should be meticulously washed from hands, secateurs, etc., for safety's sake, immediately after handling such material.

FAGUS sylvatica—"Beech"
Tree; deciduous

Anyone who has travelled the A272 motor road between Petersfield and Winchester when the trees are in leaf will be familiar with an imposing avenue-like roadside planting of large "Copper Beeches" and will perhaps have been struck by the wide variation in the intensity of the leaf colour among individual trees. The explanation is, I think, that these are not all one and the same familiar "Copper Beech". There are in fact quite a number of different purple- and copper-hued varieties, of which the commonest is not the "Copper" but the "Purple" beech, *Fagus sylvatica* 'Purpurea', which starts with a coppery look in spring but develops a very dark mahogany-purple hue as the foliage matures. The true "Copper Beech" is the beautiful and less widely planted *F. sylvatica* 'Cuprea', which has a much more copper leaf colour of a lighter tint. Amongst other beeches with colourful foliage is one called 'Tricolor' with pink and white tips to the copper-coloured leaves, which may intrigue the flower arranger if not the gardener.

All the beeches are fine, stately subjects for chalk soils in particular, but over-large and spreading (both above and below ground) for the average-sized garden. The coloured foliage types are most effective in sunny positions.

Mature leaves may be pressed or glycerined. (See Chapter IX.)

Boil and soak, particularly in the case of immature foliage, which is inclined to be difficult.

x FATSHEDERA lizei—"Fatheaded Lizzie"
Shrub or Climber; evergreen

This plant is the result of an inspired cross between *Fatsia japonica* and *Hedera hibernica* (a large-leaved ivy), combining some of the most outstanding traits of both. In particular the size and pattern of the leaf are precisely half-way between those of each parent. Though often grown as a house plant it makes an attractive, rather loose-habited evergreen garden shrub for shady places or will grow as a climber against a wall. The plain green form is at least as hardy as its parents, but the very decorative *x Fatshedera lizei* 'Variegata' is not tough enough for outdoor use except in mild localities or in a specially sheltered spot in a less favoured garden.
Soak.

FATSIA japonica *(Aralia sieboldii)* (A.M. 1966)—*(Not* "Castor Oil Plant")
Shrub; evergreen

The exceptionally large, palmate foliage of *Fatsia japonica* is indispensable for flower arrangement on a big scale and as an evergreen garden ornament it has a sculptural quality which makes it specially suitable for associating with masonry, as in courtyard plantings. The seven-lobed leaves are shaped rather like those of the fig except that the tips of the lobes are pointed, and the colour ranges from a fresh, glossy light green in youth to a more matt-surfaced, duller green with age, finally fading to pale yellow when about to fall. The size ranges from a mere 5 in. in diameter to as much as 15 in. and the length of the leaf stem varies in about the same proportion. *F. japonica* makes a sturdy-looking shrub of about 8 ft. in favourable garden climates, but in my experience it is not as hardy as is often claimed. It is commonly recommended as a plant for a shady position, but except in the milder seaside gardens and in warm gardens inland it is likely to need the protection of a wall or other form of

83

shelter; and in the coldest areas I find that it does better if it get sunshine for at least half the day, preferring a west rather than a north or east wall. Even the hardest of winters may not kill it outright, but if a young plant has been badly cut back when grown against a shady wall the new growth may come too late in the following summer to harden off before another winter overtakes it. I have not seen it in bloom in this neighbourhood, which suggests that the ivory flower clusters in October to November followed by black berries are only borne freely in areas more temperate than this.

Fatsia japonica 'Variegata' is a delightful form in which the light green leaves have a cream-white margin broadening to more conspicuous splodges at the tips of the lobes. But this is no shrub for a cold climate. Like the variegated fatshedera it is usually sold as a house plant, but I know one specimen which makes a good living and flowers freely in a bed at the foot of a warm house wall in Lymington, so those with milder gardens need not be afraid to try it.

Fresh fatsia leaves last interminably in water and even the dying ones retain their soft yellow complexion in an arrangement for several days before they are overtaken by grey-black desiccation. It is one of the handsomest of all subjects for glycerine treatment. (See Chapter IX.)

FERNS, Hardy
Hardy perennials; mostly ground cover

Hardy ferns are a specialist subject in themselves and one with which I could wish to be more familiar, for many of the less common species and varieties make extraordinarily beautiful material for floral decoration, from tightly furled fiddlehead to mature frond. The eight which immediately follow are my own particular favourites among the limited number with which I am familiar.

What to Grow, and How

Matteuccia struthiopteris (*Onoclea germanica, Struthiopteris germanica*)—"Ostrich Feather Fern", "Shuttlecock Fern"
Deciduous

Both the English names are in this case well founded on fact. The leaf, at maturity, is prettily crimped and waved much like an ostrich feather, but it is when each segment of the frond is still curled into a tight little ball or crozier of its own along the young, arching stem that I find *Matteuccia struthiopteris* most enchanting. The name, "Shuttlecock Fern", is descriptive of its habit of growth which is too upright to serve as ground cover, applying to the arrangement of the fronds which spring upwards and outwards from the base in an expanding circle. I hope to persuade this beautiful, moisture-loving fern to feel at home in my waterless garden so as to have my own supply for cutting and I understand that it is not unduly difficult in a moist loam or leafy soil and light shade. (Untried, but I expect singeing would be necessary.)

Onoclea sensibilis—"American Oak Fern", "Bead Fern" of North America, "Sensitive Fern"
Deciduous

The broad, pale green fronds of *Onoclea sensibilis* contrast attractively with their reddish stems and are of an exceptionally tidy pinnate design with marginal indentation. The curious bead-like clusters of spores borne separately on stiff, erect stems are perhaps as great an attraction to the flower arranger as the finely fashioned fronds, which vary in length from 1 to 2½ ft. A kind friend who used to let me loose in her water garden full of lush variegated iris, rodgersias and ferns has, alas, long since moved house, but I still cherish an apparently indestructible store of the decorative beaded spikes picked many years ago and now dried to assorted mahogany and nigger-brown hues. This fern is happiest in moist woodland or stream-side plantings in a neutral or slightly acid soil, where it quickly increases by underground runners. It will tolerate full sun and ordinary garden positions provided its roots are kept fairly constantly moist.

85

Osmunda regalis*—"Royal Fern"
Deciduous

This has the most majestic vital statistics of any hardy British fern, with enormous but well-proportioned bipinnate leaves of a fresh green which unfurl from shaggy, rust-brown croziers. A proportion of the fronds bear curious "flowers" or fertile panicles at their tips, which turn from green to brown at maturity, unfolding from the upright into lacy scrolls and arabesques. Though usually seen in a waterside setting this noble fern will make do in waterless gardens with plenty of moisture at the roots in summer, in a peaty, lime-free soil. But to me it never looks quite so right as when grown on the margin of a pond, lake or stream and it excels itself in such surroundings, particularly alongside running, rather than stagnant, water. (See illustration facing page 128.)

Mature fronds stand well if boiled and soaked.

Polystichum setiferum 'Divisilobum' (*Aspidium setiferum* 'Divisilobum')—Form of "Soft Shield Fern"
Semi-evergreen

This is quite one of the prettiest of hardy ferns, with shaggy, rusty-stemmed, light green fronds of the most delicately patterned lacework. (See illustration facing p. 145.) The habit is more spreading than erect, with a height of about 2 ft., though the fronds themselves may measure a good deal more than this, when grown in cool, moist soil—preferably acid—and in a partially shaded spot. It has a curious method of reproducing itself by means of little bulbils which form minute plants upon the mature fronds along the main stem, and the plant can be propagated by growing these on. There are other somewhat similar and singularly decorative forms of polystichum which are not known to me by name but are well worth exploring for flower arrangement.

This one needs only to be singed.

Next in my affections come our native Hart's Tongue and a hardy Maidenhair.

Adiantum pedatum (F.C.C. 1884)—Form of "Maidenhair Fern"
Deciduous

There are two species of outdoor Maidenhair Fern in commerce, *A. pedatum* and *A. venustum*. The former is the hardiest member of the genus, with lacy fronds on rather a different pattern from those of the house plant, composed of ten to fourteen sprays of little leaf-blobs, or pinnules, arranged fanwise and poised more or less horizontally at the top of the wiry main stem, which varies from 1 to 2 ft. The bronze tinge of the young shoots is an additional attraction. Though an acid soil is not essential it is certainly preferable. In a cool, moist, shady position this species is not specially difficult, but the dwarfer and less branched *A. venustum*, which more closely resembles the indoor type, is only likely to succeed in sheltered gardens, being much more frost-tender in its early years.

Phyllitis scolopendrium (*Scolopendrium vulgare*)—"Hart's
Tongue Fern"
Evergreen

Our native Hart's Tongue is especially welcome in that the entire, narrow strap-shape is in such marked contrast to the much-divided design predominant among the commonest of hardy ferns. The obligingly reversible 18-in. fronds are a glossy bright green on the one side and a matt light green on the other, with a ladder-pattern back at maturity formed by decorative ginger-brown spores. In the type plant the leaf margin is only slightly undulating, whereas the rather dwarfer *P. scolopendrium* 'Undulatum' exaggerates this trait into a highly ornamental frilling. But the latter is fussier about shelter than the species, which will make do almost anywhere. If grown in sunshine it needs more moisture than in cool, shady spots, where the fronds will be longer and of a deeper green. Beware of slugs, which make nonsense of the epithet 'entire' as applied to the leaf margin.

87

Athyrium filix-foemina—"Lady Fern" and Dryopteris filix-mas
—"Male Fern"
Deciduous

Finally, two of the commonest of all, the "Lady Fern" and
the "Male Fern", keep each other company in vast numbers in
my garden, which sounds a very sociable arrangement, but they
are just good friends and nothing more, each being of a separate
genus. The dryopteris has bipinnate fronds up to 3 ft. long by
1 ft. broad at the lower end and the athyrium is somewhat similar but more lacily attired, as befits the lady. Indeed she is quite
a beauty although so commonplace. In this rather sunless garden
both seed themselves everywhere, including arid chinks in dry
walls, and sometimes produce odd forms with crested tips,
which, I think, do nothing to add to their attractions. If the
unwanted seedlings are not rooted out from chinks between
rocks, etc., in early youth, it often becomes a major operation
to get rid of them at a later stage.

As regards conditioning, where no special instructions have
been given above, singe and soak, including young croziers,
and avoid the use of moisture-retaining substances. Troublesome varieties may respond to stem-tipping. Most may be preserved by pressing or glycerining. (See Chapter IX.)

FOENICULUM vulgare—"Common Fennel"
Hardy perennial or annual

The Common Fennel, with its 6- to 8-ft. stems and delicate
wisps of gossamer greenery, will be familiar to many as a culinary herb, but for decorative purposes the dark-foliaged forms
are usually more popular. These are listed under *Foeniculum*,
Ferula and Fennel, with such varietal names as 'Purpureum',
'Giant Bronze', *officinale*, 'Black Form', 'Smoky' or 'Dark
Form' and appear to vary in colour from copper to almost
black.

If the lacy yellow flower umbels are removed in the first year
the plant will behave as a perennial, but it will in any case re-

main with you year after year if allowed to seed itself, which it does with abandon, particularly in light soil and sunshine. The latter is also necessary for good leaf colour. Only the smaller seedlings transplant satisfactorily.

My experience, which is limited to borrowed cut pieces of 'Purpureum', was disappointing, but flagging may have been due to immaturity at the time of cutting, in May, since it is widely grown for flower arrangement. As far as I remember I boiled only; perhaps I should also have soaked.

FUCHSIA, Variegated Forms

I have found eight or more different permutations and combinations of names for variegated fuchsias in nursery lists and have tried hard to obtain expert information on the distinctions and duplications among these, without very definite results; but my impression is that all these names cover only three, or possibly four, variegated forms. There seems to be most general agreement regarding *F. gracilis* 'Variegata', which is the gayest of the foliage varieties. Though comparatively dwarf it has quite large leaves generously variegated with deep cream-yellow and some white on light green, with a lovely coral-pink flush spreading up from the reddish stems to suffuse the lower half of the leaf in youth. The combination is delightful in itself and makes an excellent foliage foil to the vivid scarlet and purple flowers.

For foliage of a different hue there are one or two of a more smoky overall plum-purple in effect. The one which seems the most useful for cutting came to me as *F. magellanica* 'Tricolor', which I believe to be the same as 'Versicolor'. The latter kind derive from comparatively small-leaved and small-flowered types, but from this one it is possible to cut quite long shoots of finely tapered foliage in which the soft grey-green is merged with reddish-purple, with only an occasional streak of bright or light pink on the leaf margin. In view of the confusion over nomenclature among the growers it would be as well to inspect plants in the nursery before purchase if possible.

The hardy fuchsias, in which these are included, need to be

rather deeply planted and to be kept well watered in summer. Slugs must be kept at bay when the new growth is due to emerge above ground in spring and in cold districts the protection of a shovelful of weathered ashes above the roots, after the top growth has died down, will help them through the winter.

Boil and soak briefly.

GALAX aphylla*—"Fairies' Wand", "Wand Plant"
Ground cover; evergreen

It may seem surprising that a plant recommended for the beauty of its foliage bears the specific name *aphylla*, meaning 'without leaves'; but in this case it undoubtedly derives from the erect, leafless flower stems which rise to about 1 ft. above the low clumps of foliage, bearing close-packed spikes of pinkish-cream florets in midsummer. These evidently inspired the nicknames too. Nevertheless this is pre-eminently a foliage plant—and evergreen at that.

A native of eastern North America, *Galax aphylla* is fairly uncommon, even in gardens, over here, though flower arrangers in the U.S.A. are able to buy bunches of the tough, shiny, circular leaves from the florist. The serrated and sometimes lightly scalloped leaf margin becomes broadly banded with crimson when exposed to sunlight and intensifies in colour in winter, whereas plants in dense shade usually remain a constant green which deepens as the leaf ages. Size varies according to growing conditions, the largest leaves, which are about 5 in. in diameter, with wiry stalks of similar length, occurring in dense shade and in moist woodland soils—which must be lime-free.

Though galax revels in such conditions in the shrub borders it spreads only slowly and I have never found it invasive. Even though the leaves will be smaller in more exposed positions it is worth while to grow a plant or two in partial sun for the sake of the more vivid foliage colour. In her book, *Favourite Flowers*, Mrs. Spry gave the impression that this is a difficult plant which she had no hope of growing 'down south' even though, as she said, she might supply the lime-free soil. My own experience is that, given the latter condition, it is singularly obliging and trouble-free. Slugs will spoil the look of this charming evergreen ground-coverer if they are given the opportunity, at the same time rendering the leaves unusable for cutting; and if scraps of vegetation are allowed to lie rotting on the leaf surfaces they are also likely to be disfigured by brown patches.

The leaves are singularly long-lasting when cut and mature ones glycerine well. (See Chapter IX.)

GALEOBDOLON luteum 'Variegatum' (*Lamium galeobdolon* 'Variegatum')—Form of "Yellow Archangel"
Hardy perennial; ground cover; evergreen or semi-evergreen

This yellow-flowered "Dead Nettle" has charmingly variegated, somewhat glistening leafy trails in a mixture of silver and light green with a central area of bronze which becomes accentuated as the leaf ages. The shape is broadly ovate with a serrated edge and the average length of a leaf about 2½ in. It is a particularly obliging form of ground cover for dry shade and similar difficult conditions, but although its preference is for a moist root-run it also does well in full sun, which produces a more attractive yellower-green background hue in the leaf. Its rapid-spreading habit is a virtue when required to cover awkward spots where nothing else will grow, but condemns it as invasive if so placed that it may smother any less aggressive plant within reach. The long, more or less evergreen trails of prettily marbled foliage, which keep their good looks or even excel themselves in winter, provide excellent material for cutting.

The Yellow Archangel also exists in a yellow- and bronze-leaved form called *Galeobdolon luteum* 'Aureo-variegatum', which is similarly rampant.

GAULTHERIA shallon*
Shrub; ground cover; evergreen

Of the many species of gaultheria this is one of the two most familiar and has bolder foliage than *procumbens*, the other most commonly grown. It is a shrubby, ground-covering evergreen of dense habit for lime-free gardens, with broadly ovate or slightly heart-shaped, rough-textured, leathery leaves of a very dark green often tinged with maroon, measuring about 3 by 2 in., beneath which hide the pinkish-white flower bells in May and, later, edible purple fruits. The leaf shoots arch out more or less horizontally for much of their length, thus providing pleasing shapes for cutting—so long as the slugs are kept at bay.

In cool, moist, peaty woodland soil and partial or dense shade it is said to grow to as much as 6 ft., but in this poor, sandy soil it lacks the moisture to make such rampant, thicket-type growth, rarely exceeding 2½ to 3 ft. and spreading slowly, whereas in ideal conditions it may become a nuisance.

The foliage lasts interminably in water and glycerines well. (See Chapter IX.)

GINKGO biloba (*Salisburia adiantifolia*)—"Maidenhair Tree" *Tree; deciduous*

It would be difficult to point to a conifer of more recent introduction which surpasses in beauty this most ancient of living fossils, said to have survived in its present form for a million centuries. It is aptly nicknamed, for the foliage pattern bears a distinct resemblance to a much magnified maidenhair fern. The deciduous, ribbed apple-green leaves are highly un-conifer-like, being shaped like a 2-in. fan split in half through the centre almost to the base and they turn to a soft yellow in autumn. (The illustration facing p. 96 shows a young specimen.) The tree grows fairly erect in its early years but becomes spreading and roughly pyramidal in time, requiring many years to reach about 70 ft., with a 40-ft. spread. It also exists in a columnar form, *G. biloba* 'Fastigiata', which would no doubt be easier to accommodate in a small garden.

The ginkgo enjoys any deep, moist but well-drained loam, but will make do with lesser benefits so long as it is not waterlogged, which it abhors. (Untried.)

GLYCERIA maxima 'Variegata' (*aquatica*, or *aquatilis*, 'Variegata')—Form of native "Reed Grass"
Grass; evergreen or semi-evergreen

I should not expect to succeed with an ornamental grass which is really happiest with its feet in some inches of water; but encouraged by the very passable appearance of a 2-ft. clump planted in light, sandy soil, in full sun and a long way from any water in a Surrey nursery, I am trying it at the bottom of my garden, where the soil is heavier and less parched than elsewhere on the steep slope. Obviously it will not be especially lush; but the white, yellow and green pin-striping of the comparatively broad, strap-shaped leaves, which add a tinge of purplish-pink to their make-up in spring and autumn, is decorative even in the far from favourable circumstances of this waterless garden. It should reach 2 or 3 ft. and where it is well suited it may spread to become troublesome, but I doubt whether I need worry. It almost disappears here in winter, but is none the worse for this once the temperature begins to rise in spring.

Boil and soak.

GRISELINIA
Shrub; evergreen

As may be deduced from the specific epithet, *Griselinia littoralis* is an ideal subject for coastal gardens, where it is quite unharmed by salt sea winds; but it is slightly tender farther inland except in the milder areas. It is much used for evergreen seaside hedges, though so decorative a shrub seems wasted in such a role, growing to 30 ft. if left unpruned. As a foliage plant the laxer-habited female is preferable to the male, having larger, broadly oval leaves of an unusually light yellowish-green (approximately Yellow-Green 144B), which are tougher-textured that the light colour and satiny finish would suggest. The yellow bark of the leaf shoots is an additional attraction.

How unfortunate it is that variegation is so often synonymous with lack of stamina, for in gardens where *G. littoralis* may only just succeed the most decorative of the variegated sorts, *G. lucida* 'Variegata', almost certainly will not. Its broadly spoon-shaped light green leaves have a gay border of light yellow which makes this even more attractive than the hardier, green-leaved *G. littoralis*. There is also a variegated cv. of the latter species, which is hardier than *lucida*, called *G. littoralis* 'Variegata', but the leaf margin and striation are almost white and correspondingly less effective, in my estimation.

I have only tried cut foliage of *G. littoralis*, which needs no special conditioning. Short pieces also glycerine well. (See Chapter IX.)

HEBE (*Veronica*)—Shrubby "Speedwell"
Shrub; evergreen

The shrubby evergreen species of veronica have for a long time been separately classified under the generic name of *Hebe*, despite which almost all the nursery catalogues persist in listing them as *Veronica*. What, I think, is more reprehensible is the failure of some growers to warn the unwary customer of the tender nature of a number of these and all manner of other plants of doubtful hardiness, which are made to seem so infinitely desirable but would in fact be doomed to failure in the average garden climate.

Hebe x andersonii 'Variegata'

H. x andersonii 'Variegata' is one that should carry such a warning. This is one of the large-flowered, large-leaved types, with spikes of light violet in late summer and glossy foliage attractively edged and streaked with cream. It grows to 4 or 5 ft. where climate permits, making a most ornamental foliage plant for coastal gardens in particular, but certainly not for cold ones. (Untried.)

H. armstrongii (A.M. 1925)

I have written so much and so often about *Hebe armstrongii*

94

that there can be little left to say! Other people's 'musts' are usually a bit of a bore, I know, but to me this is a singularly beautiful thing. Not only is its yellowish-olive-khaki (predominantly Yellow-Green 152A) unique as a foliage colour for floral decoration, but in the garden it provides a striking contrast to silvers, coppers, blue-greens and other foliage hues; and in winter the sight of these neat hummocks lit by wintry sunshine to a gleaming old gold is to me far more heart-warming than that of most winter-flowering plants in bloom. It makes a compact mound of 2 to 2½ ft. when grown in full sun, as it must be, to do itself justice both as regards colour and habit. In shady places it becomes miserably gaunt and dingy. The stiffly feathered, spreading, whipcord shoots are curiously cypress-like and both this and *H. hectori* are indeed often mistaken for dwarf conifers except when spangled with their minute starry white flowers in early summer.

It is important to cut for indoor use with an eye to the shape of the bush, and not too much at a time, since it is rather slow to break into fresh growth from the woody stems if these are more than pencil-thick. An occasional light clipping-over is however advisable to prevent legginess.

Cut pieces are very well behaved provided the bark is stripped from the split stem-end.

H. 'Autumn Glory'

'Autumn Glory' is chiefly notable for its deep violet flowers in late summer, but the darkish evergreen foliage tipped with bronze-purple is also rather telling, both indoors and out, and it mixes particularly well in some of the earliest spring arrangements from the garden, in which pinks, mauves and purples tend to predominate at that time of year. There are always plenty of longish foliage shoots to spare, especially in spring, when this hebe should be cut back fairly hard to correct a straggling tendency.

H. x franciscana 'Variegata' (*elliptica* 'Variegata')

Those who cannot grow the tender variegated form of *H. x*

andersonii may be content to substitute *H. x franciscana* 'Varie-gata' which is of similar colouring and considerably tougher, though much smaller and less striking in effect. It is a compact dwarf rarely exceeding 2 ft. in height and the fact that its mauve flowers are only sparsely produced is no disadvantage, since they somewhat detract from the beauty of the rather short and broad green leaves with their generous cream-white markings.

H. hectori

This is another personal favourite, no doubt on account of its resemblance to *armstrongii*. In particular the whipcord con-struction is repeated here, but this time on a thicker gauge, and the spriglets which make up a shoot are more erect and are not in this case individually feathered. In size and habit it is similar, but the overall colour is a more olive green (Yellow-Green 148A), with only the tips of the polished shoots touched with much the same old gold as the other. I am always glad when the incon-gruous little flowers disappear, leaving the plant to resume its cypress-like act. Provided it gets plenty of sunshine this makes a most handsome and richly coloured dwarf evergreen, but in the shade it loses its compactness, to become an ungainly, sprawling tangle of old rope. A sunny position is also necessary for the further reason that *hectori* seems slightly less robust than *armstrongii*, though still reasonably tough.

H. pimeleoides 'Glauco-coerulea' and H. pinguifolia 'Pagei' (*Veronica pageana*) (A.M. 1958)

Close though the similarity is between these two dwarf hebes, there should be a place for both in the flower arranger's garden, if she cares for small material, because of their contrasting habit of growth. Both have tiny, fleshy, oval, glaucous leaves, nar-rowly piped with maroon at most seasons, but whereas 'Glauco-coerulea' grows semi-erect in a compact, low mound, the pros-trate 'Pagei' rolls out a carpet with a 9-in. pile. The leaf colour ranges in both cases from around Greyed Green 189B to 190A, 'Glauco-coerulea' being if anything the darker of the two. Both look their best in sunny situations but will stand a fair amount

9. A young *Ginkgo biloba*

10. *Hosta fortunei* 'Yellow Edge'

11. *Hosta sieboldiana (glauca)*

of shade. Though the rather more straggly growth which results in shade may suit us well for cutting it is not quite such a pleasing garden spectacle. The flowers (light violet, and white, respectively) should ideally be removed once they are finished and indeed the foliage effect is more satisfying if this is done even sooner. Side-shoots of *H.* 'Pagei' root almost wherever they touch the soil and may be used to form new plantings.

H. 'Snow Wreath'

At the time of writing this is a fairly recent introduction. The young specimens included in one or two trade displays at the Chelsea Show of 1967 were too small to give much idea of its possibilities, but it is chiefly remarkable for the very large proportion of white in the long, rather flimsy-looking, pale grey-green leaves. It is said to make a bush of 3 or 4 ft. and to be somewhat tender. It lasts well in water.

HEDERA—"Ivy"
Climber or Ground cover; evergreen

Lugubrious ivy-clad Victorian mansions and parterres may have testified to the utility, but suggested nothing of the beauty, of the *Hedera* genus. It has however gained much in status in recent years, thanks no doubt to the seeing eye of the flower arranger, who has discovered that ivy leaves come in an astonishing assortment of sizes, colours and shapes.

H. canariensis—"Canary Island Ivy"

Though much less popular than its variegated form, *H. canariensis* is particularly attractive in winter when the large, plain green leaves turn to a very dark bronze with green veining on the upper surface and self-coloured maroon beneath.

H. canariensis 'Variegata' ('Gloire de Marengo')

One of the most spectacular of the variegated ivies, *H. canariensis* 'Variegata' has large, leathery, slightly glossy, roughly diamond-shaped leaves (though they may vary widely on a single

G

plant) irregularly margined with cream and combining greens and grey-greens of varying intensity within the central area. If it has faults they are that the leaves are too pendent and tend to roll backwards longitudinally, giving the whole a rather droopy look. Nevertheless a long-established, well-grown specimen is a fine sight, and provides enormous leaves and long, long trails for cutting.

To achieve the best results it should be given a fairly sunny, sheltered position. This is the only ivy I propose to describe which is not entirely hardy and since it survives on a north wall here it must be reasonably tough. When I first planted mine I shared a common misapprehension that *all* ivies enjoy shade and northerly aspects. After a very hesitant start it suddenly took heart in its present position and is now, after ten years or so, quite a thriving specimen. But it would undoubtedly have made faster progress and would, I expect, suffer less winter leaf-scorch if it had been more favourably sited.

H. colchica dentata 'Variegata'

This ivy is sometimes confused with the foregoing but may be identified by its heart-shaped leaf, which is further distinguished by a very faintly toothed margin. The bold variegation is a more primrose yellow combined with green and grey-green, the texture more matt and slightly thinner and I would say that the leaf is presented at a better angle on the stalk—altogether a highly ornamental large-leaved ivy and one of the best for ground cover between shrubs.

H. helix cultivars—Forms of "Common Ivy"

I have eight varieties of *Hedera helix* in this garden, but there are a great many more in commerce with which I am less familiar. One of my own favourites is the small-leaved, yellow 'Buttercup' ('Flavescens', 'Golden Cloud' or 'Russell's Gold'). Despite one grower's recommendation to put this in the shade I have found plenty of light, if not of sunshine, to be essential for the bright yellow leaf colour. My own plant gets only morning sun on a low north-east wall, and those parts of it growing in full exposure are brilliantly coloured, particularly when young, whereas shoots which have wandered into the shade of a dense hydrangea have permanently become a quite unremarkable green.

'Congesta' is an uncommon little ivy of curious appearance, with stiff, upright shoots closely packed with short-stalked, tiny, dark green leaves with lighter veining. Most of the foliage is roughly triangular, becoming larger and more definitely lobed towards the base of the shoots. Grown as an erect, open-ground shrub it slowly reaches about 2 ft. I know nothing of its performance as a climber.

'Glacier' is another small-leaved cv., aptly named and properly deserving of the overworked epithet 'dainty', with white variegation on lobed grey-green leaves.

In 'Jubilee' ('Goldenheart') the more usual pattern of variegation is reversed, as the alternative name suggests, with a very bright yellow centre offset by the very dark green of the small, lobed leaf.

'Marginata' ('Silver Queen') has a larger leaf and more vigorous habit than the other forms of *H. helix* described here. The shape is variable but roughly triangular, sometimes with sharply pointed lobes and sometimes with an entire margin. It is generously variegated with white on a combination of dark green and light grey-green and is a graceful climber or carpeter.

Of the plain green sorts 'Sagittaefolia' ('Feastii') is densely furnished with small, sharply lobed arrow-heads. The leaf design is attractive and the closely packed habit weed-smothering when used as ground cover. 'Sagittaefolia Variegata' is prettily margined with white on green and grey-green.

The three-colour effect in 'Tricolor' ('Elegantissima') is most marked in winter, when the marbled grey-green leaf-centre with its irregular white trimming adds a purplish-pink or red border to its attractions. This is yet another small-leaved cultivar.

Ivies are for the most part encouragingly easy and if failures occur among hardy varieties it is probably for the reason that they have been bought from a florist. Those sold as house plants will have been grown under glass and will not have been hardened off for outdoor planting. Even in such circumstances they should succeed if planted out in early summer to become acclimatized before the onset of winter. A friend who grows many varieties from cuttings tells me that small, newly rooted pieces get away better if allowed to trail in contact with the soil for a time after planting out, regardless of whether they will subsequently be required to climb.

For cut foliage soaking is beneficial and when using single leaves of the large-leaved types I find them much more amenable if a small stitch is made with a rose-wire across the central vein towards the base of the leaf and the ends of the wire wound round the stem. (See also Chapter IX.)

HELICHRYSUM
Shrub; evergreen

H. petiolatum

I was about to say that *H. petiolatum*—to my mind the most desirable of all the shrubby helichrysums for cutting—does not really qualify as a hardy foliage plant, but am reminded of Mrs. Underwood's surprising experience in Colchester during the winter of 1962–3, when six plants were found covered with shoots in April 1963, after having been thrown on a rubbish heap during the previous November. She attributes their survival throughout that notorious winter to the dryness of their roots; but even in the driest of soils it cannot normally be said to be hardy except in the mildest districts. However a very small plant will quickly develop a quantity of long, spreading, sinuous wands of small, velvety, heart-shaped silver leaves during the summer months if planted out in May and for those who must forgo it as a permanent garden plant a year-to-year supply can be maintained either by potting it up from the garden and bringing it indoors for the winter or by taking cuttings (which strike very readily) and growing these on a warm window-sill for planting out the following year.

By the end of the season cut sprays need no special conditioning beyond scraping an inch or two of the split stem-end, but boiling is advisable if the shoots are soft at the tips. It quickly wilts in moisture-retaining substances.

H. plicatum 'Elmstead'

The foliage sprigs of *H. plicatum* 'Elmstead' are of carnation-like construction, but with narrower, woollier leaves of a vivid silver-white on a compact dwarf bush. Given a really well-drained soil and the open, sunny position which all such grey foliages demand this helichrysum is said to be tough enough for any ordinary garden. It has a reputation for greater hardiness than any of its shrubby relations, but this has not yet been put to the test with my new young plants in this colder-than-average garden. (See also Chapter IX.)

I have nothing big enough to cut from as yet, but have Mrs. Underwood's assurance that it is well-behaved. (Untried.)

HELLEBORUS—"Hellebore"
Hardy perennial; evergreen

H. foetidus (A.M. 1969)—"Stinking Hellebore"

Whether in flower or in seed this native hellebore has the appearance of being in bloom from January right into summer, with its large, tall-stemmed clusters of light green flowers piped with maroon, followed by flower-like green seedheads. Both the flower colour and that of the pale green leaf-stalk are in sharp contrast to that of the exceptionally dark green foliage, which often has a black-bronze overtone. The leaves are sharply toothed and many-fingered, the narrow, tapered segments meeting at the base to form a roughly circular shape varying in diameter from a few inches to 1 ft. An evil smell which is said to be emitted by the leaves when crushed is supposed to have earned this plant its unsavoury common name; but I think it largely undeserved—and which of us would wish to crush these fine leaves anyway?

H. foetidus is hardy and easy-going, doing equally well in sun or shade and reproducing itself with abandon. It seems particularly partial to a position at the foot of a rock offering a cool, moist, but well-drained root-run. It often becomes heavily infested with greenfly, without noticeable damage. The current season's woody flower stems need cutting to the ground when they have finished fruiting (or sooner, if seedlings are unwelcome) before they turn black and unsightly, to be replaced by the new growth.

The leaves of this species need singeing or boiling, and soaking.

H. lividus subsp. corsicus (*argutifolius*) (A.M. 1930, F.C.C. 1960)

It is not easy to keep pace with the name changes of the hellebore which we used to know as *H. corsicus*, later as *argutifolius* and more recently as a subspecies of *lividus*, with the threat of yet another change of name in the offing. This is the one with the huge clusters of pale apple-green flowers of a larger size than those of *foetidus* and much more solidly sculptured leaves. These have a thick, waxy texture and are divided into three reflexed segments each about 7 in. long and 2 in. wide with a sharply toothed margin and tapering gradually to a sharp point, borne on strong 5-in. stalks. The colour charts at a soft Greyed Green 194A—or more nearly the Lavender Green of the old chart.

We are commonly advised to grow this hellebore in the shade but I am not sure of the wisdom of this in a cold garden, for I have in the past lost several plants by doing as I was told and have only begun to succeed since trying it in sheltered but open situations—the shelter being chiefly necessary for the top-heavy, woody-stemmed types such as this and the foregoing, to prevent wind-rocking. Personally I like to stake *corsicus*.

The foliage needs no special conditioning and glycerines well. (See Chapter IX.)

H. orientalis (A.G.M. 1925)—"Lenten Rose"

Helleborus orientalis hybridizes freely in the garden, producing considerable variation in the foliage as well as in the flower colour, which ranges from deep maroon-purple to greenish-white. The leaves differ in the extent to which they are divided and in the size of the segments, which are larger and less numerous than those of *H. foetidus*, forming a rough circle or open fan-shape of up to 1 ft. in diameter. Some are much more conspicuously serrated than others and leaf surfaces vary from smooth to rugose. The foliage colour is a more or less uniform, occasionally bronze-tinted, deep green, though much less dark than that of *foetidus*, and each leaf springs from ground level on a stiff 9- to 12-in. stalk.

Herbaceous types of hellebore such as *orientalis* greatly prefer dappled shade and benefit from deep planting and a top dressing of leaf-mould after flowering. They should be left undisturbed to form colonies until these become so overcrowded as to need splitting up.

The leaves of *H. orientalis* and its hybrids need to be boiled and soaked.

All hellebores appreciate a rich, well-drained soil and are particularly happy on limy soils, seeding themselves freely in favourable circumstances.

Finally, I should like to add a word of encouragement to those flower arrangers who may be tempted to give up growing them from despair of making the flowers last satisfactorily in water, thus depriving themselves of the foliage at the same time. This is not strictly to the point, since hellebore leaves are not difficult as cut material, but those unfamiliar with the secret of success with the cut flowers are always delighted to learn the trick of first boiling the stem-end, then making a *shallow* incision with a sharp-pointed knife the entire length of the stem, starting as close to the flower head as possible, and then immersing stem, flowers and all in water for several hours.

HEMEROCALLIS fulva—Form of "Day Lily"
Hardy perennial

Growers of the fine modern American hemerocallis hybrids probably no longer cultivate the less spectacular species still found in old-fashioned gardens. No doubt many of the former, with which I am unfamiliar, are also equipped with splendid leaves;

but those of an old favourite, the mahogany-orange *H. fulva*, are I think among the best of all spring foliages, partly on account of their graceful strap-shape which provides such a welcome contrast of form, but above all for the enchanting delicate lime-green of the leaves in youth (Yellow-Green 150C, soon changing to 145B). It throws up large clumps of foliage, with several arching blades to a shoot, at the first premature hint of spring—indeed it is altogether too eager to get started, constraining one, perhaps unnecessarily, to protect the tender-looking growth from the threat of frost for many weeks, although the young greenery is much tougher than it looks. Even if the more precocious shoots get damaged they will usually have served to protect newer growth beneath. Slug bait must be regularly applied from earliest spring onwards, as the short, erect, emerging shoots gradually increase in length, throwing their gracefully arching blades out sideways in a cascade of glistening yellow-green ribbons.

This hemerocallis is very easily grown and is indifferent to sun or shade, though some shade is perhaps advantageous on very light soils, particularly if the mahogany flower colour is important.

The foliage lasts better when soaked and when whole shoots are to be used in an arrangement it is advisable to hold the cut end together with a small elastic band or to bind it with florist's wire or wool, to prevent the leaves falling apart.

HIERACIUM waldsteinii—Form of "Hawkweed"
Hardy perennial

The furry silver-grey leaf rosettes of *Hieracium waldsteinii*, which are about 1 ft. wide or rather less, might possibly be mistaken for those of *Verbascum bombicyferum* seedlings, but these are clump-forming and the individual leaves are greyer, smaller and proportionately broader and have a wavy margin. I feel sure that this is a plant which I coveted for its foliage (but not for its yellow daisies) years ago on a trade stand at a Chelsea Show but was warned at the time that it was not for a cold garden such as mine. But I have since seen it growing locally and can find no mention of undue tenderness and to me this seems a foliage plant of sufficient beauty to be well worth a risk. All it is said to need is a sunny position and a poor, well-drained soil. A seedling from a local source survived the winter well here.

Although I have not yet been able to test it as cut material I feel sure its needs in this respect must be carefully studied, for I have sometimes seen it looking fresh and fair and sometimes drooping in summer exhibits in the hot R.H.S. Halls. Probably it would respond to conditioning in hot water before arranging. (Untried.) (See also Chapter IX.)

HOSTA (*Funkia*)—"Plantain Lily"
Hardy perennial; ground cover

Species and varieties of hosta probably run into several dozens, but not all are of equal value for flower arrangement and many are very much alike. The following selection is made from those that I grow and includes most that are likely to be of interest for cutting.

H. crispula 'Aurea Maculata'

This uncommon variety has broad, wavy green leaves oddly streaked and splashed with yellow. The effect, though striking, is perhaps more freakish than beautiful.

H. fortunei

The species has a large, long-stalked, useful, plain green heart-shaped leaf, and several of its cultivars are among my favourite hostas, whether for garden or indoor decoration.

H. fortunei 'Aurea'

One such is *H. fortunei* 'Aurea', which has elegantly shaped medium-sized leaves of a clear light yellow (Yellow 8C). The colour is particularly good in spring, but unfortunately the younger the leaves the less reliable they are when cut. The texture of this beautifully coloured leaf is rather flimsier than average, which makes the plant more susceptible to drought.

For the same reason the cut foliage needs more careful conditioning than most. Stem-tipping is advisable during immersion.

H. fortunei 'Albopicta' (A.M. 1960)

In this version much the same pure yellow (Yellow 10C at its best) is surrounded by a two-toned margin of lime and darker green in spring, gradually fading at maturity to a less beautiful but still pleasing mixture of dark and light yellowish-green. The leaf is rather broader than that of 'Aurea' and both are comparatively short in the stalk. This, too, is rather thin-textured in youth and may be badly battered by rough spring weather. I still chuckle to recall the desperate tactics of a friend who rushed into her garden during a severe hailstorm on the eve of our Flower Club's annual exhibition to hold an umbrella over her newly unfurled clump of 'Albopicta'.

Stem-tip and soak.

H. fortunei 'Hyacintha'

The strongly constructed leaf on a long, firm stalk is typical of the species, but in colour *H. fortunei* 'Hyacintha' is much more glaucous. For those who cannot accommodate the very large-leaved and still bluer *sieboldiana* this may serve as second-best, but *sieboldiana* would be my choice where space permitted.

H. fortunei 'Yellow Edge'

One of the newest among my *fortunei* cvs. is a recent introduction called 'Yellow Edge'. This has a large and sturdy green leaf of a broad heart-shape effectively trimmed with a neat yellow margin and it comes on a good strong stem. To my surprise the attendant on the Chelsea Show stand who sold it to me seemed to regard it as a monstrosity suited only to the depraved taste of the flower arranger! But even as a garden plant I find it charming in the shrub borders and for cutting it is one of the best. (See illustration facing p. 97.)

H. lancifolia

The foliage of *H. lancifolia* is more narrowly elliptical and altogether more miniature than any of the foregoing, but with a disproportionately long stalk. For smaller arrangements this provides glossy, rather deep green leaves with conspicuous longitudinal ribbing where most hosta foliage would be out of scale.

H. sieboldiana (*glauca*)

It would be helpful if it were true, as is sometimes claimed, that *glauca* rather than *sieboldiana* is the more correct specific epithet for this most glaucous of hostas, but the latter seems to be in current favour. In size this one comes at the other end of the scale and, as in the case of all hostas, the moister the soil the larger the leaf. When grown as a waterside plant the broadly heart-shaped, often rather cupped leaf of *H. sieboldiana* is immense. The colour is the bluest of blue-grey-greens, with a surface bloom which needs careful handling when cut. The foliage is intriguingly furrowed and puckered, rather as though rows of stitching had been botched by an ill-adjusted sewing-machine, except that the result is decorative rather than maladroit. (See illustration facing p. 97.)

The seedheads are particularly good, whether green or dried, so long as untidy remnants of the decaying flower trumpets are extracted from among them at an early stage, before they stain the pods.

H. 'Thomas Hogg'

H. 'Thomas Hogg', which is often sold under the name of *albomarginata*, is one of those most familiar to the flower arranger, with medium-sized, ovate, white-edged leaves on longish stalks. I understand that the true *albomarginata* is the one with much smaller, narrower leaves of altogether dwarfer habit and with a narrower edging of cream-white.

H. undulata

This, too, is an old ally of the flower arranger—and one which is sometimes forced into premature leaf as a house plant. The specific name derives from the characteristic wavy outline of the rather small leaf, in which the variegation consists of a conspicuous white central zone bound by a pale green margin. Catalogue descriptions may suggest that this is synonymous with *H. crispula* (A.M. 1959), but I understand that the true *crispula* is larger-leaved and is a much scarcer species than would appear from the lists.

H. undulata 'Univittata'

'Univittata' is very similar to *undulata* except that the leaf-centre is more cream than white, the green margin darker and the size appreciably larger, providing a useful choice if both these attractively contorted shapes are grown.

All hostas bear elegant mauve or white flower spikes, made up of little trumpets grouped on three sides of the stiffly erect stalks and rising above the clumps of foliage.

As regards cultural needs, all require a rich, moist soil for the best results and most thrive in the shade, though those of yellow colouring need plenty of light to achieve the most vivid effect. Constant applications of slug bait are necessary from spring to late autumn and protection from earwig damage may also be required in late summer.

In the confusion at present prevailing regarding hosta nomenclature I have done my best to give the correct names, as far as these can be ascertained. But one has only to compare names and varieties on display at a Chelsea Show, for instance, to see what an abysmal muddle exists in the trade.

I have given a lot of space to the hostas, but there are so many to choose from that I hope it will not be thought disproportionate when it is remembered that these leaves are some of the chief stock-in-trade of the flower arranger from spring to late autumn.

Where no special conditioning instructions have already been recommended only a preliminary soaking is necessary. Older leaves may do without, but for young foliage it is essential. (See also Chapter IX.)

HUMULUS lupulus 'Aureus'—"Golden Hop"
Climber; deciduous

The "Golden Hop" is a rampant herbaceous climber like its commoner green relative and resembles it in almost all respects, including the drooping clusters of hop "flowers" which appear in late summer. The difference lies in the so-called golden leaf colour, which is more accurately an acid lime-yellow. The long, twining ropes of rough-textured, vine-like foliage make as much as 15 ft. of growth in a season, needing a good deal of training and tying in if grown on a fence, but able to take care of themselves if allowed to clamber over a hedge or to festoon the branches of a tree. Plenty of sunshine is necessary for a good crop of hops, but if foliage is the main consideration some shade for a part of the day will produce an intense *chartreuse* hue, whereas a cruder yellow and a tendency to scorch result from too much sun. If, on the other hand, the shade is too dense, the leaf colour is too green to be interesting. The tangle of withering tentacles should be cut to ground level in late autumn to make way for the new growth which renews itself annually from the steadily increasing rootstock.

The tender, sinuous trails of vivid lime-yellow in spring are delightful material for cutting and as the size of the leaves increases, later in the season, these are individually useful. In either case stem-tipping and a brief preliminary soaking are necessary. It dislikes moisture-retaining substances.

HYDRANGEA macrophylla, variegated cvs.
Shrubs; deciduous

Most hydrangea foliage makes good cutting material and a chlorotic shoot of a yellower green than it should be or one burnished by the sun brings added colour interest to an indoor arrangement. But whereas these contributions are incidental from shrubs grown for floral effect, there are several hydrangeas with variegated leaves which qualify as foliage plants in their

109

own right. Discounting *H. macrophylla* 'Maculata', or 'Variegata', which has green leaves margined and spotted with white, we are left with two much superior forms, explicitly named 'Quadricolor' and 'Tricolor' respectively.

The foliage of the former combines a fairly deep yellow, cream-white, and grey-green variegation on darker green, and the latter is a mixture of deep green, light grey-green and deep cream. The flowers are of the lacecap type, pale blue or pale pink according to the acidity or alkalinity of the soil, either colour being pleasingly set off by the unusual foliage. Neither is quite as hardy as the majority of the green-leaved types, but they are not unduly tender, requiring only the shade and shelter of adjacent trees, shrubs or walls—and, of course, the plentiful moisture which is essential to all—to make tall, healthy specimens. Provided that they are kept constantly watered and free from greenfly and that the roots are protected from freezing, these make interesting and unusual subjects for tubs and garden vases.

ILEX—"Holly"
Tree or shrub; evergreen

Hollies vary widely in the degree of prickliness of their foliage, from the fiendish pin-cushion-spines of *Ilex aquifolium* 'Ferox', the "Hedgehog Holly", to the almost and entirely spineless. To me 'Ferox' and its variegated forms are more curious than decorative, the overcrowded prickles which invade the entire leaf surface being altogether too muddled for beauty—and for floral decoration they would be as 'horrid' aesthetically as in the botanical sense.

Among the many less ferocious variegated types *I. aquifolium* 'Golden King' (A.M. 1898) is generally considered the best for yellow variegation and the somewhat more prickly 'Silver Queen' for cream-white. Illogically the king is a female, and so capable of fruiting if fertilized, and the queen a non-berrying male! I have however recently come across a holly of exceptional beauty as a foliage plant, which I think outshines all others of green and yellow colouring. Its name is *I. aquifolium*

'Lawsoniana' and it has unusually large, broad, shining and rather sparsely spined leaves in a vivid combination of canary yellow and rich green, more closely resembling *Elaeagnus pungens* 'Maculata' than a typical holly in its overall effect. In habit also it is more akin to the elaeagnus, making a spreading bush of moderate size rather than a tree. Unfortunately it takes its time about doing so, eventually reaching about 5 ft. It is said to be perfectly hardy, which makes one wonder why this spectacular holly is not more frequently seen.

Some of the spineless, or almost spineless, plain green hollies also provide elegant evergreen foliage for winter decoration. If I had room for one of these I think it would be *I. aquifolium* 'Pyramidalis Fructu-luteo', which is very nearly devoid of prickles and bears plentiful yellow berries which are a tremendous extra attraction so long as a male pollinator is grown near by— that is to say, one would have to find room for two trees if berries were of as much concern as foliage. Other good smooth-margined hollies include the beautiful, large-leaved and aptly named *I. x altaclarensis* 'Camelliaefolia' (A.G.M. 1931), which has only an occasional prickle and *I. aquifolium* 'Scotica', the "Dahoon" or "Smooth-leaved Holly", which has none.

All the above are hardy and obligingly adaptable evergreens, doing equally well in smoke-polluted, clean country, or salt sea air, in sun or shade and in any kind of soil. The fact that they are slow-growing subjects is probably the chief reason why they are not more frequently planted in these days of 'instant' gardening. (For glycerining see Chapter IX.)

IRIS

Hardy perennial

I. foetidissima 'Variegata' (A.M. 1965)—Form of "Gladwyn Iris", "Roast Beef Plant"
Evergreen

Iris foetidissima 'Variegata' is unusual in that its foliage is evergreen, growing in flat, fan-like clusters of grey-green blades more or less broadly margined with white down one side, the

outer leaves often taking on a sickle shape. Being much less
free-flowering than the species it will not provide nearly as many
of the ornamental seed pods. The foliage of *I. japonica* 'Variegata' looks very similar, but the plant is a good deal more
troublesome than the variegated *foetidissima*, which is hardy and
unfussy, though giving the best results where shade and moisture
are present.

I. kaempferi 'Variegata'* and I. laevigata 'Variegata'

These beautiful irises are somewhat alike, but only *kaempferi*
requires acid soil conditions. Without growing experience of
either I have the impression that *laevigata* is the more amenable.
The water's edge is perhaps the proper place for both, but they
may also be grown in the ordinary garden border. In the first
case the foliage is boldly variegated with white and in the other
with deep ivory-yellow from spring until well into summer, finally darkening to a more or less uniform green. All such plants
as prefer to grow beside the water should be kept as moist as
possible if planted in drier positions.

I. pseudacorus 'Variegatus'—Form of "Water Flag", "Yellow
Flag"

This also goes for *Iris pseudacorus* 'Variegatus' which must, I
think, be the universal favourite among flower arrangers, with
its spectacular ivory-yellow applied in such broad longitudinal
bands that little room is left for any green. These lovely leaves
grow taller and finer with their feet in a few inches of water, but
they do remarkably well in much less accommodating surroundings. Unfortunately they too lose most of their light yellow
colour towards the end of the summer.

JASMINUM officinale—"Jasmine" or "Jessamine"
Climber; deciduous or semi-evergreen

Though I am familiar with only one of the variegated jasmines it may be worth while to bring them to the notice of those
who are unaware that they exist.

112

12. *Lonicera nitida* 'Baggesen's Gold'

13. *Mahonia lomariifolia*

14. *Mahonia repens rotundifolia*

The foliage of the tough, winter-flowering evergreen *J. nudi-florum* is not perhaps sufficiently ornamental for us to concern ourselves with its variegated form, in which the leaves are splashed with yellow in competition with the flowers. But the summer-flowering *J. officinale*, with its white flowers set off by elegantly shaped green foliage, is quite another matter. This species exists in both yellow- and white-variegated forms. According to Mrs. Margery Fish, who grew one form of each, the latter is much the more attractive, combining silver, pink and pale green. Having seen the one with the bright yellow markings I am sure I should agree with her, for I am not at all enamoured of the sickly leaf colour of *J. officinale* 'Aureum'. Unfortunately the better-looking one is much slower than the other.

None is fussy as to soil, but full sun produces maximum flower-power. (Untried.)

KALE, Ornamental—See under Cabbage

KERRIA japonica 'Picta' ('Variegata')—Form of "Jew's Mallow"
Shrub; deciduous

The variegated kerria is very much dwarfer and less rampant than the type, rarely exceeding 2 ft. in height, with delicate, branching wands of foliage in a mixture of pale grey-green edged with white. The small leaves are narrowly tapered and serrated, and when they fall they leave behind a clump of the slenderest green twiggery. Some find the appearance of this kerria unattractively sickly—and it is perhaps on the anaemic side—but I think it looks quite at home in a planting of mixed foliage, though less so in an ordinary shrub border. The foliage effect is both prettier and healthier-looking in the shade than in full sun, where it often has an unpleasantly screwed-up appearance. I should prefer to dispense with the rather spotty little yellow flowers, if this were possible, for they are undistinguished in themselves and only interfere with the natural pallor of the foliage effect while they last.

The plant seems quite hardy despite its fragile appearance and is not fussy about growing conditions, though it is happiest in the shade. Any foliage shoots which revert to plain green should be cut out to the base and flowered shoots should get the same treatment in early summer when the small single blooms are over.

LAMIUM maculatum—"Spotted Dead Nettle"
Hardy perennial; ground cover; evergreen

Hitherto my chief grouse against *Lamium maculatum* had been that it is just about as perpetual-flowering as gorse and, to me, the muddy magenta-purple flower colour is one of the unloveliest in nature. In association with the dull green of the much-netted, neat little heart-shaped leaves with their broad central flash of grey-white the effect seems to me so frowsy that I had thought of passing over *L. maculatum* in silence, though I know that there are plenty who admire it and find the foliage sprays useful for cutting. But I had not then seen the pink-flowered variety, *L. maculatum* 'Roseum', in which the flower colour is a delightfully warm, light rose-pink which looks altogether charming against the identical foliage background. The white-flowered 'Album' is merely dull, but at least an improvement on the purple one. 'Aureum', which has yellow leaves on the same pattern, is too dwarf and compact to be useful for cutting and is not especially hardy. The others speedily carpet large expanses of bare soil in all kinds of inhospitable circumstances, including dense, dry shade. In dry conditions I believe they flower with rather less persistence. Whatever one's opinion of the lamiums I think they can hardly compare in beauty with their near relation, *Galeobdolon luteum* 'Variegatum', which has an equally accommodating nature.

LAURUS nobilis—"Bay Laurel", "Sweet Bay"
Tree or shrub; evergreen

All good cooks will be familiar with the bay leaf, if only in a dried state, in which nothing remains of the fine dark green colour of the elegantly tapered leaf. *Laurus nobilis* is not commonly thought of as a flowering plant, but the handsome foliage further serves as an ideal setting for the small cream-yellow flowers in April or May, providing additionally fine cutting material when flowers and foliage are combined.

Though the 'green bay tree' (which comes from the Mediterranean area) is proverbially reputed to flourish it cannot be guaranteed to do so in all parts of the British Isles, young plants in particular being vulnerable to frost damage. I believe that many older trees also came to grief in the winter of 1962–3, but generally speaking an established specimen should survive average winter temperatures in a sheltered position in all but the bleakest districts. It thrives exceedingly at the seaside and does well in chalky gardens, other conditions permitting. Shade is usually recommended, but I fancy that in all but the kindest climates some sunshine would be acceptable to remind it of home. Its ultimate size depends largely on growing conditions, reaching 20 or 30 ft. in the milder areas, but it is more commonly seen as a dense pyramidal shrub of about 10 ft. It is a favourite subject for topiary, but when this aristocratic foliage plant is clipped into geometrical and other unnatural shapes it seems to me to forfeit all its natural 'nobility'.

It also exists in a rather more spreading yellow-leaved form called *Laurus nobilis* 'Aurea', which I have not seen.

LEUCOTHOË catesbaei* (*Andromeda catesbaei*)
Shrub; ground cover; evergreen

I think few flower arrangers who can provide the acid soil required by *Leucothoë catesbaei* would willingly forgo it. I cast envious eyes on the lush growth of plants grown in really moist woodland conditions, with leaves almost twice as large as those of my own rather thirsty specimens; but even on this poor soil (enriched over the years by leaf mulching) there is year-round beauty in the graceful, ground-covering, closely massed wands of narrow, tapering, glossy, evergreen leaves, from the time that the new growth masks the clump with pale pinkish-copper in late spring, through the light, shining green of summer to the claret and maroon hues which intermingle with the green throughout autumn and winter until the new shoots appear. The drier and more exposed the conditions the dwarfer the growth—in this garden the height is not above 2 ft., but in really well-grown clumps the branched, arching shoots may reach 5, or even 6, ft. It is by nature a shade-loving subject, but grows perfectly well, if less vigorously, in full sun, with more pronounced winter colour in such positions. It spreads only slowly by underground rootstocks and here, at any rate, never outgrows its welcome.

A new cv. of *L. catesbaei* called 'Rainbow' combines red, yellow, green and, surprisingly, white in the leaves. The copper-red of the young growth streaked with the lighter hues is magnificent on approaching maturity.

L. catesbaei is one of the most enduring of foliages for flower arrangement, lasting for many weeks in water; and even the soft young growth stands well if previously boiled. This is one of the best subjects for glycerining. (See Chapter IX.)

LIGULARIA dentata (*Senecio clivorum*)
Hardy perennial

Though most commonly grown as waterside plants, where no doubt they are happiest, these giant groundsels will put up quite a creditable performance in dryish soils and may be grown in sun or shade. The two worthiest varieties are 'Desdemona' and 'Othello', the former having the better coloured foliage. Both have rounded, leathery, sharply toothed, glistening leaves which, in ideal circumstances, may measure as much as 18 in. across, on 6- to 12-in. stems. In 'Desdemona' they are of an overall purplish-maroon, and in 'Othello' the leaf surface is green above with purple veining and reverse. The large, ragged, droopy-petalled orange daisies are borne in branching heads on 4-ft. stems in late summer, but to me these have an untidy, hang-dog look which is unworthy of the noble foliage. (Untried.)

LIGUSTRUM—"Privet"

L. ovalifolium 'Aureo-marginatum'—"Golden Privet"
Shrub; semi-evergreen

When grown as a fine, free-standing, open-branched shrub of 12 ft. or thereabouts, *L. ovalifolium* 'Aureo-marginatum' is hardly recognizable as the tight-clipped "Golden Privet" of suburban hedges and other mutilated, man-made shapes. For one thing the close trimming results in an over-concentrated, garish hue, whereas the unpruned plant—unpruned, that is, except at the hands of the flower arranger—is of sufficiently loose construction to trap light and shade among the branches, thus producing a varying intensity of colour from pure bright yellow variegation in fullest exposure, to a subdued yellowish-green where little or no sun has penetrated, with some self-coloured or variegated lime-yellow in between.

Though classed as deciduous it is more nearly evergreen; it puts up with any kind of soil; it is bone-hardy; and it stands any amount of indiscriminate cutting, so that one can select the line of the branch and the colour of the leaves to suit oneself, without concern for what the plant can best afford. Common it may be, but it earns its keep, both indoors and out, a good deal better than many a more aristocratic horticultural 'treasure'.

L. lucidum 'Tricolor'
Shrub; evergreen

Of several less familiar (and less vigorous) variegated privets in cultivation the evergreen and rather larger-leaved *L. lucidum* 'Tricolor' includes a youthful pink tinge to the white-margined green leaf to account for the cultivar name. But this is only likely to succeed in the milder areas.

L. sinense 'Variegatum'
Shrub; deciduous

L. sinense 'Variegatum' is a rather hardier deciduous variety with light grey-green leaves pleasingly margined with white.

117

LOBELIA

Hardy or half-hardy perennial

Lobelia cardinalis

Of the tall-growing, mainly scarlet-flowered, herbaceous lobelias the two best-known species are *cardinalis* and *fulgens*, and it is unfortunate for our purposes that the former is the hardier of these two not very hardy species, because it lacks the intense beetroot-purple foliage colour of *fulgens*. There are however one of two tougher *cardinalis* hybrids with dark-hued leaves, of which two of the hardiest and most colourful are 'Queen Victoria' and the still hardier 'Bee's Flame', both of which have mahogany-crimson foliage topped by vivid scarlet flower spikes. The latter is said by the growers to have withstood 16 degrees of frost and to send up fresh growth from the base if frost-damaged.

Lobelia fulgens

My own experience of these lobelias is limited to an unsuccessful experiment with the rather too tender *fulgens*, which has such fine, glistening plum-coloured leaves, but was unable to endure the prolonged freeze-up of a normal winter here and probably suffered a great thirst at other seasons. For it requires a tremendous amount of moisture, a deep, leafy soil and preferably a shady position. It disappears altogether in winter, when it should be covered with weathered ashes or some other form of protection until it is due to push up its rosette of colourful leaves (of great slug-appeal) in spring, to be followed by the 3-ft. scarlet flower spikes of late summer. In the case of my own plant I admit that few of these requirements were met. These lobelias should be planted in the spring and, given the other essentials, should survive the winter out of doors in milder gardens. (Untried.)

LONICERA—"Honeysuckle"

L. japonica 'Aureo-reticulata'

Climber; evergreen or semi-evergreen

It is not to its discredit that this honeysuckle flowers only sparsely or not at all, for its small, prettily dappled leaves are the real attraction. These are rounded or ovate, with a network of bright yellow veining on a yellow-green, sometimes pink-flushed ground. The pink tinge is most pronounced in winter, where the foliage persists. The leaf colour is most effective when exposed to sunshine and the warmer the position the more wholly evergreen it is likely to be. It is perfectly hardy nevertheless and will grow with equal vigour in any aspect except north, making a fairly rampant climber from which to cut graceful trails of foliage.

As cut material it will almost certainly let one down if it has not been carefully conditioned, often spoiling exhibition entries when this has been neglected. I think it safest to boil before stem-tipping and soaking for a short period, since the tips of the shoots are almost always immature.

L. nitida 'Baggesen's Gold'

Shrub; evergreen

The plain green *Lonicera nitida* (A.M. 1911) is much used as a hedging plant though perhaps not always recognized as a honeysuckle—and indeed this shrubby species bears little resemblance to the climbing members of the tribe. The type plant, with its tiny, shining, ovate, dark green leaves on slender branching shoots, has given rise to a much more uncommon and wholly delightful yellow-leaved cv. called 'Baggesen's Gold'. When left unpruned this grows to about 4 ft., throwing out long, densely branched wands of unusually dainty, gaily coloured evergreen foliage which may conveniently be cut to improve the shape of the bush. Its habit is clearly shown in the illustration facing p. 112. It does not make such rapid growth as the type, but I have found it much less slow-growing than is sometimes

119

suggested. My largest specimen, planted as a minute rooted cutting about six years ago is now quite 4 ft. high. It should be given plenty of sun, not only to do justice to the colour but also because it is slightly less hardy than its green-leaved parent, needing some shelter in its earliest years in cold districts.

L. pileata (A.M. 1910)
Shrub; ground cover; evergreen

This is a dwarf, shrubby evergreen species with rather larger (½- to 1½-in) and more elongated, oval, glossy, bright green leaves neatly set upon slender, horizontally spreading branches. It has clusters of dark violet berries in late summer, but these are not very freely borne here. Though recommended as ideal ground cover for shade, in this garden it makes a much better-looking plant in at least partial exposure, which prevents legginess. If conditions are too dry it shows a tendency to leaf-drop. It rarely exceeds 3 ft. and the densely tiered habit fits ideally as ground cover at the base of a leggy type of shrub or short-trunked tree. The semi-prostrate lower branches readily root new plants from suckers, particularly in the decaying leaf mulch of the shrub borders.

As cut foliage the habit is excellent and its behaviour impeccable. It also glycerines well. (See Chapter IX.)

MACLEAYA (*Bocconia*)—"Iodine Plant", "Plume Poppy"
Hardy perennial

From the point of view of foliage the species, *Macleaya microcarpa* (*cordata*), does not differ sufficiently from that of its cv., 'Kelway's Coral Plume', to make it necessary to grow both if space is limited and I prefer the latter for the exquisite pinkish-coffee of its flowers as compared with the paler ivory-buff of the type. The inflorescence is plume-like though far from poppy-like (albeit of the Poppy family), and is borne in late summer on an immensely tall stem above the large, deeply lobed foliage, though leaves of all sizes are found on a single plant. (See illustration facing p. 64.) The latter is somewhat similar in shape to a fig leaf, but smooth, thinner and of a more complicated and even more ornamental outline. The upper surface is a dull grey-green, turning to an interesting gamboge yellow as it fades, with a grey-white underside. Spreading rapidly in all directions by underground suckers, it is a difficult plant to contain in a herbaceous border. The name "Iodine Plant" derives from the bright orange juice which stains anything it touches, from one's fingers to the bath in which the tall flower spikes need to be immersed after cutting. Both flowers and foliage should be singed before soaking and the leaves in particular will rapidly wilt in water without these attentions. They object to moisture-retaining substances.

MAGNOLIA grandiflora
Tree or shrub; evergreen

'Goliath' (A.M. 1931, F.C.C. 1951) beats all other named varieties of the evergreen *Magnolia grandiflora* for flower size and it is a bitter disappointment to me to find that, after cherishing it for some years to a flowering stage on my south wall, the petals have turned brown almost before the flowers open during the past two seasons. This may of course be due to lack of moisture, or some other remediable cause. At the time of planting I was undoubtedly more interested in flowers than foliage and, fine though the leaves are, it is an even greater blow to me today to have to admit that the striking ginger-brown indumentum of some of the other evergreen varieties is lacking, or nearly so, in the case of 'Goliath'. If I could start again I would grow 'Ferruginea' instead. Even though I might have to wait a good twelve years for its flowers it would be worth it for the sake of the vivid rusty felting on the backs of the leaves. For those who prefer to compromise, 'Exmouth Variety' will flower at a much younger stage than 'Ferruginea' and has similarly coloured but rather less spectacular foliage. There is not a wide variation in the leaf pattern between one evergreen variety and another: some are broader and some more wavy than others, some blunt-nosed and some more elegantly tapered, but all are large and solid, with glossy bright green uppers.

121

All forms of *M. grandiflora* are lime-tolerant, 'Ferruginea' being a particularly good doer in chalky soils. Although all these are hardy they are most often trained against a south or southwest wall, where a maximum ration of sunshine encourages production of the large ivory flower chalices in late summer and the shelter prevents wind-scorching. Since all magnolias dislike being moved they should be bought as pot-grown specimens so as to reduce root disturbance to a minimum when transplanting. Greenfly find the tender new leaves and leaf buds especially delectable and will seriously damage the appearance of the foliage unless they are promptly exterminated.

An established young wall-plant will soon begin to thrust out a branch or two which cannot easily be trained into position and these are the ones we should cut for floral decoration in the earlier years. The foliage is immensely long-lasting in water and is a good subject for preservation. (See Chapter IX.)

MAHONIA
Shrub; evergreen

M. aquifolium (A.G.M. 1960)—"Holly-leaved Barberry", "Oregon Grape"

There are a good many mahonias of interest to the flower arranger and not least of them is the humble *M. aquifolium*, which may be accorded no more than 'game covert' status by the fastidious plantsman, but has many virtues notwithstanding. This is the familiar holly-like evergreen with glossy, spiny, pinnate dark green leaves, often turning crimson or bronze from autumn onwards, particularly when grown in full exposure in a hungry soil. The bright yellow flower clusters in earliest spring make more interesting cutting material when in yellow-green bud and the ink-blue fruits which follow are an additional bonus. The foliage is often tiresomely nibbled, but I doubt whether slugs are the culprits in this instance. If not the work of caterpillars (and I have never caught these on the job) it looks to me like that of leaf-cutter bees and I do not know how these are to be dissuaded. This is a good subject for glycerining. (See Chapter IX.)

M. aquifolium 'Atropurpurea'

Rooted suckers of the type plant are usually to be had for nothing from gardening friends and mine came to me in this way; but if I were to buy one I would go for the form called 'Atropurpurea', for which it is claimed that the foliage retains most of its fine plum-purple and bronze complexion at all seasons and in sunless situations. In other respects it is similar to the type, the height varying in both cases from 5 ft. in moist soil and shade to 3 ft., or less, in dry, sunny positions.

M. japonica (often misnamed *bealei*)[1] (A.G.M. 1962)

M. japonica is constructed on an altogether more massive scale, the tough, bold, glossy, pinnate leaves being sometimes as much as 18 in. long, arranged in great whorls of truly sculptural aspect, on a shrub of 7 ft. or thereabouts. A wide range of leaf colour is usually found on a single plant, from very dark to light green, through lime-yellow, flame and scarlet to crimson-maroon according, mainly, to the degree of exposure—that is, the foliage of the crowning whorls being more highly coloured as a rule than the shaded portions lower down the shoots. I suspect that the drier, the hungrier and the more exposed the site the more hectic the red will be, though the plant itself will probably have an unhappy, starved appearance. Even in ideal conditions of partial shade, adequate moisture and preferably a lime-free soil, the lower portions of the erect shoots become gaunt and leggy after a time and although the removal of whole whorls of foliage for a massive indoor arrangement is sometimes regarded as vandalism the surgical operation does more good than harm if performed when the winter-blooming sprays of fragrant primrose-yellow flowers are over. This, in my view, provides the finest cutting foliage of the genus, with the possible exception of *lomariifolia*, the massive cartwheels being just as long-lasting as the individual leaves when cut. The latter glycerine beautifully.

[1] See *Shrub Gardening for Flower Arrangement*

M. lomariifolia (A.M. 1938, F.C.C. 1939) and *M. x* 'Charity'

Other choice mahonias with foliage based on the same design are the much more tender *lomariifolia* and 'Charity', which is tougher. In the former case the much narrower leaflets are elegantly tapered and spaced fish-bone-fashion, with mathematical precision, averaging around fifteen pairs on a strong stalk up to 2 ft. long. Though it has fewer spines than *japonica* they are even more formidable, concentrating most of their venom into the recurving, claw-like, needle-tips of the leaflets. The illustration facing p. 113 shows a particularly well-grown and long-established plant. This is too tender for me and as a garden plant in less than ideal circumstances it is often unattractively gangling in appearance, but the leaves are magnificent for cutting purposes, including glycerining. (See Chapter IX.) *M. x* 'Charity', a recent cross between *lomariifolia* and *japonica*, shows the influence of both parents, and of the former in particular, in the leaves, and whereas much of the bright yellow flower colour is derived from *lomariifolia* it inherits a commendable hardiness from the other parent.

Mahonia repens rotundifolia—Form of "Creeping Barberry"

Having come across this mahonia recently at Wisley, I feel certain that it will become one of my favourites for cutting when my newly acquired plant has grown big enough. The smooth, matt-surfaced leaves are fairly similar to but considerably larger than those of *M. aquifolium* and the remarkable thing about them is that they are entirely spineless. The smooth, rounded margins give the leaves a most pleasing and unusual appearance and the foliage colours attractively. The whorl-like construction apparent in the mature plant was more distinct than in *aquifolium* but less so than in *japonica*, forming a dense, suckering clump 5 ft. high, though 2 or 3 ft. is quoted by Messrs. Hillier as the normal height for this "Creeping Barberry". (See illustration facing p. 113.)

For the present I have had to limit my experiments with the cut foliage to the preservation of a few good-sized leaves with a terminal leaflet of 3 by 2 in. and two smaller pairs, which seems typical of the general leaf pattern. All mahonias glycerine particularly well and this is no exception. (See Chapter IX.)

MENTHA—"Mint"
Hardy perennial; ground cover

M. rotundifolia 'Variegata'—"Apple Mint", "Pineapple Mint"

This is a variegated mint with conspicuous cream-white markings on the small, roundish, wrinkled leaves which are prettily crimped at the edges and clothed in woolly hairs. Being an edible variety it will not be out of place in the kitchen garden if considered too invasive elsewhere, though it makes good ground cover, in sun or shade, wherever sufficient moisture is present.

M. x gentilis 'Variegata'

In this case an unusually bright yellow striping and splashing on bright green amounts to an intensely acid lime-yellow in effect, in a moist, sunny position. The first of these prerequisites seems essential for survival and the second for a good colour. Both this and the previous mint are about 1 ft. in height and are equally enjoyed by slugs. This one is invasive.

The rather flimsier texture of the yellow-variegated leaf stands less well in water than the other, unless given a preliminary soaking, and both dislike moisture-retaining substances.

MISCANTHUS sinensis (*Eulalia japonica*)
Grass

Of the two variegated forms of this tall, graceful grass which I grow I prefer the long, grey-green-and-white-striped arching ribbons of *M. sinensis* 'Variegatus' to the curious transverse yellow banding on the green leaves of 'Zebrinus', though the latter further earns its keep with large, silky, pinkish-bronze tassels on 6-ft. stems in the autumn. These are hardy and unfussy perennial grasses, forming non-invasive clumps of tall-stemmed, cascading foliage which needs to be cut to ground level in late winter, before new shoots start pushing through among the old. Boil and soak.

MYRTUS bullata—New Zealand "Ramarama", form of "Myrtle"
Shrub; evergreen

My miserably inhospitable garden climate deprives me of one of the foliages I covet most for flower arrangement—that of the strangely rugose, reddish-bronze-leaved *Myrtus bullata*. This looks like a real gem for cutting: evergreen, finely coloured and distinguished above all by the intriguingly quilted or blistered appearance of the small, round leaves; but, alas, this is a shrub for mild districts only. It is said to succeed in parts of south-west Britain, where it reaches an average height of 15 ft., bearing small, cream-white flowers with a central fuzz of stamens much like those of the common myrtle, but with purplish calyces.

I have seen it used for flower arrangement and would not expect it to be difficult. (Untried.)

ONOPORDUM—Form of "Thistle"
Hardy biennial or perennial

In case this spelling causes surprise I should explain that the terminal *um*, rather than the more usual *on*, has now been officially declared the more correct.

These giant thistles are equipped with large, prickly-lobed, silver-grey leaves on flanged, spiny stems with an overall coating of matted white hairs. *Onopordum arabicum* may well attain 8 ft., reaching out with ferociously sharp-spined branches which require a wide berth. And *O. salteri* is even more massive. And so, for most of us, the branching 5 ft. or more of *O. acanthium* (A.M. 1962) is quite enough of a good thing. This is commonly known as the "Scotch Thistle" and is another of those biennials which may develop a perennial character if prevented from flowering. The ovate, wavy-edged leaves are of a much finer silver-white and are also larger on a young plant before it reaches the flowering stage, often measuring 18 by 12 in. and sometimes much more. As the flowering stems develop from the original leaf rosette the foliage is attached to them with flange-like extensions, so that it is necessary to cut away part of the base of the leaf on either side of the midrib in order that this may serve as a stalk when using the foliage for floral decoration.

All these onopordums require sunshine and good drainage.

I have always thought it necessary to soak these leaves, but Mrs. Underwood recommends only that they should be stood in water directly after cutting.

ORIGANUM vulgare 'Aureum'—Form of "Dittany", "Marjoram"
Hardy perennial; ground cover; evergreen

This gaily coloured form of our native marjoram makes efficient weed-smothering pools of sunshine in the front of a border, forming dense mats of slender 9- to 12-in. stems of small, ovate, bright yellow leaves about 1 in. long interspersed with greener and still smaller leaves at their bases, creating an overall effect of vivid lime-yellow. Its flavour is just the same as that of the more sober-looking herb used for cooking and it is ridiculously easy to grow, given a sunny position and preferably a well-drained one.

As cut material it is equally untroublesome.

PACHYSANDRA terminalis*—"Japanese Spurge"
Ground cover; evergreen

The nickname is apt in this case, for the low-growing, 6-in. wide, evergreen rosettes of *Pachysandra terminalis* do indeed suggest those of the ground-covering *Euphorbia robbiae*, though in no way related to the spurges. They are, however, of a lighter, glossier green, with faintly lobed leaf tips, are more loosely put together and are borne on a more sprawling pale green stem. I have marked it with an asterisk because although the general opinion seems to be that it has no soil fads Mr. Graham Thomas states that it is calcifuge. I am only familiar with its performance on a variety of acid soils and in such conditions it makes a first-rate, easy carpeter under trees and between shrubs, even in dense shade. Indeed the deeper the shade the richer the green will be. The true beauty of the shining evergreen carpet can only be assessed when a fair-sized clump has become established, such as that shown in the illustration facing p. 145; so do not be disappointed if a young plant straight from the nursery looks pretty dull to start with, for it will not take long to spread. Pachysandra is more likely to be found in the shrub section of a catalogue, though it does not seem to me to be markedly shrubby in character.

(For glycerining see Chapter IX.)

P. terminalis 'Variegata' ('Silveredge')

A less common variegated form of the species, *P. terminalis* 'Variegata' also bears some resemblance to one of the spurges—this time to the green and white annual, *Euphorbia marginata*, or "Snow-on-the-Mountain". The variegation is a pleasant mixture of cream and white edging the light grey-green foliage, but being smaller and narrower than those of the species the leaves make a meaner rosette of a somewhat muddled, screwed-up appearance. It spreads more slowly than the other and its comparative lack of vigour makes it a less effective colonizer of empty spaces. My plants are too new to provide reliable data, but those growing in the shade appear to be making rather better growth than the others. Pinching out the tips of the shoots of young plants of either kind helps to counteract the legginess which may result in shady positions. Both need protection from slugs.

PAEONIA—"Peony"

Species: P. delavayi (A.M. 1934), P. lutea ludlowii ('Sherriff's Variety') (A.M. 1954, A.G.M. 1963)
Shrubs; deciduous

P. mlokosewitschii (A.M. 1929, A.G.M. 1955)—"Molly-the-Witch"
Hardy perennial

15. *Osmunda regalis*

16. *Paeonia lutea ludlowii*

Among the species the large, compound, light green leaves of
P. delavayi and *P. lutea ludlowii* are of a similar, much divided
pattern, the former being the more solid and with a pinkish
stalk and the latter having a more delicately fringed outline to
its leaflets. (See illustration opposite.) Both are comparatively small-flowered, an intense maroon-red in the case of the
former and a clear yellow cup-shape in that of *lutea ludlowii*.
They seed themselves liberally and although the foliage is
always good the flowers of some of the *delavayi* seedlings in
particular vary widely in quality, both as regards colour and
size, the best forms providing striking material for flower
arrangement though apt to get lost among the luxuriant leaves
on the growing plant.

As a foliage plant *P. mlokosewitschii* bears very little resemblance to either of the foregoing, the lovely leaves being much
less lobed and all rounds and curves where before were tapered
points and laciniation. In colour the newly unfurling leaves are
of a beauty beyond description, first emerging in an ineffable,
soft, smoky, brownish-pink guise with brighter pink stalks and
veining. These gradually become suffused with a still lovely
grey-green as they mature and they colour well in autumn. The
small, cupped, cream-yellow flowers are also delightful, as are
the scarlet and midnight-blue seed pods. Altogether a plant
most devoutly to be wished for flower arrangement but lament-
ably scarce in commerce at the time of writing, and has been
for some years. This is one for which we should keep pestering
the growers.

P. suffruticosa Hybrids

Shrubs; deciduous

The *suffruticosa* hybrid tree peonies are invariably equipped
with beautiful leaves designed more on the lines of *P. delavayi*,
but less divided and often suffused with grey-pink or
purplish tinges. But these are pre-eminently flowering shrubs,
and of such magnificence that they must be selected for the

colour and shape of the bloom, taking the fine foliage as it comes.

Herbaceous Varieties
Hardy perennials

Much the same is true of the herbaceous types, in which the quality of the flower is also likely to be of the first importance in making one's selection. And if one follows one's fancy in the matter of the bloom a supply of first-class foliage will automatically result, from the rich, copper-red, close-furled shoots in early spring to the boldly ornate compound design of the mature leaves with undivided leaflets. Most, though not all, varieties include fine autumn foliage colour.

Boiling and standing in warm water is usually sufficient by way of conditioning, but if not, follow up by stem-tipping and soaking. Moisture-retaining substances are unsuitable for any peony foliage.

PELTIPHYLLUM peltatum (*Saxifraga peltata*)—"Umbrella Plant".
Hardy perennial

Familiarly known as the "Umbrella Plant" on account of its massive circular leaves, *Peltiphyllum peltatum* is, as a rule, sufficiently funnel-shaped to suggest rather an umbrella blown inside out. The foliage is borne on single stems up to 3 ft. tall and is often 1 ft. or more in diameter. It is much netted and glossy-textured, with decorative lobing and scalloping round the perimeter, and the colour ranges from bronze in spring, dark green at maturity and crimson in autumn, to pale green on the underside. The large corymbs of bristly-stemmed pink saxifrage-flowers appear in early spring before the leaves. I believe that this may be grown in any really moist soil, but it is above all a plant for the waterside, where these great sculptured saucers really look as though they belong.

Though I have not had an opportunity to try the cut foliage in water I have seen it used in good condition at maturity, but the young leaves look dangerously soft. I am told that it is essential to put it into water *immediately* after cutting if a straight stem is required. It is most impressive when used with other plant material in scale with its bold design. (Untried.)

PHALARIS arundinacea 'Picta' ('Variegata')—"Gardener's Garters", "Ladies' Garters", "Ribbon Grass"
Grass

One or two growers describe this grass as having "golden" variegation, but unless there is a second distinct form of which I am unaware (and which should bear a separate varietal name) the adjective seems hardly applicable, since the broad white striping of the leaves has barely a hint of cream. The foliage is popular for cutting, but the exaggerated droop of the leaves does not always suit our purpose and my own feeling is that the similar, but firmer leaf of *Glyceria maxima* 'Variegata' serves a more useful purpose, though admittedly a little more fastidious in its requirements. Indeed the phalaris is much too easy to please and I have been forced to root mine out—with considerable difficulty—in desperation at its abuse of my hospitality. It spreads enthusiastically in all directions, worming its way into the heart of other plants as it goes and growing to about 2½ ft. high in ordinary circumstances, but in rich, moist soils its stature may be almost doubled.

Boil and soak.

PHILADELPHUS—"Mock Orange" (but *not* "Syringa")
Shrub; deciduous

P. coronarius 'Aureus'

Generally speaking philadelphus foliage is downright dull, but that of *P. coronarius* 'Aureus' is a strikingly colourful exception. The acid lime-yellow leaf colour is most brilliant in the new growth in spring (Yellow-Green 150B), but plants grown

131

in the shade will retain an attractive though slightly greener lime throughout the summer, whereas too much sunshine bakes the leaves to a harsh, true yellow, frequently scorching them brown at the edges into the bargain. This is a comparatively dwarf variety, usually about 6 ft. tall, but depending somewhat on growing conditions and on the amount of pruning it receives. A good many of the long, gracefully curving sprays are likely to be cut for pedestal work and other large arrangements, but the thinning of confused twiggery in late summer or autumn is also necessary to help the production of the more elegantly shaped pieces. I believe in cutting out some of the oldest wood to ground level every other year or so for the same reason. The ovate, serrated leaves vary a good deal in size, the largest being about 3½ in. long by 2½ in., and they are often borne on rather awkwardly forking side-shoots growing at stiff angles to the main branches, but even these, with a little judicious trimming in the hand, can be shaped to suit the flower arranger's needs. Philadelphus is not fussy as regards soil, but foliage varieties should not be allowed to become parched, particularly if they are required to provide well-behaved cutting material.

Being somewhat thin-textured, especially in spring, the cut foliage of *P. coronarius* 'Aureus' needs to be boiled and soaked for a few hours only.

P. coronarius 'E. A. Bowles' ('Bowles Variety'), P. coronarius 'Innocence' and P. coronarius 'Variegatus'

These are comparatively rare forms of *P. coronarius,* one of which was given to me by a connoisseur as *P. coronarius* 'Variegatus'. It has rounded light green leaves measuring about 2 in. by 1½ in., of much the same shape as 'Aureus', but broadly margined and streaked with cream-white and an occasional touch of pale grey-green. I believe this and the one sold as 'E. A. Bowles' or 'Bowles Variety' to be identical, as is borne out by the fact that 'Variegatus' features in the planting known as "Bowles's Corner" at Wisley. At maturity it makes an exceptionally cool-looking, delightful foliage plant, but young nursery stock may look disappointingly scruffy (probably as a result of growing in full exposure) at least until the leaves develop to their proper size. The foliage effect of a well-grown plant is much more attractive than that of 'Innocence', which has smaller leaves in a mixture of deep cream and fairly dark green.

'Variegatus' is not a very vigorous or rapid grower and newly emerging leaves in spring may get badly scorched by frost, wind, or late spring drought, so a sheltered, shady spot and attention to watering are advisable if this charming and unusual phila-delphus is to do itself justice in the years ahead.

My young plant has not been able to spare more than an 18-in. spray for testing as cutting material, but this was put into hot water and lasted well over a week.

PHLOX paniculata 'Norah Leigh'
Hardy perennial

The recently introduced phlox with the elegantly tapered, variegated leaf of primrose yellow on two shades of green caused something of a stir in flower arranging circles and indeed the foliage is strikingly attractive when the plant is in good heart, as may be judged from the illustration facing p. 144. But al-though the growers are fairly unanimous in hailing it as vigorous I have heard it rumoured that 'Norah Leigh' is a bit of a miff. Without personal experience I can neither confirm nor deny this, but it is only fair to say that I have seen several healthy-looking clumps of this 3-ft. foliage plant, particularly at Wisley, where it no doubt gets the 'good light soil' it is said to need. There it grows in full sun, though it is said to like shade and to need plenty of moisture. (Untried.)

PHORMIUM tenax—"New Zealand Flax"
Shrub; evergreen

This majestic evergreen not only provides a spectacular con-trast of form among the prevailing rounded contours in the garden scene but is also of inestimable value to the flower arranger for its immense, rigid sword-blades of indestructible, slightly glaucous greenery often thinly outlined in maroon. These rise from ground level in clumps composed of assorted sizes: some leaves may be as much as 8 or 9 ft. long, some very much less, most of them 4 or 5 in. wide and some are conveniently twisted into a barely perceptible arc or incipient spiral, which makes them much more adaptable as cut material than an uncompromisingly straight, erect blade—for they are not at all malleable.

P. tenax 'Purpureum'

The purple-leaved and variegated forms, though less commonly grown, are at least equally noble garden ornaments and are perhaps even more desirable than the species for floral decoration. The coloration of 'Purpureum' is a subtle, glistening blend of dull purple and bronze faintly shot with red on a grey-green foundation. My own experience bears out the suggestion that there may be two distinct varieties, one having much longer, broader and more erect leaf blades than the other, which answers to the description of the much rarer *P. tenax alpinum* 'Purpureum'. Whereas both have their separate uses in flower arrangement the smaller one is slightly less effective out of doors, not only on account of its lesser stature but also because the more flaccid leaves are inclined to sprawl. Nevertheless it seems to produce its foliage in greater profusion than the other, making a densely furnished clump when conditions are to its liking and here it would appear to be slightly hardier than the larger-leaved version. In either case the foliage colour is a fascinating ingredient in a grouping of off-beat hues.

P. tenax 'Variegatum' and P. tenax 'Veitchii'

The leaf colour of 'Variegatum' is made up of almost invisible hairstripes of light and medium green, interspersed and bordered with wider bands of cream. Some leaves barely carry any variegation, some are almost all cream and the majority have a broad cream margin thinly piped with reddish-brown. The amount of striation varies considerably from plant to plant, so it is as well to do one's shopping in person, or at least to insist on adequate variegation if ordering by post. I have not seen the other variegated cultivar, *P. tenax* 'Veitchii', in which the green blades have a broad central stripe of yellow.

P. colensoi (*cookianum*)

Lastly, if these are all on too massive a scale for you, *Phormium colensoi* may fill the bill, for this is a much more miniature species, with greener leaves than those of *P. tenax* and a height of only 2 to 3 ft. and other vital statistics proportionately reduced. It is a particularly hardy one but is nothing like as spectacular as the bolder types.

All the above have immensely tall spikes of orange-mahogany flowers except *P. colensoi*, which has dwarfer, yellower ones. Phormiums are said to prefer thoroughly moist situations and yet I know some huge specimens of *P. tenax* which flourish in light sand at the top of a hot, dry bank; and my own plants get by with very little moisture, with the help of the leaf mulch in the shrub borders. I have found 'Purpureum' the least hardy in our exceptionally cold winters here and this one, in its large-leaved form, is therefore given the protection of a warm south wall, while the rest mostly chance their luck in the open garden, where they suffer some, but not fatal, damage in a bad winter. Much superficial harm is caused here by the weight of snow and the force of the wintry gales, which bend the foliage beyond repair and leave the clumps looking miserably dejected until the battered blades are replaced by new ones. I have recently tried to defeat this by bunching the clump together and tying it to a stake at different heights with old nylon stockings (which combine strength with a soft, elastic texture), during the winter; results have been most encouraging, providing frost as well as snow protection.

The leaves of all these phormiums are almost indestructible when cut and may also be preserved. (See Chapter IX.)

PHYSOCARPUS opulifolius 'Luteus' (*ribesifolius* 'Aureus')
(*Spiraea opulifolia* 'Lutea')
Shrub; deciduous

Physocarpus opulifolius 'Luteus' is not a collector's piece. But
to the eye of the flower arranger, which sees differently from that
of the plantsman, this shrub has sterling qualities: nor, I believe,
would the gardener with a keen colour sense side with the horticultural snobs in condemning it as common or coarse. It is tall,
vigorous and erect-habited, with leaves of a splendid lime-yellow
or lime-green hue, retaining much of the *chartreuse* colour of the
young spring foliage throughout the season and developing burnished tips to the shoots in late summer. The coloration is much
the same as that of *Philadelphus coronarius* 'Aureus', but the
physocarpus needs a sunnier position to get the best colour—
that is, a bright lime-yellow—whereas too much shade will dim
this to a more ordinary light yellowish-green. One can cut at the
big bush quite savagely for huge, pedestal-size wands of foliage
reminiscent of that of the currant in shape. Indeed the quality of
the foliage is improved by hard pruning of overcrowded growth
in mid-or late summer if this has not already occurred at the
hands of the flower arranger.

Rare, in the connoisseur's sense, it will never be; but scarce
it may well be before very long. This is not the first time that I
have rallied to its defence—nor have I any personal axe-grinding
in view; two plants are plenty for my needs, but unless demand
keeps pace with supply the dwindling band of growers who continue to list it are likely to drop it as uneconomic pretty soon,
as so many of their colleagues already appear to have done.
Boil.

PIERIS* (*Andromeda*)
Shrub; evergreen

Pieris formosa forrestii (A.M. 1924, F.C.C. 1930)

This is perhaps even more renowned for the brilliance of its vermilion young leaf shoots than for the refined beauty of the clustered panicles of pitcher-shaped ivory-white flowers accompanying them in spring, on a slow-growing shrub which eventually reaches 8 ft. or thereabouts. 'Wakehurst Form' (A.G.M. 1944) is commonly acclaimed the best on both counts, with translucent scarlet leaves thrusting up like flaming torches and expanding into flat flower-like heads which gradually fade through coral-pink to plain dark green at maturity, sometimes putting on a second show in the autumn. Growers lightheartedly sum up its cultural requirements as being the same as for the rhododendrons to which it is related, but it is in fact far more difficult to please than many of the latter. Given a moist, acid soil and sufficient shade to prevent the tender young leaves being scorched and to prolong the scarlet leaf colour, it still requires very special placing to protect this stupendous spring foliage display from wind damage and frosting. The plant is hardy enough to withstand severe winter cold when dormant, but the bud-tenderness of both flowers and foliage render it very vulnerable to spring frosts, especially if the early morning sun is able to get at the swelling buds.

P. x 'Forest Flame' ('Flame of the Forest')

P. x 'Forest Flame' is a comparatively recent hybrid between *formosa forrestii* and *japonica*, which combines much of the remarkable young leaf colour of the former parent with the more compact habit and hardier constitution of the latter. It, too, is slow-growing. The foliage is of a slightly less intense, pinker scarlet, but has the advantage of opening rather later, thus suffering less risk of frost damage. A small plant has weathered two winters here without damage, so it may well succeed where the other can barely be said to exist, lingering on as a pitiful, stunted relic unadorned by flowers in all the years I have had it and almost equally devoid of fiery foliage.

P. japonica 'Variegata'

The other parent of 'Forest Flame', *Pieris japonica*, has such lovely fan-shaped clusters of drooping sprays of ivory bells, tinged brownish-pink in bud, that I feel they deserve a plain-coloured backcloth of foliage to display them to advantage, whereas in its variegated form flowers and foliage tend to cancel one another out. *P. japonica* 'Variegata' has comparatively small, narrowly elliptical leaves which combine a light greyish-green with cream-white and a tinge of pink. Most people consider it a pretty foliage plant, but for my taste there is too much variegation chasing too little space in this dense, leafy little shrub and the effect is merely confusing. I believe it is not very hardy.

P. taiwanensis (A.M. 1922, F.C.C. 1923, A.G.M. 1963)

This is a reasonably hardy species of dwarfer and more spreading habit than most, with delightfully tinged young foliage shoots of a glistening coppery pink. Though less arresting than some it is well worth growing both for the flowers and for the youthful foliage, though it needs a sheltered position to save its early spring blooms from frosting.

Although the translucent shoots look too tender to stand satisfactorily as cut material I believe that they give no trouble if boiled and given a brief soaking. I have not been able to try any of the above but expect that all would respond to conditioning of this kind. (Untried.)

PITTOSPORUM
Shrub; evergreen
P. tenuifolium (A.M. 1931)

This is, I suppose, the most popular—or at least the most available—of all purchasable foliage, from the street barrow to the classiest florist's shop, but it has little charm for me. The waxy, wavy little grey-green leaves on their wiry black stems are pretty enough in themselves, but the habit is uncomfortably stiff and unyielding for cutting material, at least as sold to the public. I have a suspicion that a home-grown bush might yield much more attractively shaped pieces than are ever offered for sale, but that since these are awkward to bunch and pack for market only the straightest of the leafy branches find their way to Covent Garden and thence to shops, barrows and street stalls. Perhaps because it may be the only greenery in the shop the slender, small-leaved evergreen sprays are too often obliged to keep incongruous company with florists' flowers which are entirely out of scale—with big, blowsy tulips or chrysanthemums, or with such unsuitable blooms as daffodils, irises or hyacinths, whereas they might look most at home in an arrangement of mixed foliage.

It makes an attractive, tall hedging plant in mild areas, particularly in seaside gardens, but it is not entirely hardy in colder districts inland.

P. tenuifolium 'Silver Queen' (A.M. 1914) and P. x 'Garnettii' (*barrettii*)

Of several variegated pittosporums 'Silver Queen', with white-edged, very pale grey-green leaves, is the most widely grown; but a more uncommon recent introduction from New Zealand known as *P. x* 'Garnettii' is superior for a number of reasons. I am uncertain of the parentage of this hybrid, but it lacks the characteristic wavy margins of *tenuifolium*, with larger, tougher leaves than 'Silver Queen'. Though the variegation is similar the white margin is more distinct on the broader leaf and the general effect less anaemic, including a purple tinge in winter. It is erect-habited and said to be vigorous and, most important of all, it is reputed to be hardier than the other.

P. tenuifolium 'Golden King' and P. tenuifolium 'Atropurpureum'

Other varieties of *Pittosporum tenuifolium* with unusual foliage are the yellow-leaved 'Golden King', and 'Atropurpureum', in which the leaf colour is a really good dusky mahogany brown devoid of red or purple, with some greenish undertones. Both are rare and I have seen only the latter, which I covet most among the pittosporums. Not only is the colour beautiful and subtle, but the waxy texture and the wavy leaf contour are attractively pronounced. I doubt, however, whether

139

this is any more hardy than the rather tender 'Golden King'.

PLANTAGO major 'Rubrifolia'—Form of "Plantain"
Hardy perennial

The plantain I like best is *Plantago rosularis*, on account of its weird, chunky, deep green "flowers"; but when these are absent it looks so much like the common weed that un-flowered seedlings are in constant danger of their lives in well-kept gardens. *P. major* 'Rubrifolia' runs no such risk, for the broadly ovate, heavily ribbed leaves are of an unmis-takable, bronzed, light beetroot-crimson if grown in full ex-posure. They may be up to 7 in. long and are more upstanding than the other.

If attacked by a disfiguring mildew, affected plants should be destroyed—and this is no great sacrifice, because self-sown pro-geny are always available to carry on, unless the spent flower spikes have been removed before seeding.

Soak.

POLYGONATUM multiflorum (A.M. 1957)—"David's Harp", "Jingling Johnny", "Solomon's Seal"
Hardy perennial

The old-fashioned Solomon's Seal has long been a favourite flower for indoor decoration, but is perhaps less commonly thought of as a foliage plant. Indeed the flower arranger often strips all the leaves from the sprays of elongated, pendent green and white bells with the intention of displaying the latter to better advantage, though to me the effect is as naked and unnatural as a cheap set of false teeth. The large, broadly oval deep green leaflets may measure as much as 7½ in. by nearly 3 in. and are staggered on either side of the upper half of the tall, sturdy, arching stems above the flowers. These graceful 3-ft. sprays of foliage are invaluable for large arrangements in particular and are beautiful when successfully glycerined. (See Chapter IX.)

P. japonicum 'Variegatum' (*multiflorum* 'Striatum'), ('Baker's Variegated')
Hardy perennial

The pretty little variegated Solomon's Seal, *P. japonicum* 'Variegatum', is more miniature in every part, rarely reaching 2 ft., with fewer, smaller and more rounded light green leaves borne on reddish stems. The leaflets measure about 4 in. by 2 in. and are trimmed, or partially trimmed, with a neat piping of cream, usually at the tip end of the leaf only. I only know of one form of variegated polygonatum, but perhaps it would not be safe to assume that *P. multiflorum* 'Striatum' and 'Baker's Variegated' are alternative names for the one I grow.

The larvae of the Solomon's Seal Sawfly strip the leaves of all kinds of polygonatum down to the skeleton midribs in midsummer in my garden unless I take timely precautions. Dusting the foliage and the ground beneath the plants with derris at intervals from the time that the fly lays its eggs in May, until midsummer, seems to keep the leaves free of this pest and the fat sausage-like grey grubs which swarm on the undersides of any of the foliage sprays which escape the treatment in late June or early July succumb quickly to derris (or, I believe, malathion) either in powder or spray form.
Soak both.

POPULUS alba—"Abele", "Silver Poplar", "White Poplar"
Tree; deciduous

I have never found this poplar of much value for cutting once the leaves are fully developed, since I know of no example which does not then become riddled with unsightly caterpillar holes— regrettable, because it could spare such useful lengths of the felted, dark grey-green leaves backed with white which are borne in curving sprays and arabesques. But in spring the graceful lines of the slender branches burgeoning with silver-white make them delightful cutting material. Later the leaves shimmer and quiver attractively to display their white undersides in the slightest

141

breeze and the overall silver-grey hue of this very fast-growing tree contrasts well with shrubs of bronze and yellow foliage colours in the garden. But the unbelievably wide-spreading, shallow roots can be a serious menace to buildings if the tree is planted where they can find their way into drains and foundations. (See also Chapter IX.)

POTENTILLA fruticosa 'Vilmoriniana' (A.G.M. 1926, A.M. 1965)—Form of "Shrubby Cinquefoil"
Shrub; deciduous

Of the many potentillas which are such excellent flowering shrubs *P. fruticosa* 'Vilmoriniana' is, I think, the only one with foliage worthy of special mention for flower arrangement. Quite a number have attractive silvery leaves, but most of these are dwarf varieties, whereas this is an erect, 4-ft. shrub with small, five-fingered, silver-green leaves wrapped in silky floss on branches which vary from long and straight to tortuous shapes. The foliage colour also makes an attractive setting for the primrose-yellow strawberry-flowers from June to late autumn.

'Vilmoriniana' is sometimes said to be a difficult plant, but it has never caused any trouble here. Like all potentillas, it is entirely hardy and it no doubt enjoys the rapid drainage provided in my garden. All do best in full sun and, in the case of the taller types such as this, some of the old wood should be cut out in early spring to encourage new growth from the base. My plant does not seem to object to fairly hard cutting at any time during the summer as floral decoration occasions demand and it tends to get somewhat leggy and bare at the base if not pruned fairly regularly.

PRIMULA vulgaris—"Primrose"
Hardy perennial; ground cover

The common primrose can scarcely be described as a foliage plant and yet I find the broad, round-nosed leaves extraordinarily useful for cutting. The texture is so beautifully crimpled, the colour so often a delicious lime-green and the shape can be made to curve so conveniently over the lip of the container.

The leaves should be stem-tipped and soaked and because so much water becomes trapped in the rugose surfaces they should be spread out to dry on some absorbent material for a short time before using in an arrangement, to avoid dripping and siphoning. They will not last in moisture-retaining substances.

PRUNUS

The so-called purple foliages are much in demand for flower arrangement and there are quite a number among the prunuses, but they are not ideal for the purpose because, whether or not the birds allow one to enjoy the flowers, caterpillars rarely if ever spare the leaves.

P. x blireiana (A.M. 1914, F.C.C. 1923, A.G.M. 1928)
Tree or shrub; deciduous

P. cerasifera 'Atropurpurea' ('Pissardii') (F.C.C. 1884, A.G.M. 1928)—"Purple-leaf Plum"
Tree or shrub; deciduous

P. x cistena—"Purple-leaved Sand Cherry"
Shrub; deciduous

My own preference is for the charming hybrid *P. x blireiana*— half cherry-plum and half apricot—which can be grown either as a large shrub or a small tree, with nicely coloured copper-bronze leaves and delightful little sugar-pink flower pompons. *P. cerasifera* 'Atropurpurea', which is one of its parents, is however the one most commonly planted for its dark purplish-brown foliage; but although the tender young spring growth is of an attractive light copper the colour soon darkens overmuch for my taste. It makes a larger tree than the other and can also be grown in bush form. I have long since been forced to discard both in this garden in favour of the more bird- and pest-proof cotinuses and barberries of similar leaf colour. *P. cerasifera* 'Atropurpurea' has also played a more recent part in the production of the popular hybrid, *P. x cistena*, which makes a much smaller shrub with an average height of 4 or 5 ft. and leaves of a more intense red-mahogany than either of the foregoing. Caterpillars have a way of making all of these unusable for flower arrangement.

Cut foliage consequently needs a careful going-over to remove damaged leaves and should then be boiled and soaked to defeat its tendency to wilt in water.

P. laurocerasus—"Cherry Laurel", "Common Laurel"
Shrub; evergreen

The genus *Prunus* covers a confusingly wide range of trees and shrubs, providing surprises such as the inclusion of the Common Laurel among the almonds, apricots, cherries, plums and peaches. *P. laurocerasus* makes an efficient, peep-proof hedge, but the prevalence of solid walls of close-clipped laurel in this residential neighbourhood has somewhat dulled my appetite for what is in fact an evergreen foliage plant of noble stature when allowed to grow untrammelled to its full height and spread. The oval, glossy, bright green leaves can then be had in huge lengths which make excellent background material for large winter arrangements. The foliage also responds well to glycerining. (See Chapter IX.)

P. laurocerasus 'Variegata'
Shrub; evergreen

Whatever one's feelings about the Common Laurel one cannot fail to covet its variegated form as foliage for floral decoration, for the cream or white variegation on the bright green can be strikingly ornamental, even suffusing some shoots altogether. I am at present hoping for rooted cuttings from branches which turned up as a substitute for some other foliage ordered one Christmas from the florist, but it does not strike very willingly in mid-winter in the open. (I was interested to find that the first cutting to get going was one which had been daubed with clear nail varnish and lightly scattered with glass glitter, which presumably reduced transpiration during the rooting process.)

17. *Phlox paniculata* 'Norah Leigh'

18. *Pachysandra terminalis*

19. *Polystichum setiferum* 'Divisilobum'

Until recently I had been unable to trace any source of supply for this variegated laurel, but Messrs. Hillier have lately notified me that stocks are now available. Meanwhile they warn me that it is 'of rather weak constitution', which is not of course unusual in a variegated plant; but whereas it might well be too scraggy for hedging I can testify that I am able to buy large and lovely branches of fine design for floral decoration from my florist. It seems however that in some cases the variegation is disappointingly meagre, so one needs to take one's pick. (See also Chapter IX.)

P. lusitanica 'Variegata'—Form of "Portugal Laurel"
Shrub; evergreen

This attractively variegated laurel is very different from that just described, having very much smaller oval leaves (approximately 3 in. by 1½ in. on my young specimen, but possibly bigger on an established plant), of a more matt-finished, darker green with a narrow white border, and sometimes tinged with pink, on red-barked stems. My own plant is young (and uncut) as yet and I understand that it slowly reaches 8 to 10 ft. It seems to me to be of reasonably strong constitution. (Untried.)

PYRUS salicifolia 'Pendula'—"Silver-leaved Weeping Pear", "Silver Willow-leaved Pear"
Tree; deciduous

Both the leaf shape and the weeping habit of *Pyrus salicifolia* 'Pendula' are more suggestive of a willow than of the familiar fruit tree which the word 'pear' usually brings to mind. This graceful little weeping tree grows to about 15 ft. and in the early part of the season it has intensely silver-white foliage, covered at first with silky hairs and looking all the whiter for the admixture of small, cream-white flowers in April, but later turning to a more glossy greenish-grey. Even after some of its spring glory has departed the colour mixes effectively in a foliage grouping of purple-leaved cotinus, vivid yellow *Cornus alba* 'Spaethii' and blue-green rue or *Hosta sieboldiana*. The colour is much the same as that of the White Poplar, but although the latter grows so fast that it helps to give a new garden a semblance of maturity long before this slow-growing but more elegant weeping standard would begin to pull its weight as a garden decorator, I would choose the pyrus rather than the poplar for this small garden if I could start again. (Untried.)

RHEUM palmatum 'Red-leaved Form'—Form of "Rhubarb"
Hardy perennial

It would be hard to beat the young rhubarb of the kitchen garden, with its ruby stems and tightly crumpled lime-yellow leaves, for sheer brilliance of colour; but some of its grander relations are even more imposing foliage plants. In the red-leaved forms of *Rheum palmatum* a glowing red suffuses the young growth, bunched-up leaf and all, in spring, and as the leaves uncurdle themselves they flatten into many-pointed, ornamental, palmate lobes with five main veins radiating from the stalk junction. At this stage it is the backs of the leaves which provide the chief attraction, for whereas at maturity the upper surface is more nearly green the underside retains much of the original hue, with conspicuous, raised veining of a light copper-pink standing out in marked contrast to the rich crimson ground. At present the leaves on my newly acquired young plant measure no more than 1 ft. each way, on colourful 6-in. stalks, but an ultimate height and spread of 6 ft. in each direction, with leaves about three times the size of mine, may be expected. My plant has survived several winters here unscathed and appears hardy enough to require no special protection. I feel sure that a sunny position is necessary for good leaf colour, and moisture for exuberance. Assuming that the richer the soil the more massive the result will be, I am tempted to try mine on a comparatively meagre diet with the object of keeping the size of the plant to manageable proportions in the cutting bed and that of the foliage itself to more modest dimensions for floral decoration. The immensely tall spikes of soft pink rhubarb flowers in late spring are followed by branching heads of disc-shaped seeds of equally attractive colouring.

Boil, and stand in warm water as hot as the stalk will take
without damage. Arrange in deep water if possible.

RHODODENDRON*
Shrub; evergreen

Without wishing to denigrate the hardy hybrid rhododendron
as a foliage plant—and very fine some of them can be—I think
few would dispute that it is usually among the species rather
than among the more familiar iron-clads that the most spectacularly beautiful foliage is to be found, due in most cases to a vivid
rust-brown or silver felting on the undersides of the leaves. It
seems unlikely that any flower arranger would take steps to
destroy such an ornamental trait, but it is not unknown for this
colourful indumentum to be mistaken for disease and sprayed
with all manner of fungicides in a vain attempt to cure it! Conversely, I am sometimes asked what I do to induce it. In the
selection which follows I have limited myself in the main to
rhododendrons of A and B hardiness categories: that is to say,
those tough enough to succeed in any part of the country, requiring only some shade, in the case of B ratings, to give the best
results. I need hardly add that in all cases an acid soil is essential.

R. falconeri (A.M. 1922) and R. macabeanum (F.C.C. 1935)

Considerations of hardiness should exclude the mammoths
with leaves of up to 1 yd. long—for, generally speaking, the
larger the leaf the more difficult the plant—and make borderline cases of some of the hardier large-leaved species such as
falconeri and *macabeanum*, which I think must get a brief mention for their superb foliage, in spite of their C rating. *R. falconeri* has broad, obovate leaves up to 12 in. long, with thick
rusty felting on the underside and fawn-coloured young shoots;
and *macabeanum* has red-scaled buds effectively combined with
the silvery new growth which matures to dark green leaves of a
slightly smaller size with a grey-white backing. Both make
superb tree-like foliage plants, with pale yellow, purple-spotted
flowers in spring, but would be totally misplaced in a small

garden. These are only seen at their best in a mild, moist, wood-land setting and in the absence of these prerequisites the foliage has such a dilapidated appearance that they are not worth at-tempting, especially when it is realized that other less fussy species are equipped with similar-coloured indumentum.

R. argyrophyllum (A.M. 1934)

Dealing first with the silver-backed types, the bone-hardy and slow-growing *R. argyrophyllum* has narrow, tapering leaves about 6 in. long by 1½ in. wide, with a bright silver underside and young growth totally clothed in silver-white. It makes a dense, rounded bush which will not exceed 7 ft. or so for many years. The flowers are pale pink. (A rating.)

R. niveum (A.M. 1951)

This, too, is a very hardy species, but its purple flowers come so early in the year that they are vulnerable to frost damage un-less shelter can be provided, and such conditions will also be beneficial to the young leaf shoots, which are correspondingly precocious and thus susceptible to damage by late spring frosts. The foliage is most unusual, particularly in early summer, when the white-felted new growth mingles with the mature leaf-rosettes, which are greyish above and silvery tomentose beneath. An average leaf measures about 7 in. by 2½ in. In woodland conditions it reaches about 15 ft. (B rating.)

R. arizelum and R. fictolacteum (A.M. 1953)

There is a wider choice among the hardy species ornamented with red-brown indumentum, ranging from the large-leaved and tree-like to the semi-dwarf, but the latter are not very useful in the present context since they are unable to spare much foliage for cutting. *Arizelum* and *fictolacteum* are among the tougher of the tree-like types of the *Falconeri* series, with leaves as long as those of *R. falconeri* itself (about 9 in. by 4 in. in favourable circumstances, but less in cold, dry conditions), forming large, orderly, deep green rosettes felted with orange-brown beneath and with young shoots covered in rufous hairs. The flowers of *arizelum* are pale yellow with crimson markings and those of *fictolacteum* either pale pink or white, with darker spotting. (Both B rating.)

R. bureavii (A.M. 1939)

Few acid-soiled gardens would be too small to find room for the compact 6 ft. of *R. bureavii*. This rounded, leafy shrub has leathery foliage measuring about 5 in. by 2 in. with a particularly woolly backing of spectacular ginger-brown and a dense casing of beige-coloured down on the young shoots, stems and all, making this one of the best of the easier foliage species. The flowers are pale pink. (B rating.)

R. campanulatum

Of this species the Knap Hill form is generally acclaimed the best, as having the most nearly blue flowers combined with the finest foliage—light coffee-coloured, short-piled velvet in the young shoots, deepening in colour on the undersurface of the leaf to light chestnut at maturity. The leaves average about 6 in. in length and the bush itself is usually around 15 ft. tall. It is one of the hardiest. (A rating.)

R. fulvum (A.M. 1933)

Like so many of the species, this is a very variable one, so it is advisable to make one's own selection in a specialist nursery. My own plant is from the Exbury Gardens and was recommended as a substitute for the temporarily non-available *R. campanulatum* which I had come to collect. It has oval dark green leaves from about 7 to 10 in. long by 2½ in. wide, with a backing of intense rusty-orange, and paler new growth of apricot-coloured suède. My own plant has accidentally become so densely shaded as to discourage the formation of flower buds and although it is now a fair size it has so far produced only two flower trusses of a washy blue-pink, which I can well do without. The white flowers of the form called *R. fulvum album* associate much more pleasingly with the orange leaf-backs, but the size of the plant at the time of purchase was more important to me than the flower colour and what started as a 3- or 4-ft. specimen is, happily, making fairly fast progress towards an ultimate 15 ft. This is one of the most gratifying examples of the grower's 'nearest' that I have ever been persuaded to accept and has become one of the most highly prized foliage plants in my garden and one of my top favourites for flower arrangement. (B rating.)

R. mallotum (A.M. 1933)

In addition to the spectacular, velvety, bright chestnut indumentum backing the broad, well shaped foliage of *R. mallotum* at maturity the young unfolding leaf shoots are also enveloped in dense rufous hairs. Though this species will make do in a shady spot in any but the coldest gardens the leaves are said to be much finer and larger in mild districts of high rainfall. Unless such conditions prevail some of the species of A and B ratings might possibly be more rewarding, but the intensely vivid hue of the woolly indumentum would encourage more cautious gardeners than I to take a chance. The colour of the leaf-backs is the best I know. It is a slow-growing rhododendron, making a small tree about 10 ft. high in time, and has deep crimson flowers. (C rating.)

Turning now from species with decorative indumentum we come to an assortment of rhododendrons with other varied assets as foliage plants.

R. cinnabarinum (F.C.C. 1931)

One of these assets is the glaucous leaf colour shared by such species as *cinnabarinum* and *concatenans*. The former makes a rather slender-branched shrub of 8 ft. or more, with narrow leaves of a distinctive blue-green, which is especially vivid in the young shoots, and beautiful tubular flowers of vermilion or cinnabar red. Almost equally blue leaf colour is present in some, but not all, of its hybrids, thus allowing of some choice as regards flower hues. I grow the exquisite 'Lady Chamberlain' (F.C.C. 1931), which has rather larger flowers in a combination of flame and pale tangerine and foliage only slightly less glaucous than that of the species and similarly backed with pale green.

Though rated slightly more tender than the type (C as against B), 'Lady Chamberlain' has never come to any harm in this cold garden, where it occupies a shady, sheltered nook. 'Lady Rosebery' (A.M. 1930, F.C.C. 1932) is another fine *cinnabarinum* hybrid with similarly blue-green foliage but with deep pink flowers. (C rating.)

R. concatenans (F.C.C. 1935, A.M. 1954)

R. concatenans also belongs to the *Cinnabarinum* series and if this and the foregoing species are to be judged purely on their foliage merits *concatenans* has the advantage, I think, over *cinnabarinum*. Not only are the broader, rounder leaves poised more attractively on the branch but the newly unfurled foliage in midsummer, which follows the early apricot-yellow flowers, is of a more intensely glaucous greenish-blue, with a bloom as tangible as that of a grape. But alas, this is only the bloom of youth, gradually disappearing as the leaves age to a darker, less remarkable, but still pleasing blue-green, with matt pale green undersurfaces. This beautiful species has been rather slow in reaching a height of 5 ft. here. (B rating.)

R. 'Moser's Maroon' (A.M. 1932)

The hardy hybrid, 'Moser's Maroon', is included for the beauty of its young leaf shoots in summer, which unfurl to a rich red-mahogany hue and only slowly fade to a more ordinary bronze-green at maturity. Few flowers other than *Paeonia delavayi* can match the unusually sombre maroon-red of the blooms, which add subtlety to a flower arrangement, though not so telling out of doors. Unfortunately the habit is usually too straggly to make a really handsome garden shrub—though I can think of one notably dense-habited exception—but such a fault at least allows one to cut at it, with the possibility of inducing an increased bushiness, without any sense of guilt.

R. obovata (*ponticum* 'Variegatum'), ('President Lincoln')

And now for the most controversial item on my list of foliage rhododendrons—controversial as to name and controversial

as to its right to inclusion among fine-foliaged species and varieties. I have made numerous, so far unsuccessful, attempts to
acquire the rhododendron with the rather narrow, dark green
leaves broadening at the tip and boldly variegated with white,
and also to find out its name. Exbury Gardens supplied the first
of the three names listed above, Messrs. Reuthe the second and
Messrs. Slocock thought that what I was after was a long-since
discontinued variety called 'President Lincoln'. I am not sure
whether these apply to one and the same plant, but Exbury's
obovata looks to me the same as *R. ponticum* 'Variegatum'.
Whether or not you are too much of a purist to countenance a
variegated rhododendron, *qua* rhododendron, in your garden it
would, I think, be difficult to fault it as a foliage plant for floral
decoration. My inquiries for this form have been greeted
variously by the specialist growers with faint disdain to near
indignation, but I am unrepentantly in favour of this 'monstrosity'. If, as I do, you feel that variegated foliages have a role
of their own to play in garden plantings as well as for flower
arrangement, forget that this is a rhododendron in disgrace and
judge it on its merits as an ornamental evergreen on both these
counts. (A rating?)

The above list by no means exhausts the finest foliages in the
genus, but it contains at least a bit of all sorts and to extend it
any farther would overweight the balance in favour of the
rhododendron in a general account of leaves for flower arrangement, which aims to cater alike for those who garden on lime
and those with acid soils.

Given suitable growing conditions rhododendrons are exceptionally trouble-free shrubs. It is advisable to dead-head them
before they set seed after flowering, at least until they outgrow
one's reach, and to protect the foliage from attack by the Vine
Weevil and the Clay-coloured Weevil, which ruin the leaves for
cutting purposes. A heavy dusting of Sevin or BHC on the
ground beneath the plants and a *light* dusting of either among
the foliage at intervals during spring and summer is the easiest
form of control, but if one is at all heavy-handed with the dust-
gun among the leaves the white powdering permanently dis-

figures those with coloured indumentum. If unopened flower buds turn black and hairy these should immediately be picked off and burned, and if it is thought necessary to take precautionary measures against this disease, commonly known as **Bud Blast**, malathion or BHC applied during July is said to be effective. The disease is not troublesome in this garden and I have not tried this remedy.

Young foliage shoots of any of the above should be boiled and care must be taken not to wet the coloured felting, which will leave it permanently blemished.

(For preserving see Chapter IX.)

RODGERSIA
Hardy perennial; ground cover

R. aesculifolia (A.M. 1950)

The specific name of this rodgersia is appropriate to the large, seven-fingered foliage, borne singly on a 12- to 18-in. stem, which closely resembles a larger and more nearly circular horse chestnut leaf in design, each leaflet measuring up to 9 in. long. The fine bronze or copper tinge is most pronounced in spring and autumn and the cream flower panicles in summer are also ornamental. All rodgersia seedheads dry well.

R. pinnata

The leaves of this species are 1 ft. or more in diameter, with a much wrinkled surface, five-fingered as a rule but not quite so deeply lobed as those of *aesculifolia*. I am not sufficiently familiar with the rodgersias to distinguish *R. pinnata* from its cv. 'Superba', which is said to be superior in the chestnut-bronze colour of the leaf and also in the pink flower colour.

R. podophylla (F.C.C. 1890)

The five large, smooth lobes of *R. podophylla* terminate in three points with jagged edges and are grouped in palmate fashion on a tall stem. This is the one most often grown, with a characteristic and attractive bronze hue to the leaf and with cream flower spikes.

What to Grow, and How

Because the rodgersias are so frequently described as suitable for marsh or waterside planting one is apt to be scared of trying them elsewhere; but it seems unnecessarily defeatist to deny oneself such handsome foliage for lack of a pool or stream, when they need only a reasonably moist soil, not necessarily a boggy one. My own fast-draining sandy slopes are so patently unsuitable that I have not attempted them, but I think one may assume that, although they are said to be equally happy in sun or part-shade, the less watery the site the more necessary it would be to provide some shade and a deep, leafy soil by way of compensation, though the splendid leaf colour would be less good in shade. This handsome foliage also needs shelter from the wind. All these rodgersias spread only slowly and are unlikely to become a nuisance. (Untried.)

ROSA rubrifolia (A.M. 1949)
Shrub; deciduous

The rose-breeders' 'novelties' come and go in bewildering profusion, but when the "blue" roses, bicolours and fluorescent scarlets have done their jostling for popularity and been forgotten we shall all go on planting *Rosa rubrifolia*. For it is not the flower but the foliage which counts in this case—and one does not readily tire of lovely leaves. This is a graceful, loose-habited, 6-foot species, with long, almost thornless maroon-red wands of subtly tinted foliage which can only be described by a string of contradictory colour adjectives. Dusky, glaucous, greyish, mauvish-plum, overlaid with a fruit-like bloom, just about sums it up, but the redder tinge provided by the spraying stems also affects the overall colour.

It is obligingly trouble-free, but a sunny position is required to develop the distinctive leaf colour and it needs to be in good heart to yield the finest foliage. One must therefore keep it free of greenfly and other pests, feed and water it well, and prune it hard to promote the strong new arching shoots which are so lovely for cutting. It is mistaken kindness to curb one's predatory instincts in this respect, for the more incidental

154

pruning it receives throughout the season the better it seems to like it.

Boil and soak the young growth in particular.

RUTA graveolens 'Jackman Blue'—Form of "Rue", "Herb of Grace"

Shrub; evergreen

The improved form, 'Jackman's Blue', which is bluer and slightly taller than the Common Rue, is the one most often grown for flower arrangement. It makes a neat sub-shrub of about 2 ft., packed with erect, leafy sprigs of vividly glaucous and curiously aromatic little lacy fans. (See illustration facing p. 176.) The strong smell of the foliage is by no means to everybody's taste, but its colour and design cannot fail to please.

I have never seen it suggested that this rue is not entirely hardy, but I have a bit of a struggle with mine in various positions in this cold garden and often lose plants in a bad winter. In gardens where growth is vigorous they need a fairly severe clipping-over annually in early spring to keep their compact, rounded shape and the little yellow flower spikes in summer should be removed for the same reason, unless the pleasantly neat seedheads are required for drying.

R. graveolens 'Variegata'

Shrub; evergreen

Since I have trouble in keeping the plain blue-leaved rue going I suppose I am foolish in attempting *R. graveolens* 'Variegata' which, as is the way of so many variegated plants, is likely to be a bit of a miff. But the charming combination of blue-green, edged and streaked with cream-white, cannot be forgone without a trial and it may possibly succeed here in a sunny bed against a house wall. This bed is no thing of beauty, but is the warmest one I have for the ill-assorted medley of none-too-hardy foliage plants which I try my best to please in order to be able to cut from them. The variegation in this rue improves in colour as the season advances and the new growth develops, but plants I have

155

seen in mild Dorset gardens are much better-looking than those in colder districts and when it is not well suited the foliage looks a sorry mess. So if I fail once I shall not try again.

All rue foliage is very well-behaved in water.

SALVIA—"Sage"

S. argentea—"Silver Clary"
Hardy biennial or perennial

The boldly ornate, shimmering, silky silver foliage rosettes of *Salvia argentea* are to me unquestionably the loveliest of all the large silver leaves for cutting. Individual leaves are about 15 in. by 9 in. at maturity, roughly ovate heart-shaped and appear to be made of ruched and scalloped plush. They are at their best in youth, losing some of their silver-white sheen with age. Though this beautiful foliage looks almost too good to be true it is in fact reasonably hardy in a sunny spot with good drainage and, preferably, an alkaline soil. By cutting out the comparatively uninteresting, tall white flower spikes at an early stage each year this salvia can be induced to exchange its biennial habit for a more perennial one. Slug-bait should be regularly applied.

Put into warm water when cut.

S. officinalis cultivars
Shrubs; evergreen

Though the pleasant, shrubby, grey-green culinary sage is usually relegated to the kitchen garden it has given rise to several garden varieties with more colourful foliage of similar flavour, but unfortunately none is quite as hardy as the species. *S. officinalis* 'Icterina' makes a compact mound of pleasing grey-green and yellow variegation and, being the least robust of any, would probably need a sun-baked spot at the foot of a wall in many gardens, whereas the rest might be content in full sun and a light soil on the verge of a well-drained shrub border. 'Purpurascens', the "Purple-leaved Sage", is more accurately named than the majority of so-called purple foliages, with larger, velvety leaves of a smoky grey-purple without a hint of bronze or brown. While whole plants often remain a uniform grey-purple, others put forth a number of shoots attractively splashed with light pink and white, earning for them a separate cv. name of 'Purpurascens Variegata' or 'Purple Variegated' in certain catalogues. These two purple forms are less compact in habit than 'Icterina' or 'Tricolor', but can be kept neat and bushy at about 2½ ft. by regular pinching out of the tips of the shoots during the summer.

Despite its name, the lovely little 'Tricolor' includes four or five different hues in its make-up, mixing cream-white, pink, red and purple veining and streaking on a grey-green ground, but with a clearly demarcated light margin and with pink predominant in the overall hue of the small, narrowly ovate leaves. Neither this nor 'Icterina' could ever become very bountiful providers of foliage for cutting, except for quite small arrangements.

The cut foliage of the shrubby sages needs boiling and soaking.

SAMBUCUS—"Elder"
Shrub; deciduous

S. nigra 'Aurea'—"Golden Elder"

The "Golden Elder" differs from the species in the vivid yellow colour of the pinnate foliage, which is made up of four or five narrowly ovate, tapered leaflets in opposite pairs, finished with a terminal one. It is especially useful for chalk soils and any situation, retaining its colour throughout the season.

S. racemosa 'Plumosa Aurea' (A.M. 1895)—"Golden Cut-leaved Elder"

S. racemosa 'Plumosa Aurea' resembles the other in colour, but in this case the pinnate leaves are heavily and ornately fringed. The finely cut leaf margins make this the more decorative of the two, but it is considerably less vigorous than the other, taking a long time to make a shrub of a size to cut from with any freedom. I understand that it grows faster and more vigorously in the northern half of the country.

Both are happy in sun or shade, indifferent as to soil and tolerant of drought, but the leaf colour will of course vary according to situation, being yellowest in full sun. (Untried.)

SANTOLINA—"Cotton Lavender", "Lavender Cotton"
Shrub; evergreen

S. chamaecyparissus (*incana*)

While I very much like its low mounds of vivid silver in the front of the shrub borders, I personally do not rate the value of *Santolina chamaecyparissus* very highly for cutting purposes; but since a number of flower arrangers seem to do so I feel that I cannot pass it over. The feathery little silver-green leaves are closely packed right the way up the erect, slender shoots, which erupt at the tips into bright yellow flowers in July (if allowed to do so). Hard pruning in spring is necessary to keep the plant bushy and I also like to remove the flowers before their yellow buttons detract from the fine foliage effect of the dense, neat silver cushion. I think the truth is that if one keeps this dwarf shrub cut back sufficiently to preserve its beauty as a garden plant there is perhaps not much left of a useful length for cutting; but it soon becomes unsightly if allowed to straggle and compactness increases its frost-resistance. It is in fact one of the hardiest of silver-leaved shrubs, but full sun and sharp drainage are nevertheless required to do it justice.

S. neapolitana

S. chamaecyparissus has a very similar relative with rather taller and even more feathery foliage shoots of a slightly greener grey and much more attractively coloured light sulphur-yellow daisy-buttons, for which I believe the correct name to be *Santolina neapolitana*, but those listed as *sulphurea*, *italica sulphurea*, *neapolitana sulphurea* and *pectinata* appear to be very similar or even identical. Cultivation is the same as for *S. chamaecyparissus*.

Boil both and stand in hot water.

SARCOCOCCA hookeriana—Species of "Christmas Box", "Sweet Box"
Shrub; ground cover; evergreen

This is indeed related to the Box. But the 3-in., finely tapered, narrowly elliptical leaf shape is about as different as possible from the almost circular foliage of the "Common Box", the arching sprays of glossy, willow-like dark green leaves seeming much more nearly akin to those of a smaller *Danae racemosa* or *Leucothoë catesbaei*, though rather more densely and less elegantly branched. I have singled out the Himalayan species as being taller-growing than most of the genus and thus better able to spare useful pieces for cutting; but it also exists in a Chinese form called *Sarcococca hookeriana digyna* (A.M. 1936), which is only slightly dwarfer, with similar foliage borne on purplish-red shoots and with pink flowers instead of cream. In both cases the insignificant flowers, which appear in late winter, have an unusually strong, sweet scent which pervades the air on sunny days in particular. These shade-loving evergreens will grow in any ordinary soil, slowly spreading by suckers to provide useful ground cover without becoming invasive and yielding pleasing and immensely long-lasting foliage for cutting. They also glycerine well. (See Chapter IX.)

SCROPHULARIA aquatica 'Variegata' (*nodosa* 'Variegata')
—Form of "Figwort", "Water Betony"
Hardy perennial; evergreen

My own feeling is that the proper place for *Scrophularia aquatica* 'Variegata' is in the picking border, for although the basal clump of heart-shaped evergreen leaves strikingly mottled with pale yellow and white is good enough to look at almost all the year round the effect is usually spoiled by the tall, rigid flower stems only sparsely clothed with smaller, scruffier leaves and topped by ridiculously insignificant little brown flowers which one has somehow neglected to remove. If the flower spikes are not cut out the plant soon becomes scraggy and untidy and it also needs regular applications of slug bait to keep the foliage fit for floral decoration. Like our native figwort, this one appreciates plenty of moisture, but it will do well enough in any good, rich soil.

The late Mrs. Margery Fish tried hard to persuade the horticultural public to discard the specific adjective *nodosa* for *aquatica*, which she claimed to be the more correct; but almost nobody, she found, took any notice. *Nodosa* is applied to this garden variety in the *R.H.S. Dictionary of Gardening* and *aquatica* appears on the plant label in the R.H.S. Garden.

Boil and cut in only moderate lengths, i.e. a 9-in. stem of young foliage will be dependable when one twice as long may not.

SEDUM—"Stonecrop"
Hardy perennial

S. albo-roseum 'Variegatum' ('Foliis Medio-variegatus')

The sedums include some first-class foliage plants for flower arrangement and also for garden decoration. Of these *S. albo-roseum* 'Variegatum' is one of the showiest, with a vivid yellow leaf centre (Yellow 10A) merging to light and medium blue-green at the edges. The shape is mainly obovate, somewhat contorted, and serrated at the tip end of the fleshy leaves. These measure about 4 in. by 1½ in, encircling a pale, 12- to 15-in. stem for most of its length and finishing in a loose rosette. The foliage is so good that one could wish it had no flowers, but these at least refrain from intruding on the display until late in the season. One is sometimes advised to grow this sedum in the shade for most telling effect, but in this garden I find it needs all the sun it can get, not only for the richest yellow variegation but also for the sake of sturdy growth. It has an irritating habit of throwing up plain blue-green shoots, which need to be removed, but in other respects it is easy and trouble-free and immensely rewarding. The name *Sedum spectabile* 'Variegatum' appears to apply to the same plant.

20. *Senecio cineraria* 'White Diamond'

21. *Tellima grandiflora* foliage in late summer

S. maximum 'Atropurpureum' (A.G.M. 1963, A.M. 1964, F.C.C. 1967)

This is an equally firm favourite of mine for cutting and in the garden it makes an ideal contrast to the foregoing, when the two are grown side by side. It is rather taller than *albo-roseum* 'Variegatum' and even fleshier, with less conspicuously serrated oval leaves which develop an increasingly rich purple-mahogany bloom as the season advances. The succulent 18-in. foliage shoots are crowned in late summer with rather loose flower heads of a deep pink only slightly less brown than the leaves and stems. The flowers dry well.

S. x 'Ruby Glow' (A.M. 1962)

'Ruby Glow' is a fairly recent cross between *S. cauticola* and the fine-flowered hybrid 'Autumn Joy'. Whereas the flat, glowing ruby flower heads inherit some of the beauty of 'Autumn Joy', the leaves are more characteristic of the other parent. This is a variety of semi-prostrate habit with smaller, more rounded leaves with a waxy finish, suffused with greyish plum-purple and borne on reddish 12-in. stems.

S. 'Autumn Joy' ('Herbstfreude'), (A.M. 1959, F.C.C. 1961)

Finally one must I think, include 'Autumn Joy', which is so outstandingly beautiful in flower, with its huge, flat bronze-pink flower heads in late summer, that the beauty of its foliage tends to get overlooked. Reputedly a cross between *S. telephium*, which itself has attractively tinted foliage, and *spectabile*, which has broader, decoratively serrated glaucous leaves, 'Autumn Joy' takes after the latter most noticeably in its bold, compact whorls of rounded, fleshy foliage, but with an attractive rubicund tinge derived from *telephium*. These flowers, too, dry well.

All the fleshy sedums are equally attractive to slugs.

SENECIO
Shrub; evergreen

S. cineraria (*Cineraria maritima*) 'White Diamond' and 'Ramparts'

Having failed in the past with *Senecio cineraria* I am happy to find that I can sometimes keep its cultivar 'White Diamond' throughout the winter here. In less cold districts it regularly seems to survive, for it is one of those obliging plants which are not only a visual improvement on the type but are also of a tougher constitution. It is, I think, the whitest of the genus, with broad, thickly felted leaves about 5 in. long, roughly egg-shaped but much indented, particularly at the stem end, rather on the lines of a more solid chrysanthemum leaf. (See illustration facing p. 160.) Having too few sunny spots to go round, I have not tried the equally esteemed 'Ramparts', which seems to be slightly taller, with still more deeply cut-up foliage, and which I believe to be equally hardy. Mrs. Underwood recommends that both should be pruned hard in early May to produce a compact 2-ft. clump of young shoots in early summer and warns us that the tender young growth which results from cutting silver-leaved shrubs late in the season is particularly vulnerable to frosting.

Singe or boil.

S. laxifolius (A.G.M. 1936)

There is widespread confusion about the two very similar species, *greyi* and *laxifolius*, and although *laxifolius* appears to be the rarer I have now satisfied myself that this is the one which does so surprisingly well in this cold garden and corresponds with the species so labelled in the R.H.S. Garden. Without comparing specimens of each it would be impossible to say whether mine has the larger leaves characteristic of *laxifolius*, but they are not even faintly wavy, as those of *greyi* are said to be, and their undeniable hardiness further weights the scales in favour of *laxifolius*. For good measure the 4 ft. attributed to the latter fits my plants much more nearly than the 8 ft. said to be attained by *greyi*. The oval, 2½- to 3-in. leaves are a semi-matt, darkish grey-green on top and smoothly felted white below, well distributed along the somewhat curving shoots and finished at the top with a loose rosette formation. Though the slender sprays of silver flower buds are also delightful for flower arrangement the shrub looks much more decorative and grows more strongly if the crude yellow daisy-flowers are removed. They should not in any case be allowed to weaken the plant by setting seed. Fairly severe pruning in April produces fine, densely leafy 3-ft. bushes when grown in full sun and well-drained soil, but it is worth while growing one or two plants in half-shade without much regular pruning—bad horticultural practice no doubt, but there will be longer and more sinuous shoots for cutting if some straggling is allowed. This senecio is in fact sometimes recommended as a shrub for shady situations, but mistakenly, I think; for although it will not object to shade it cannot achieve the compact, mounded appearance which best becomes it except in full exposure.

It is one of the best-behaved of all grey foliages as cut material even when arranged in moisture-retaining substances rather than in water. (For preserving see Chapter IX.)

S. leucostachys

The finely cut, spidery-leaved *Senecio leucostachys* is one of the most brilliant silver-whites and the poorer the soil the whiter the feathery shoots will be. The deep cream flower-buttons are fairly attractive, as senecio flowers go, but it is wiser to remove them nevertheless, in order to get better sprays of the delicate white tracery. Even in full sun and poor, sandy soil it tends to sprawl, reaching out sideways rather than upwards to a bare 2 ft. in height. It will not overwinter in the open here, but can be kept going from year to year in milder gardens. Any shoot with a heel to it grows roots in water, so there is no difficulty in keeping a winter supply of cuttings going on a sunny window-sill, to be planted out in May.

Singe or boil.

SILYBUM marianum (Carduus marianus)—"Blessed Thistle",
"Holy Thistle", "Our Lady's Milk Thistle"
Hardy annual

The big, broad, prickly leaves of *Silybum marianum* are some-
where between those of onopordum and *Acanthus spinosus* in
outline and are further ornamented by a broad white mid- and
side-ribs branching into a network of smaller white veins on a
glistening green ground. The foliage forms large, flat rosettes
and is topped by tall thistle flowers. It is a vigorous, unfussy,
annual (with occasional biennial tendencies) and will become
naturalized in any well-drained soil by seeding itself from year
to year. (Untried.)

SKIMMIA
Shrub; evergreen

As far as foliage is concerned *Skimmia japonica* 'Foremanii'
is probably the finest of the genus, with bold, obovate, leathery
light green leaves. Although the shade-loving character of skimmias is commonly stressed, I find the foliage of 'Foremanii'
more interesting for floral decoration when grown in the sun,
which induces a yellower-green leaf colour fading attractively
to an unexpected silver at the margins. It makes a dense, spreading evergreen mound from 3 to 5 ft. high.

Though berries are not our concern in the present context,
most of us who grow skimmias feel that we have a right to expect these, at least as a fringe benefit, along with the evergreen
foliage and the pleasant greenish-cream flower clusters (best in
male forms) in earliest spring. But we are all too often disappointed. The trouble is, I think, that horticultural writers and
nurserymen will keep telling us that *S. japonica* 'Foremanii' is
hermaphrodite, or self-fertile, when it is nothing of the sort. And
so we mistakenly expect this solitary female to bear a crop of
sealing-wax-scarlet berries, which it is physically incapable of
doing except when pollinated by a nearby male plant such as

S. japonica 'Fragrans', or *S. rubella* (A.M. 1962), which has attractive red-brown flower buds in place of the usual greenish-cream. A male form of *S. japonica* itself (this species provides both males and females) would do equally well as a pollinator. The only hermaphrodite form that I know of is *S. reevesiana* (*S. fortunei*),* but its berries are far less spectacular, being more crimson than scarlet—and this species will not tolerate lime.

The rest are less fussy, enjoying a moist loam, preferably on the acid side, and are excellent shrubs for shady spots, though shade is not essential.

SMILACINA racemosa (A.M. 1947, F.C.C. 1956)—"False Spikenard"
Hardy perennial

If you do not know *Smilacina racemosa*, at first sight you will hardly believe your eyes, for the big, broad, soft green leaves which clothe the tall, arched stem look so very much like Solomon's Seal and the terminal whipped cream panicles of flower so much like an astilbe that the outcome seems an unbelievable freak, undeniably beautiful though it is. The leaves are just a little lighter in colour and a little more sharply tapered than those of *Polygonatum multiflorum*, or Solomon's Seal, to which it is related. The smilacina enjoys similar conditions of cool, moist soil and shade, though it will put up with a less comfortable billet. Having no creeping rhizomes it is much less spreading than the polygonatum.

SORBUS aria—"Whitebeam"
Tree or shrub; deciduous

Our native whitebeam may be grown as a large bush or as a rather pyramidal tree which quickly reaches 30 ft. or so. The vivid white felting and the chalice-like shape of the expanding leaf buds in spring create an effect almost as flower-like as that of the leafless *Magnolia denudata*, or Yulan Magnolia, in bloom.

165

As the broadly oval, serrated and deeply veined leaves unfold the upper surface turns green at maturity while retaining the tomentose white underside. The full-grown leaf measures about 4 in. by 2½ in. The tip-tilted S bends to be found among the branches of older trees are splendid for pedestal work in particular, providing side-pieces of gracefully flowing line. Delightful though it is as a garden plant, to me it looks most right in an untamed setting, surpassing itself in beauty, for instance, as it lights up the landscape amid the sombre yews of the chalk downs of Goodwood, in Sussex. Even in acid-soiled districts it seeds itself so freely in the wild that roadside supplies for cutting are not hard to find.

The selected form, *S. aria* 'Lutescens' (A.M. 1952), is perhaps rather more of a garden tree, differing from the species in the yellowish-white down which covers the upper surface of the young foliage in spring.

Boil and soak.

STACHYS lanata—"Donkey's Ear", "Lamb's Ear", "Lamb's Lug", "Lamb's Tongue", "Rabbit's Ear", "Sow's Ear"
Hardy perennial; ground cover; evergreen

The string of nicknames above—and I expect there are plenty more—is proof, if proof were needed, of the widespread popularity of this old cottage-garden favourite. Although I once heard a demonstrator describe these charming, furry, silver ears as 'rubbish', many of us discern true beauty in the texture, colour and shape of the foliage of this humble plant.

S. lanata 'Silver Carpet'

The chief fault of *S. lanata* is that the tall, rather gawky, wishy-washy mauve flower spikes spoil the appearance of the silky ground-covering mat of shimmering greenish-silver. This has recently been remedied in a non-flowering variety called 'Silver Carpet', which also has longer-stemmed leaves—a further asset from the flower arranger's point of view.

Both these need replanting every other year or so to keep them in good condition, and they are better-looking in sun than in shade.

Boil.

STEPHANANDRA incisa and S. tanakae
Shrubs; deciduous

Both of these are more attractive in leaf than in flower and although *S. tanakae* is the one most enthusiastically boosted for flower arrangement the slender, elegant, smaller-leaved foliage sprays of *incisa* may please some tastes equally well. The latter has long, arching or semi-weeping red-brown stems clothed with deeply-cut, slimly pointed leaves attractively flushed red-bronze in spring and has good, if less brilliant autumn colour than the other. *S. tanakae* is a more vigorous grower, with larger, less-divided, roughly triangular, three-lobed, bronze-green leaves borne on equally graceful spreading wands. The stems are a brighter red-brown than those of *incisa* and if cut to the ground annually in early spring the bark of the new shoots will be almost as colourful as that of some of the willows and dogwoods. It also has vivid orange or yellow autumn colour which persists late into the season.

Much as I admire their foliage for flower arrangement I would not say that either is a very effective garden decorator except in autumn. I know one flower arranger who advises against hard pruning, but this is usually said to produce better foliage sprays, prevent them from building up into tangled thickets and keep *incisa* to a height of about 4 ft. and *tanakae* to 6 or 7 ft. They thrive in any ordinary soil, in sun or shade—though I suspect that the delightful spring foliage tints will be less in evidence in shady surroundings.

S. tanakae needs no special conditioning, but I have not tried *incisa*, which I would expect to be equally well-behaved.

SYMPHORICARPUS orbiculatus 'Variegatus'—Form of "Coral Berry" or "Indian Currant"
Shrub; deciduous

My disdain for the normal, flimsy, dull green foliage of even the best of the snowberries is such that I strip the lot when using the decorative moth-ball sprays of fruit (not only because the leaves are uninteresting but because they quickly shrivel in a hot atmosphere indoors) and in my ignorance I had until recently supposed that a variegated member of the genus could hardly be worth chasing after, unaware that the symphoricarpus in question was not a "Snowberry", but a "Coral Berry"—that is, an entirely separate species, with very different foliage. It was not until a kind friend recently offered me a plant that I discovered my mistake. I have never seen the small pink berries which give rise to the nickname, but I understand that the variegated form is not very fruitful. When they do appear, they should make a lively combination, for the dainty little oval leaves of *S. orbiculatus* 'Variegatus' are bright green in the centre with a broad and equally vivid yellow margin. Only the arched, wiry stems of this engaging little 3-ft. shrub bear any resemblance to the larger, coarser, white-fruited *S. albus laevigatus* (*rivularis*) which, even in the magnificently berried form 'Constance Spry', is still very boringly equipped as regards leaves and suckers much too freely for the average small garden.

Established plants should be cut back fairly hard in spring and if plain green shoots appear these should immediately be removed. I imagine that the leaf colour would be less gay in a shady position.

There is another variegated form of *S. orbiculatus* with a narrow white margin to the leaf, but this is much less effective than the yellow-edged form.

TELLIMA grandiflora—"False Alum Root"
Hardy perennial; ground cover; evergreen

Never a great one for botanical Latin names, the friend who first acquainted me with the delights of *Tellima grandiflora* kindled such a spark that she has referred to them as "Sybil's leaves" ever since. I have indeed the greatest affection for these deeply waffled, intricately veined, subtly mottled and faintly bristled leaves for floral decoration, as well as for the tall, slim wands of little greenish-yellow bells in spring. The rounded, heart-shaped leaf has a prettily scalloped border and varies in size from 1 to as much as 6 in. across, with a slender stem up to 9 in. long, but often a good deal less. The foliage colour ranges from dark bronze-brown mottling on green, or lime-green edged with salmon, to an all-over coral, the orange-pink tinge being most pronounced in exposed positions and usually from late summer onwards, and the brown marking in the shade. The plant shown in the illustration facing p. 161 was beginning to develop the brown veining and mottling of the autumn and winter foliage. I find that it pays to grow these evergreen clumps in both positions to get the full gamut of foliage hues for cutting.

T. grandiflora 'Purpurea'

There is also a darker-leaved form of *Tellima grandiflora* called 'Purpurea', with a smooth crimson-bronze upper surface and hairy beetroot-purple backing; but although the colour is rich, particularly in autumn and winter, the smoother, thinner texture lacks body as cut material and lasts less well in water.

Clumps of either kind slowly crowd their centres out of the ground as they increase, thus requiring division every few years, and seedlings are so prolific that one always has quantities of spares on hand, including chance hybrids with foliage half-way between the two in colour and texture. Beloved though the tellimas are of flower arrangers they figure in so few catalogues nowadays that maybe the very ease of propagation which should

169

be the nurseryman's ally is doing him out of business in this instance and driving him to drop them from his repertoire. Slugs are a constant menace.

Cut leaves of either kind tend to flop unless they are actually cut, not picked, so that the tenuous thread inside the stem is neatly severed with the stalk, and are then stem-tipped under water during the soaking process. Properly conditioned foliage lasts a long time. To prevent the stems twisting and curving overmuch when soaking I bunch a number of leaves together and bind the stems with wool, or pack as many stems as possible into a cigar tube or plastic toothbrush-case before submerging.

TEUCRIUM fruticans (*latifolium*)—"Shrubby Germander"
Shrub; evergreen

The lax, spreading habit of *Teucrium fruticans* produces a mass of long white wands of dainty evergreen foliage with engagingly light and graceful qualities as cut material. The small, rather sage-like, ovate leaves are 1 in. or more in length, silver-grey above and backed with white. Unfortunately it hates the cold, needing a hot, dry position backed by a sunny south wall in all but the mildest areas. It is particularly happy in seaside gardens, where it will romp away either as a wall-shrub or in full exposure in the open, rapidly reaching about 5 ft. Those flower arrangers who can succeed with it will probably prune away many of the airy foliage sprays, but they should also remove the lavender flower heads before they seed.

I know this to be satisfactory cutting material but have no experience as to the type of conditioning required. (Untried.)

THALICTRUM glaucum (*speciosissimum*)—Form of
"Meadow Rue"
Hardy perennial

The soft yellow-flowered thalictrum is one of the most undemanding and yet the large, triternate blue-green leaves of a lacy, fern-like design are among the most decorative of the

170

genus, with something of the maidenhair and something of the rue leaf in their make-up, but on a larger, looser pattern. The tall-stemmed, fluffy Easter-chick flower panicles are also good for flower arrangement, but more luscious foliage can be had for cutting if one is willing to sacrifice at least some of the bloom by removing a number of flowering shoots as soon as they emerge above the low-growing leaf clump in late spring. *Thalictrum glaucum* will grow anywhere, without any sort of attention and the rigid flower stems need no staking.

Soak.

THUJA occidentalis 'Rheingold'—Form of "Arbor-vitae"
Shrub; evergreen

Though regularly included among the dwarf conifers and, as often as not recommended for rock garden work, the lovely *Thuja occidentalis* 'Rheingold' will eventually make a dense, bushy, broad-based cone of 6 ft. or thereabouts—quite big enough, that is, to be considered as a foliage plant for cutting. The feathery evergreen fronds are warm yellow in summer but achieve their greatest beauty in autumn and winter, when the colour deepens to orange-bronze. An open situation is necessary to achieve a good colour, but otherwise this thuja is very easy. It is said to be slow-growing, but in ten years mine has outgrown neighbouring dwarf shrubs in what started as a small rock garden and it has now gone to join a border of mixed foliages, where its proportions are more in keeping and its shape and colour contrast pleasingly with other foliage plants.

VERATRUM nigrum—Species of "False Hellebore"
Hardy perennial

The bold, oval, light green leaves of *Veratrum nigrum* expand in spring from tightly folded fans into broad, recurving blades which retain their permanent pleating throughout their life-span and are sometimes as much as 1 ft. long by 7 or 8 in. wide. The erect, branching 4-ft. spikes of minute, starry flowers in late

171

summer are also valuable in that they bring a sombre note of darkest maroon-brown to the flower arranger's colour range. The significance of the common name given to the genus escapes me, for neither the handsome, undivided leaves nor even the greenish-white flowers of *Veratrum album* (A.M. 1958, F.C.C. 1962) are remotely reminiscent of any hellebore known to me.

This lovely and unusual foliage is too good to feed to garden pests, but its emergence in spring tends to catch us unawares and the slugs may get at it before we do if we do not keep watch for the young shoots. Both species prefer moist soils, but opinions differ as to whether sun or part-shade is to be recommended. I think this may depend upon the garden climate, for the plant of *V. nigrum* which I have tried to grow in a semi-shady position has fared so ill that I have never been able to use these lovely leaves for cutting. The veratrums hate disturbance and should be left to develop into large clumps such as that illustrated opposite p. 177, which they will do in time if conditions are to their liking. (Untried.)

VERBASCUM bombicyferum ('Broussa')—Species of "Mullein"
Hardy biennial or perennial

There are not many silver leaves of really imposing dimensions and *Verbascum bombicyferum* ranks with *Salvia argentea* and the onopordums as the biggest and best of the true silvers or silver-whites. The foliage plays a dual role, for it starts life as a large, ground-hugging, silky silver rosette, persisting through the winter to add glamour to indoor arrangements, and in spring it becomes whiter and woollier as the leaves gradually increase in size, eventually clothing the lower part of the tall, downy spikes studded in late summer with pale yellow flowers. Some of the huge, obovate leaves measure as much as 16 in. by 8 in. Like *Salvia argentea*, this biennial verbascum can be kept as a perennial if it is not allowed to flower and it is in fact most commonly listed by growers among the hardy perennial plants. When treated as a biennial it will still keep the foliage supply going if the flower heads are left to seed themselves, which they delight to do, though seedlings are somewhat variable as regards leaf colour, some being more green than silver. This is one of the hardiest of grey foliages and should succeed in any sunny, well-drained spot.

Put the cut stem-tip into hot water.

(For preserving see Chapter IX.)

VIBURNUM
Shrub; evergreen

The deciduous viburnums hardly warrant inclusion as foliage plants, though many of the delightful early spring-flowering varieties also have attractive sprays of light green leaves (which last well in water if boiled) and some are noted for autumn leaf colour. But one or two of the evergreen species have specially handsome leaves.

V. davidii (A.M. 1912)

V. davidii makes a dense, spreading mound barely exceeding 2 ft., broader than it is tall, with elliptical, leathery, dark olive-green leaves about 6 in. long by less than half as wide, deeply channelled with three longitudinal veins. Those who can find room for several plants of assorted sexes will also enjoy the lovely, turquoise-blue berries which persist well into the autumn.

V. rhytidophyllum (F.C.C. 1907)

This is a tall, vigorous species which rapidly attains 10 ft. or more. The long, narrow, ovate leaves (about 9 in. by $2\frac{1}{2}$ in.) are deeply wrinkled, dark, shining green above and covered with a thick, off-white felting below. The only fault I have to find with this highly ornamental foliage is its somewhat pendulous habit. The leaves have been likened to those of a large rhododendron, but their drooping deportment gives the bush a faintly hangdog look, as of a rhododendron reacting to intense cold. It may lose its leaves in a severe winter, but it is unquestionably hardy; nevertheless it needs shelter and shade to look its best.

173

To get the huge clusters of red berries which ripen to black several plants should be grown together.

It also exists in a delightful variegated form with cream marginal markings, but I have never seen this listed by the trade. (For preserving see Chapter IX.)

V. tinus (A.M. 1961)—"Laurustinus", and V. tinus 'Variegatum'

Our old friend "Laurustinus" is not to be despised as an evergreen foliage plant, especially in gardens unsuitable for rhododendrons and other calcifuge evergreens. (See also Chapter IX.) But *V. tinus* 'Variegatum' has infinitely more elegant foliage in two tints of light green broadly streaked and bordered with cream. Though a Haslemere nurseryman considers it perfectly hardy, Messrs. Hillier and others do not support this view and in this garden I dare not put it where I would most like to grow it, in an open border of mixed foliages. Even in a warmer and more sheltered nook my plant shows a fair amount of winter browning on the leaf margins, but this at least is the extent of the damage in the course of three or four winters here. It should slowly reach a height of 9 or 10 ft., so one has to wait a good many years to cut much more than an occasional snippet. I understand that there is also a larger-leaved variety of *V. tinus* called 'Lucidum Variegatum', in a combination of cream-white on glossy dark green; but what I most admire in the other is its remarkably light, delicate air (something of which may be seen in the illustration facing p. 176); so I doubt whether the rarer and, to me, unknown, 'Lucidum Variegatum' would supplant it in my esteem.

VINCA—"Periwinkle"

Ground cover; evergreen

V. major 'Variegata' ('Elegantissima')

The variegated form of *Vinca major* is the finest of the variegated periwinkles for flower arrangement, with much bolder, showier leaves than *V. minor*. The young growth is colourfully splashed and bordered with rich cream or pale yellow on bright green occasionally streaked with a much paler tint, standing erect to start with and gradually extending to long, slender, prostrate trails of glossy foliage with pale cream markings. The leaves are broadly ovate, the largest measuring about 2½ in. by 1½ in., and getting progressively smaller towards the tips of the shoots. Slugs are especially partial to the foliage of *V. major* 'Variegata'.

It is often seen in deplorable condition in flower arrangements for lack of careful preparation, but it will last perfectly well in water (though not in moisture-retaining substances) if boiled, stem-tipped and only briefly soaked—not long enough, that is, to saturate the leaves.

V. minor 'Variegata'

Nomenclature runs riot in the case of the variegated "Lesser Periwinkle", for which I have come across no less than eight different names, to be shared out between, as I understand it, two distinct forms—one with yellow variegation and the other with cream or white. *V. minor* 'Variegata' ('Argenteo-variegata') has small, narrow, oval leaves of light grey-green edged and streaked at first with pale cream which fades to white, rather than silver, as the foliage matures.

V. minor 'Aureo-variegata'

This and other name variants embodying the word *aurea* refer to a separate form with strong yellow leaf coloration which I find much less pleasing. Whereas this exists in both a blue- and a white-flowered form, I only know of a blue-flowered form of the green-and-white-leaved variety.

V. minor varieties need only a brief soaking after cutting.

Commonly recommended as rock garden subjects, all periwinkles, whether *major* or *minor*, are far too exuberant to be let loose anywhere near the average alpine plant and once they root into rock crevices or in the heart of other tough-rooted subjects they are there to stay. Indeed I have often found them more than a match for shrubs many times their size. The minor is the worse offender. Whereas *V. major* roots only at the tips of the shoots *V. minor* roots wherever it comes in contact with the soil, smothering and strangling evergreen azaleas, for instance, almost to death with its dense cat's cradle of foliage strands, or stealing necessary moisture from hydrangeas if used to carpet the ground around them in the shrub borders. I think the proper use for these pretty trailing plants is as ground cover beneath trees and tall, vigorous shrubs, or on banks, dry walls, or bare ground in isolation. They are ideal for such a purpose, thriving in any kind of soil and in difficult spots in dry shade. The variegated forms need more light than the green ones to get the best effect, and a rich soil makes for leaf rather than flower production, which suits me in the case of *V. major* 'Variegata' in particular. All should be cut back in spring to get a profusion of young shoots and to keep them neat; and *V. major* can only be kept presentable by regular applications of slug bait.

VITIS—Ornamental "Vine"
Climber; deciduous

V. coignetiae

Vitis coignetiae is perhaps chiefly remarkable in the autumn, but the plain green summer foliage is sufficiently impressive in size and shape to deserve a mention here. The bold leaves of rounded heart- or shield-shape are up to 12 in. in diameter, matt green above, rough to the touch and deeply veined and wrinkled, with a felted light dun-coloured under-surface. This is too rumbustious a climber for confined spaces, rapidly draping itself over large outbuildings and reaching the tops of tall trees. Though it will grow vigorously in any position, south or west aspects are most likely to encourage the brilliant flames, yellows and scarlets in autumn. It also takes a long time to establish itself in poor soil. (Untried.)

V. vinifera 'Purpurea' (A.M. 1958)—"Teinturier Grape"

I wish that this highly ornamental vine might borrow some of the superfluous vigour of the foregoing, for this is the one I

22. *Ruta graveolens* 'Jackman's Blue'

23. *Viburnum tinus* 'Variegatum'

24. Spring foliage of *Veratrum nigrum*

covet most for cutting; but unfortunately it makes scant pro-gress from one season to the next in this bleak garden. On a sunny wall in a warm district it is a splendid foliage plant—and sometimes even a fruiting one. The bunches of little black grapes may not often ripen, but the clusters of immature fruit are as good, if not better, for floral decoration. The leaves are of typical vine design, about 5 in. across, three- or five-lobed and decora-tively toothed and the young shoots are covered with a white farina at first, developing wine-red leaves which later darken to maroon-purple, shading out to near-silver at the tips of the shoots.

Instructions are that once a plant has been carefully trained to fill the required space the lateral growths should be spurred back to two or three eyes in early winter. Would that I might practise what I preach, but the winters here do more than enough spurring back, regardless of the fact that the required space has not yet been nearly covered!

Foliage must be mature when cut and should be singed or boiled, followed by a brief soaking in tepid water.

WEIGELA (*Diervilla*)
Shrub; deciduous

After one or two name switches the genus is now known once more as *Weigela*, though still often listed as *Diervilla*. The plain green-leaved garden hybrids sometimes produce magnificently burnished foliage shoots in sunny positions, but it is really to those with more unusual leaf colour that we turn for floral decoration.

W. florida 'Foliis Purpureis'

The purple-leaved form of *Weigela florida* is a comparatively dwarf, slow-growing cultivar of a compact 4 ft. with a dark, brownish-purple tinge to the foliage. It seems to have earned good reports, but the foliage colour strikes me as rather muddy and the flowers a not very pleasant purplish-pink. It would no doubt be unfair to base my judgment on the appearance of a

M   177

new and very tiny specimen in my own garden, but I was no more favourably impressed by the overall effect of larger plants seen at Chelsea and elsewhere.

W. florida 'Variegata' (A.M. 1968)

Two separate forms of *Weigela florida* 'Variegata' apparently share the same name, one with rather muddled yellow variega-tion and the other with cream and white, which is the one most usually grown and much the prettier foliage plant. It is to my mind one of the most attractive of all variegated shrubs when well grown, with elegantly tapered leaves broadly banded and streaked with deep cream in youth, the variegation paling to white with age. These make a charming setting for the apple-blossom pink and white flowers in early summer and in autumn they become slightly tinged with pink at the edges, clinging on the bush almost until Christmas as a rule. The specimen shown in the illustration facing p. 192 was photographed in late autumn, when many deciduous foliage plants had already be-come distinctly shabby. It is a good deal more vigorous than 'Foliis Purpureis', though less so than the green-leaved types, usually reaching about 5 ft. and offering a choice of the straight, strong new growth with the larger, more cream-coloured leaves, or more tortuous, smaller-leaved sprays with paler variegation. It is well able to part with a good deal of either kind, but more orthodox pruning consists of removing spent flower heads in summer and confused, spindly twiggery in winter and of occa-sionally cutting out some of the old wood altogether.

W. japonica 'Looymansii Aurea'

Whereas the yellow-leaved form of *W. florida* has little to commend it, I have recently come across one of a different species which looks to me a most desirable foliage shrub. This is the very uncommon *W. japonica* 'Looymansii Aurea', which bears graceful sprays of broader, well shaped leaves of a soft yellow hue tipped with a hint of bronze. Although its height is no more than that of 'Foliis Purpureis' it appears to be laxer in habit, with longer and much larger-leaved foliage shoots arching out laterally rather than the denser and somewhat stiffer growth of the latter. The flower colour is a pleasant warm pink.

Weigelas are easy-going shrubs, but they give better results in a moist, rich soil. 'Foliis Purpureis' should be a better colour in a sunny spot; 'Variegata' may be grown in sun or shade, though I find some shade and shelter beneficial here to prevent leaf-scorching, whether by sun or by wind; and I understand that 'Looymansii Aurea' needs a partially shaded position for the best foliage effect.

In all cases the young foliage in particular needs boiling and a brief soaking when cut.

YUCCA filamentosa 'Variegata'
Shrub; evergreen

The yuccas are all equipped with sword-like leaves, some rigid and needle-sharp as in the case of the tropical-looking, stout-trunked *Yucca gloriosa* ("Adam's Needle"), and others of floppier habit. But judged on the merits of their foliage rather than their flowers none of the green-leaved types can compare in majesty with the great sword-blades of *Phormium tenax* as material for floral decoration. There is however a rare, varie-gated form of *Yucca filamentosa* which should be of the greatest interest to the flower arranger who can offer it a really hot, arid spot. The leaves of my struggling plant average only 18 in. in length, but it does much better than this in more suitable condi-tions. The variegation is spectacular. Reversing the usual for-mula, a broad central yellow ribbon occupies almost the whole of the leaf area, with only narrow stripes of vivid green, mainly by way of outline. The curious, curling threads on the leaf margin, which are typical of the species, are less in evidence in *Y. filamentosa* 'Variegata'. (See illustration facing p. 193.) In this garden it merely survives at the draughty foot of a south wall, which is the best I have to offer. It has only once flowered in eighteen years, but I count this all to the good, if it is putting all its questionable energy into the manufacture of leaves, for I am able to get a few superb ivory flower spikes from some of the less difficult green-leaved yuccas in late summer. This should not be confused with the much less attractive dark green and white variegated form of *Y. gloriosa*.

All yuccas do best in mild climates and arid situations—the hotter and drier the better—and this should virtually count me out; but I would not willingly forgo the flowers of the various species or the vividly striped foliage of the variegated form of *filamentosa*.

ZEA mays—Species of "Maize"
Hardy or half-hardy annual

The long, broad, recurving, undulating blades of the variegated maizes are so beautifully marked and so gracefully shaped as to rank high among leaves for flower arrangement. Their beauty stems largely from the irregular striation which varies in width from broad ribbons to pin-stripes, with a high proportion of light banding amid the green. And there are a number of colour combinations to choose from.

Zea mays 'Gracillima Variegata' is comparatively dwarf at around 3 ft., in green and cream. *Z. mays japonica* is taller, conspicuously banded and striped with white on green. And its cv. 'Gigantea Quadricolor' combines green, white and yellow with pink, or sometimes red-brown or reddish-purple. This is indeed the giant of the party, but its height of 5 ft. or more can be reduced by removing the centre shoot when the laterals begin to develop, thus obtaining a dwarfer, bushier plant. The same treatment can of course be applied to any of those described above.

In warm districts it is probably feasible to sow the seed in the open, but elsewhere it is more satisfactory to start them under glass in order to speed things up, and to plant them out in early summer into a rich soil, earthing up the curious prop-roots at the base of the main stem as these develop. They appreciate all the sunshine they can get and copious watering.

Boil and soak.

CHAPTER VI

Where to Get It

The purpose of this chapter is to spare the reader the frustration of unsuccessfully chasing after the hard-to-get item, which becomes increasingly desirable in proportion to the difficulty of discovering a source of supply. I would not deny that there is also, at the back of my mind, the craftier incentive of saving myself some correspondence later on!

Having had some experience of the shrub nursery business from both sides of the counter I was able some years ago to learn more than the average customer is likely to know about where to try for certain scarce or unusual trees and shrubs; and I have currently collected nearly one hundred catalogues and price lists (1966–7) from general nurserymen, specialist growers, seedsmen, etc., in order to locate the less commonly listed foliage plants of all kinds described in Chapter V.

Many of those mentioned below are by no means 'rare' in the usual sense, but for one reason or another have become comparatively scarce in commerce—the very unpretentious yellow-leaved physocarpus is a case in point. Others are not even scarce if one knows where to look for them, but are included because the growers may not be widely known. It also seems to me helpful to give a fair number of alternative sources of supply, so that would-be shoppers may obtain the goods as near home as possible, thus reducing the ever-mounting cost of carriage and also the length of time spent by plants in transit when consigned by rail. Nevertheless the geographical odds are somewhat uneven, because the milder climate and more suitable soil of the southern counties has attracted most of the big shrub nurseries in particular to this part of the country.

181

Where to Get It

Even the humblest of local nurseries may well be worth an an exploratory visit. Unless one is looking for some particular item one is unlikely to come away empty-handed. The owner is often single-handed and his time is sure to be precious, so he will probably—but not certainly—be glad to let you prowl around on your own. Even so, past experience in the business prompts me to mention that he will *not* be pleased to see visitors during his lunch hour or within a few minutes of closing time! I know of several local one-man nurseries where the owner is in it not so much for the money as for the sheer love of growing plants, concentrating on such oddments as take his fancy rather than on best-sellers. One gives me preferential treatment because he feels that, horticulturally speaking, the plants which are his hobby as much as his livelihood are going to a loving home. These people do not advertise outside their own locality. Indeed they do not want to attract any but local custom, having no facilities for correspondence and accounting or for elaborate packing. The resulting absence of overhead expenses is often reflected in their remarkably cheap prices for the personal shopper and their stock is usually all the sturdier for being carefully and often lovingly home-grown, in all likelihood by the proprietor himself without hired help.

I cannot resist this opportunity of uttering a word of warning, before it is too late, about the danger threatening the connoisseur, whether gardener or flower arranger, with the rapidly growing popularity of 'instant' gardening. No doubt every nurseryman welcomes a quick turnover, but to the owner of a Garden Centre this is the essence of the business. He must therefore play safe by stocking only such trusty old favourites as are in constant demand, or some showy novelty widely publicized as 'new', either of which is likely to be quickly disposed of at any time of year to make room for more.

The nursery trade in general has recently become aware of the vast possibilities of the market created by the spread of the flower arrangement movement and has shown signs of eagerness to cash in on it. For the moment we are in luck, but I believe our good fortune to be perilously insecure. Faced with an ever-increasing burden of overhead costs and deprived by the Garden Centre of much of his bread-and-butter custom, the nurseryman may soon find it impossible to cater any longer for rarefied tastes; so that unless we are constantly creating a demand for the choice and the unusual his *à la carte* service will give way to cafeteria standards. In particular I fear for many of the foliage plants whose subtle refinement of colour, texture, shape or habit is so much less eye-catching than a bicolour rose, a double pink cherry or a hardy hybrid rhododendron, or which may prove uneconomic if too slow-growing or especially difficult to propagate. Only by resolving never to take no for an answer and by pestering the growers for what we want can a sufficient demand be created to save the less commonplace subjects (and unusual foliage in particular) from disappearing for ever into the limbo of the 'discontinued'.

I must stress that I have no personal experience of many of the nurseries mentioned in my plant-by-plant directory and am not answerable for the quality of their wares. If certain well-known firms appear to have been overlooked they will more probably have been omitted for the reason that they are not much concerned with unusual foliage plants. To avoid repetition only the supplier's name will appear alongside the plant, the relevant addresses being given at the end, together with those of some of the bigger general nurseries and specialist growers. Names in brackets refer to seedsmen as distinct from nurserymen.

The Scarcer Plants and Their Suppliers

Agapanthus campanulatus 'Albus': de Jager, Hillier, Kelway, Notcutt, Prichard, Sale, Scott, Slieve Donard
— Headbourne Hybrids: Bressingham, Hillier, Jackman, Margery Fish Nursery, Plantsmen, Russell, Sunningdale, Washfield Nurseries
Anglica archangelica: Ingwersen, Jackman, Margery Fish Nursery, Notcutt, Scott
Artemisia gnaphalodes: Hillier
— *arborescens:* Burkwood & Skipwith, Hillier, Notcutt, Treseder, Underwood

—*pontica:* Ingwersen, Margery Fish Nursery, Poland, Toynbee

—*purshiana:* Hillier, Underwood

Arum italicum 'Pictum': Hillier, Ingwersen, Prichard, Sunningdale

Aspidistra, and variegated: House plant specialists, via florist

Astrantia major 'Sunningdale Variegated': Sunningdale

Aucuba japonica 'Goldenheart': Treseder

Ballota pseudo-dictamnus: Barnham, Bressingham, Hillier, Ingwersen, Old Court, Plantsmen, Poland, Treseder, Underwood

Berberis thunbergii 'Atropurpurea Rose Glow': Hilling, Plant Novelties International, Sherrard, Slocock, Toynbee

Bergenia purpurascens: Margery Fish Nursery

Buxus sempervirens 'Aurea Maculata': Hillier

— — 'Aurea Marginata': Hillier, Notcutt

— — 'Elegantissima': Hillier, Jackman, Knap Hill, Notcutt, Scott, Sherrard, Waterer

— — 'Latifolia Maculata': Hillier, Hilling, Treseder

Buddleia davidii 'Harlequin': Haworth-Booth, Plant Novelties International, Sherrard, Treseder

— — 'Royal Red Variegated': Margaret Fish Nursery, Treseder

Cabbage, Ornamental: (Carter, Dobie, Sutton, Thompson & Morgan, Unwin)

Calluna vulgaris cvs: See list of heath and heather specialists

Centaurea gymnocarpa: Barnham, Toynbee, Treasure, Underwood (Carter, Sutton, Thompson & Morgan)

Chard, Ruby: (Dobie, Thompson & Morgan)

Colchicum autumnale: Hillier, Mars, Pennell, Wallace

Cornus mas 'Elegantissima': Hillier

— — 'Variegata': Hillier, Hilling, Reuthe, Russell, Scott

Cotoneaster horizontalis 'Variegatus': Burkwood & Skipwith, Everton, Hillier, Hilling, Ingwersen, Reuthe, Scott, Slocock, Sunningdale, Treseder

Crambe maritima: Charlton, Jackman, Sale, Scott (Sutton, Thompson & Morgan, Unwin)

Cynara cardunculus: Daniel, Hillier, Scott

184

Elaeagnus macrophylla: Burkwood & Skipwith, Cheal, Hillier, Hilling, Marchant, Notcutt, Reuthe, Slocock, Sunningdale, Treseder

— *pungens* 'Dicksonii': Hillier, Hilling, Scott, Slieve Donard, Treseder

Elymus arenarius: Eldon, Hillier, Hilling, Margery Fish Nursery, Prichard, Russell

Eomecon chionantha: Hillier, Ingwersen, Margery Fish Nursery, Perry, Prichard

Eryngium bourgatii: Bressingham, Hillier, Plantsmen, Prichard, Scott, Sunningdale, Washfield Nurseries

— *variifolium:* Bressingham, Hillier, Plantsmen, Poland, Prichard, Scott, Sunningdale

Erythronium revolutum 'White Beauty': Blom, Broadleigh Gardens, Hillier, Mars

Eucalyptus perriniana: Bayles, Hillier, Plant Novelties International, Toynbee, Treseder

Euphorbia characias: Charlton, Hillier, Margery Fish Nursery, Plantsmen, Scott, Toynbee

— *lathyris:* Hillier, Ingwersen Margery Fish Nursery (Thompson & Morgan)

— *marginata:* (Sutton, Thompson & Morgan, Unwin)

— *myrsinites:* Bressingham, Hillier, Ingwersen, Margery Fish Nursery, Poland, Prichard, Scott, Treasure (Thompson & Morgan)

— *robbiae:* Hillier, Margery Fish Nursery, Old Court, Plantsmen, Prichard, Sunningdale, Treasure, Washfield Nurseries

— *sibthorpii:* Plantsmen

Fagus sylvatica 'Tricolor': Hillier, Hilling, Sherrard, Slocock, Treseder

x Fatshedera lizei: Hillier, Reuthe, Scott (variegated form from house plant specialists, via florist)

Fatsia japonica 'Variegata': From house plant specialists, via florist

Ferns, hardy: See specialist list

Foeniculum vulgare, purple-leaved forms: Barnham, Bressingham, Hillier, Jackman, Margery Fish Nursery, Plantsmen, Prichard, Sale, Scott

Galax aphylla: Hillier, Kaye, Marchant, Perry, Reuthe

Griselinia, variegated cvs.: Cheal, Everton, Hillier, Hilling, Marchant, Toynbee, Treseder

Hebe armstrongii: Hillier, Hilling, Jackman, Pennell, Prichard, Russell, Toynbee, Treseder

— *hectori:* Hillier, Hilling, Russell, Scott, Slocock

— 'Snow Wreath': Haworth-Booth, Slieve Donard

Hedera helix 'Congesta': Burkwood & Skipwith, Hillier

— — 'Glacier': Margery Fish Nursery, Russell, Scott, Slocock, Sunningdale, Waterer

— — 'Jubilee': Barnham, Jackman, Margery Fish Nursery, Notcutt, Reuthe, Toynbee, Treseder

— — 'Marginata': Charlton, Daniel, Hillier, Hilling, Sherrard, Slocock

— — 'Sagittaefolia': Daniel, Hillier, Hilling, Margery Fish Nursery, Sunningdale

Helichrysum petiolatum: Sherrard Toynbee, Treasure, Underwood

— *plicatum* 'Elmstead': Underwood

Hieracium waldsteinii: Hillier, Washfield Nurseries (Thompson & Morgan)

Hosta, various: (Growers listing 8 or more kinds): Bressingham, Eldon, Hillier, Ingwersen, Jackman, Plantsmen, Poland, Russell, Sale, Slieve Donard, Sunningdale

Humulus lupulus 'Aureus': Hillier, Hilling, Slocock, Toynbee

Hydrangea macrophylla 'Quadricolor': Haworth-Booth

— — 'Tricolor': Haworth-Booth, Sunningdale, Treseder

Ilex x altaclarensis 'Camelliaefolia': Hillier, Hilling, Jackman, Treseder, Waterer

— *aquifolium* 'Lawsoniana': Treseder

— — 'Pyramidalis Fructu-luteo': Hillier, Hilling, Scott, Treseder

— — 'Scotica': Hillier

Iris foetidissima 'Variegata': Bressingham, Eldon, Hillier, Margery Fish Nursery, Old Court, Perry, Sale, Scott, Sunningdale

186

— *kaempferi* 'Variegata': Highlands, Mars, Prichard

— *laevigata* 'Variegata': Highlands, Mars, Newlake, Notcutt, Perry

— *pseudacorus* 'Variegatus': Newlake, Old Court, Perry, Slieve Donard, Treasure

Jasminum officinale, variegated cvs.: Hillier, Margery Fish Nursery, Treseder

Kale, Ornamental: (Blom, Carter, Dobbie, Dobie, Sutton, Thompson & Morgan, Unwin)

Lamium maculatum, pink form: Barnham, Hillier, Ingwersen, Margery Fish Nursery, Sunningdale

— — white form: Margery Fish Nursery, Sunningdale

Leucothoë catesbaei 'Rainbow': Treseder, Wyevale

Ligustrum lucidum 'Tricolor': Hillier

— *sinense* 'Variegatum': Hillier

Lobelia cardinalis 'Bee's Flame': Bees, Highlands

— *fulgens*: Bressingham, Newlake, Perry (Roberts, Thompson & Morgan)

Lonicera nitida 'Baggesen's Gold': Barham, Charlton, Margery Fish Nursery, Notcutt, Old Court, Plant Novelties International, Toynbee, Wallace

— *pileata*: Hillier, Hilling, Ingwersen, Margery Fish Nursery, Reuthe, Sale, Sherrard, Treseder

Magnolia grandiflora 'Ferruginea': Haworth-Booth, Hilling, Jackman, Marchant, Pennell, Reuthe, Slocock, Treseder

Mahonia aquifolium 'Atropurpurea': Haskins, Notcutt, Russell, Treseder, Waterer

— *x* 'Charity': Hillier, Marchant, Russell, Slieve Donard, Treseder

— *lomariifolia*: Hillier, Ingwersen, Marchant, Reuthe, Russell, Scott, Sunningdale, Treseder (Thompson & Morgan)

— *repens rotundifolia*: Hillier

Mentha x gentilis 'Variegata': Margery Fish Nursery

Miscanthus sinensis 'Variegatus': Bressingham, Eldon, Everton, Jackman, Sale, Sunningdale

Myrtus bullata: Hillier, Reuthe

Onopordum acanthium: Carlile, Hillier, Margery Fish Nursery (Dobbie, Sutton, Thompson & Morgan)

Orach, Giant Red: (Thompson & Morgan)

Origanum vulgare 'Aureum': Bressingham, Daniel, Hillier, Ingwersen, Margery Fish Nursery, Plantsmen, Sunningdale

Pachysandra terminalis 'Variegata': Hillier, Jackman, Perry, Plant Novelties International, Reuthe, Sunningdale, Treasure, Treseder

Paeonia mlokosewitschii: Charlton, Hillier, Kaye, Old Court, Perry, Scott (Thompson & Morgan)

Philadelphus coronarius 'E. A. Bowles' ('Variegatus'): Plant Novelties International

Phlox paniculata 'Norah Leigh': Blom, Bressingham, Old Court, Plantsmen, Poland, Russell, Treasure

Phormium colensoi: Hillier, Marchant, Reuthe, Sunningdale, Treseder (Thompson & Morgan)

— *tenax* 'Purpureum': Jackman, Marchant, Reuthe, Scott, Sunningdale, Treseder (Thompson & Morgan); alpine form: Washfield Nurseries

— — 'Variegatum': Jackman, Marchant, Reuthe, Sunningdale, Treseder

— — 'Veitchii': Hillier, Treseder

Physocarpus opulifolius 'Luteus': Bees, Hillier, Notcutt, Russell, Sale, Treseder

Pittosporum x 'Garnettii': Treseder

— — 'Golden King': Everton, Treseder

— — 'Atropurpureum': Treseder

Plantago major 'Rubrifolia': Hillier, Margery Fish Nursery

Polygonatum, variegated: Bressingham, Mars, Newlake, Pennell

Prunus laurocerasus 'Variegata': Hillier

— *lusitanica* 'Variegata': Hillier, Knap Hill, Treseder

Rheum palmatum, red-leaved forms: Bressingham, Hillier, Hilling, Perry, Plantsmen, Poland, Treasure

Rhododendron ponticum 'Variegatum': Haskins, Hillier; for *R.* species, etc., see specialist list

Ruta graveolens 'Variegata': Sherrard, Treasure, Treseder

Salvia officinalis 'Tricolor': Hillier, Margery Fish Nursery, Old Court, Plant Novelties International, Poland, Treasure, Treseder

Sedum albo-roseum 'Variegatum': Margery Fish Nursery, Plantsmen, Poland, Sunningdale

— *maximum* 'Atropurpureum': Hillier, Ingwersen, Old Court, Plant Novelties International, Plantsmen, Poland, Prichard, Scott, Sunningdale, Treasure, Washfield Nurseries

Senecio cineraria 'Ramparts': Margery Fish Nursery, Treasure, Treseder, Underwood

— *leucostachys:* Burkwood & Skipwith, Hillier, Pritchard, Slocock, Treasure, Underwood

Silybum marianum: (Thompson & Morgan)

Smilacina racemosa: Bressingham, Eldon, Hillier, Old Court, Perry, Prichard, Scott, Sunningdale (Thompson & Morgan)

Stachys lanata 'Silver Carpet': Bressingham, Margery Fish Nursery, Poland, Sunningdale

Tellima grandiflora: Hillier, Margery Fish Nursery, Plantsmen, Prichard, Sunningdale (Thompson & Morgan)

— — 'Purpurea': Bressingham, Eldon, Margery Fish Nursery, Poland, Sunningdale, Washfield Nurseries

Veratrum nigrum: Bressingham, Prichard, Sunningdale (Thompson & Morgan)

Viburnum tinus lucidum 'Variegatum': Treseder

— *tinus* 'Variegatum': Hillier, Jackman, Plant Novelties International, Russell, Treseder

Weigela japonica 'Looymansii Aurea': Burkwood & Skipwith, Charlton

Yucca filamentosa 'Variegata': Jackman

Zea mays 'Gracillima Variegata': (Carter, Sutton, Thompson & Morgan)

— — *japonica* 'Gigantea Quadricolor': (Thompson & Morgan, Unwin)

Where to Get It

Some Specialists

N.B. (+ G) = Also general nursery stock

BOG PLANTS AND FERNS
  Haig
  Highlands Water Gardens
  Hillier
  Kaye
  Newlake Gardens
  Perry
  Prichard
  Sunningdale (chiefly ferns)

RARE BULBS, ETC.
  Mars

HEATHS AND HEATHERS
  Aldenham Heather Nursery
  Davis, P. G. (*no* postal business)
  Dolley's Hill
  Letts
  Maxwell & Beale
  Oliver & Hunter
  Underwood & Son

PERENNIALS, GROUND COVER, ETC.
(See also (+ G), under Trees and Shrubs)
  Bressingham
  Carlile
  Eldon
  Margery Fish Nursery (+ some shrubs)
  Plantsmen
  Poland
  Prichard
  Washfield Nurseries

RHODODENDRON SPECIES
Exbury
Hillier
Hydon
Reuthe
Slocock
Sunningdale

SEEDSMEN
Carter
Dobbie
Dobie
Roberts
Sutton
Thompson & Morgan
Unwin

SILVER FOLIAGE PLANTS
Mrs. D. Underwood

TREES AND SHRUBS
Barnham (+G)
Burkwood & Skipwith
Everton (+G)
Haworth-Booth
Hillier (+G)
Hilling (+G)
Jackman (+G)
Knap Hill
Marchant
Notcutt (+G)
Pennell (+G)
Reuthe
Russell (+G)
Scott (+G)
Sherrard
Slieve Donard (+G)

191

Slocock (+G)
Sunningdale (+G)
Toynbee (+G)
Treseder
Waterer (+G)
Wyevale

Addresses

Aldenham Heather Nursery, Round Bush, Aldenham, Watford, Herts.

Barnham Nurseries Ltd., Barnham, Nr. Bognor Regis, Sussex.

A. J. T. Bayles, Grey Timbers, Chapple Rd., Bovey Tracey, Newton Abbot, South Devon.

Bees Ltd., Sealand, Chester.

W. Blom & Son Ltd., Leavesden, Watford, Herts.

Bressingham Gardens, Diss, Norfolk.

Broadleigh Gardens, Sampford Arundel, Wellington, Somerset.

Burkwood & Skipwith Ltd., Lane End Nurseries, Hookley Lane, Elstead, Nr. Godalming, Surrey.

Thos. Carlile (*Loddon Nurseries*) *Ltd.*, Twyford, Berks.

Carters Tested Seeds Ltd., Raynes Park, London, S.W.20

A. Charlton & Sons, Ltd., Summervale Nurseries, Tunbridge Wells, Kent.

J. Cheal & Sons, Ltd., Stopham Bridge, Pulborough (also Crawley and Handcross), Sussex.

Daniel Bros. Ltd., Norwich, Norfolk.

P. G. Davis, Timber Tops, Marley Common, Haslemere, Surrey (strictly for personal shoppers).

P. de Jager & Sons Ltd., Marden, Kent.

Dobbie & Co. Ltd., Edinburgh 7.

S. Dobie & Son Ltd., 11 Grosvenor St., Chester.

Dolley's Hill Nurseries, Normandy, Guildford, Surrey.

Eldon Nurseries, Corfe Mullen, Wimborne, Dorset.

Everton Nurseries Ltd., Everton, Nr. Lymington, Hants.

Exbury Gardens Ltd., Exbury, Nr. Southampton.

L. Haig & Co. Ltd., Beam Brook, Newdigate, Nr. Dorking, Surrey.

25. *Weigela florida* 'Variegata', cream and white variegated form

26. *Yucca filamentosa* 'Variegata'

Where to Get It

Haskins Nurseries Ltd., Trickett's Cross, Ferndown, Dorset.

M. Haworth-Booth, Farall Nurseries, Roundhurst, Nr. Haslemere, Surrey.

Highlands Water Gardens, Rickmansworth, Herts.

Hillier & Sons, Winchester, Hants.

T. Hilling & Co. Ltd., Chobham, Woking, Surrey.

Hydon Nurseries, Hydon Heath, Nr. Godalming, Surrey.

W. E. T. Ingwersen Ltd., Gravetye, East Grinstead, Sussex.

G. Jackman & Son, Woking Nurseries Ltd., Woking, Surrey.

R. Kaye Ltd., Silverdale, Carnforth, Lancs.

Kelway & Son Ltd., Langport, Somerset.

Knap Hill Nursery Ltd., Barr's Lane, Lower Knaphill, Woking, Surrey.

J. F. Letts, Foxhollow, Westwood Rd., Windlesham, Surrey.

C. J. Marchant, Keeper's Hill Nursery, Stapehill, Wimborne, Dorset.

Margery Fish Nursery, East Lambrook Manor, South Petherton, Somerset.

Lt.-Col. J. A. Mars, Dereen, Bell Vale, Haslemere, Surrey.

Maxwell & Beale, Corfe Mullen, Wimborne, Dorset.

Newlake Gardens, Copthorne, Crawley, Sussex.

R. C. Notcutt Ltd., Woodbridge, Suffolk.

Old Court Nurseries Ltd., Colwall, Nr. Malvern.

Oliver & Hunter, Moniaive, by Thornhill, Dumfriesshire.

Pennell & Sons Ltd., Lincoln.

Perry's Hardy Plant Farm, Enfield, Middlesex.

Plant Novelties International, Primrose Hill Nursery, Bunch Lane, Haslemere, Surrey (personal shoppers preferred).

The Plantsmen, Buckshaw Gardens, Sherborne, Dorset.

R. Poland, Brook House Nursery, Highbrook Rd., Ardingly, Sussex.

M. Prichard & Sons Ltd., Riverslea Nurseries, Christchurch, Hants.

G. Reuthe Ltd., Fox Hill Nurseries, Keston, Kent.

G. B. Roberts, Faversham, Kent.

L. R. Russell Ltd., Richmond Nurseries, Windlesham, Surrey.

Sale & Son Ltd., Wokingham, Berks.

Where to Get It

John Scott & Co., The Royal Nurseries, Merriott, Somerset.

J. O. Sherrard & Son, Shaw Nursery, Newbury, Berks.

Slieve Donard Nursery Co. Ltd., Newcastle, Co. Down, N. Ireland.

W. C. Slocock Ltd., Goldsworth Nursery, Woking, Surrey.

Sunningdale Nurseries, Windlesham, Surrey.

Sutton & Sons Ltd., Reading, Berks.

Thompson & Morgan Ltd., Ipswich, Suffolk.

Toynbee's Nurseries, Barnham, Nr. Bognor Regis, Sussex.

Treasure's of Tenbury Ltd., Tenbury Wells, Worcs.

Treseders' Nurseries Truro Ltd., Truro, Cornwall.

G. Underwood & Son, Hookstone Green Nurseries, West End, Nr. Woking, Surrey.

Mrs. Desmond Underwood, Colchester, Essex.

W. J. Unwin Ltd., Histon, Cambs.

R. Wallace & Co., The Old Gardens, Tunbridge Wells, Kent.

Wallace & Barr Ltd., The Nurseries, Marden, Kent.

Washfield Nurseries, Hawkhurst, Kent.

J. Waterer Sons & Crisp, Bagshot, Surrey (shrubs) and The Floral Mile, Twyford, Berks (perennials, etc.).

Wyevale Nurseries, Hereford.

To be accurate, lists such as the foregoing need constant revision. But since the grower can only gauge demand by what he gets asked for it is up to us to keep on asking, now that so many of the rarer items are being dropped in the general trend towards retrenchment. Plantsmen will no doubt regret the demise of the Plant Finder Service operated for a time by the Horticultural Trades Association; but Fellows of the R.H.S. may still seek help in the column included in its Journal under the head *Fellows Wishing to Obtain Plants Rare in Cultivation*, which lists particulars of the seeker and the plants sought.

CHAPTER VII

Where to Grow It

I am not at all convinced of the wisdom of tackling this subject, which is full of dangerous pitfalls for the amateur garden-maker. Having expended great thought and labour on the planning and planting of my own meagre one-third of an acre of shrub garden, I admit to being somewhat in love with my creation. But it was not achieved in six days, nor was there any rest on the seventh day or any day thereafter! Many nights over the years I have lain awake wrestling with some intractable problem of how to fill a particular gap in a shrub border with regard to colour, size, habit, flowering time, constitution, suitable aspect and soil requirements; and I have worked upon the whole in my mind without let-up to bring about improvements, constantly reorganizing by trial and error over the last eighteen years. It follows, therefore, that I would hardly presume to tell others what to do with the ground at their disposal had I not been persuaded that it would be helpful to include one or two plans for foliage plantings here. Nevertheless I beg to disclaim any pretensions to being a garden designer.

In my own garden I do not believe in working to scale plans on paper, finding the eye a surer guide than the tape measure or the slide-rule. For me planning consists of assembling a number of selected plants on a prepared site and shuffling them around on the surface until they are grouped to my satisfaction and, I always hope, to theirs. It proceeds preferably in instalments, getting the most important features positioned at the outset and adding others in a supporting role when it is seen what additional sizes, shapes, colours and textures are required to fill in the design.

Where to Grow It

Horticultural writers are fond of warning the reader that certain foliage plants 'need careful placing', but we are rarely told how they themselves would solve the problem. It is true that extremes of dark and light leaf colour, such as the so-called purples and conspicuous cream or white variegations, attract too much attention to themselves in plantings designed for maximum flower-power; but these come triumphantly into their own in a border or grouping planned for contrasting foliage colour. I do not know whether this is the kind of solution the above-mentioned writers have in mind, but it is surprising to me that plantings of this kind are so rarely undertaken. Whereas it is not uncommon for whole shrub gardens and arboretums to be specifically planned for ephemeral autumn leaf colour the more permanent foliar contrasts of bronze, wine, purple, yellow, lime, old gold, blue-green, silver and different variegations—in many cases actually evergreen—are much less often seen, though possibly even more satisfying to those with a taste for quieter blends of colour and certainly of greater value to the flower arranger.

For some time past I have included small foliage groups of contrasting hues in my shrub beds and more recently I have given over a whole border some 56 ft. long by 12 ft. wide to foliage plants in as varied an assortment of colours, shapes and textures as I can contrive. This has been built up piecemeal over the last few years, with annual extensions as my enthusiasm grew and the more established sections now give me as much pleasure as any part of the garden planted for more eye-catching flower colour. I have therefore attempted to plan a shrub border on similar lines for the benefit of foliage addicts among the flower arrangers who may welcome suggestions for grouping these plants in such a way as to derive enjoyment from them both out of doors and in. (See pages 200–201.)

The border is intended for a south or south-west aspect and would only be effective if it received the sun for a good part of the day, because the majority of leaf colours are dependent on sunlight for depth and richness, purples and bronzes becoming a dingy brownish-green, most limes and yellows turning green, and silvers losing much of their lustre in shady conditions.

Where to Grow It

Special consideration has been given to effective juxtaposition of colour, preponderance of evergreen over deciduous subjects (to avoid a winter nakedness), varying heights and habits and individual cultural needs. Calcifuge plants have been purposely omitted in order to suit all types of soil. Plain green hues have also been omitted, for reasons which will be explained later. It will also be seen that little or no allowance is made for carpeters and ground-covering plants such as hostas, bergenias, *Hebe* 'Pagei', epimediums and the variegated ivies and vincas, valuable though most of these are as finishing touches. The reason is that it is as finishing touches that such plants are most convenient to place, serving as fillers on the perimeter wherever gaps arise in the final stages of the planting. Such marginal spaces as appear on the plan may look very small, but whereas these cannot be accurately assessed on a scale plan it will be found in practice that some subjects tuck in comfortably at the feet of others, such as *Hebe* 'Pagei' beneath *Hebe armstrongii*, hostas and bergenias at the base of phormiums, or variegated and purple sedums of the large-leaved types around *Ruta graveolens*, and so on. Where soil permits, some of the colourful calluna foliages in lime-yellow, bronze or flame should certainly be included along the sunny verges.

I have included one item, *Berberis thunbergii* 'Atropurpurea Nana', which is too dwarf and compact to be of much use for cutting, especially if the taller forms of purple-leaved berberis are also grown; but the neat little hummock of dark copper makes such a rich and telling colour contribution among the other verge plants that the effect would be much the poorer without it. If the flower arranger grudges even a little of her garden space to anything which will not be very useful indoors, something of the same colour contrast and lowly stature for the front rank might be achieved with small rooted pieces of purple-leaved cotinus planted in clumps (these, rather surprisingly, can be kept to a height of 12 or 18 in. without much trouble), with *Tellima grandiflora* 'Purpurea', with additional groups of *Sedum maximum* 'Atropurpureum', or with the carpeting *Ajuga reptans* 'Multicolor'.

Where to Grow It

I dare say there will be plenty of head-shaking over the spacing, on the familiar grounds that the plants have not room to display their individuality. But this is not what I want of them in most cases. I am aiming rather at a backcloth of close-woven tapestry in which each block of colour merges into the next as part of the whole, and concentrating variety of form into the foreground, where sword-blades of phormium and yucca contrast with the bold heart-shapes, egg-shapes and circles of hosta and bergenia, with whipcord hebe, fleshy sedum, feathery cassinia, lacy rue and so on. I have long since proved to myself that a certain amount of what the critics regard as overcrowding pays, especially in a cold climate. Apart from the advantage in this case of achieving the widest possible assortment of foliar hues there are a number of sound utilitarian reasons for the 'close boscage' type of gardening in general: it helps to provide shelter for the less hardy subjects; encourages faster growth; leaves no bare soil to be invaded by weeds; and offers the flower arranger a large selection from which she may cut sooner and more freely than if each plant were grown as a specimen in its own right. Cutting should of course be done intelligently as a form of pruning and to prevent overcrowding.

It may cause some surprise that no plain green has been included among the mixed foliage colours. This is, I suppose, a purely personal foible; but my own feeling is that it detracts somewhat from the colourful effect of bronzes, yellows, cream or white variegations, purples, blue-greens, old golds and silvers, and since true greens in any case look so much at home among flowering plants they may just as well find a place in the herbaceous or flowering shrub borders.

Alternatively plain greens and cream or white variegations may be associated on their own in beds at the foot of house walls or in adjoining areas such as terraces, courtyards and patios, where bold leaf patterns and interesting textures may be effectively contrasted. I therefore include some plans for beds of this kind, with emphasis on evergreens and on architectural leaf forms, which are as appropriate for flower arrangement as they are for formal plantings around the house. (See pages 202–3).

198

It would not be possible to plan on these lines without including flowering subjects and in order to avoid the distracting effect of other colours during the comparatively brief period when the plant is in bloom the choice has been limited as far as possible to those with white or green flowers, which would merge without undue self-advertisement into this foliage scheme. One could not however omit the spectacular blades of *Phormium tenax* (not, in any case, very free-flowering in most circumstances), the sculptural leaf whorls of *Mahonia japonica* or the bold, solid shapes of bergenias and hostas, for instance, notwithstanding the mahogany, primrose, pink and light violet of their flowers. And in making a choice among the dwarf ever-green azaleas several of the more brightly flowered varieties might qualify on the grounds that their foliage is finer than that of the whites. In particular I would be tempted to include the beautifully tiered dark green pattern of *amoenum* 'Coccineum' and enjoy its crimson flowers for a week or two in spring, even though these would temporarily upset the master-plan.

So valuable are the positions at the foot of house walls—both culturally and aesthetically—that it is worth while going to some trouble to do away with paths which hug the walls of a building. The ground should be cleared of rubble and other rubbish and topped up with good soil if necessary, before planting begins and the plants nearest the wall should thereafter be kept care-fully watered if overhanging eaves prevent rain from reaching them. Not only does a house look infinitely more attractive when surrounded by greenery, but the warmth and shelter pro-vided by walls makes it possible to grow a number of plants not sufficiently hardy for the open garden. The small group of ever-greens shown in the illustration facing p. 208 serves a practical as well as an ornamental purpose in helping to hide my dustbins and will be still more effective when the young pyracantha against the wall spreads sufficiently to be trained over the un-sightly drainpipe. A small-leaved ivy (the yellow-variegated 'Jubilee') has also been recently planted to mask the front of the screen. In limy areas it may sometimes be possible to replace the natural soil in small house beds with acid soil suitable for

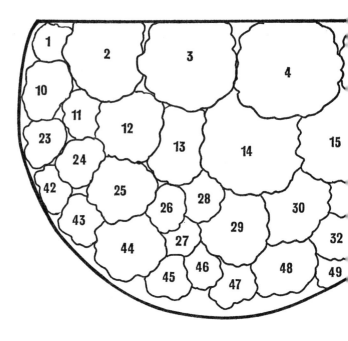

1. *Phormium tenax* 'Purpureum'
2. *Viburnum tinus* 'Variegatum' or a variegated laurel
3. *Eucalyptus perriniana,* bush form
4. *Ligustrum ovalifolium* 'Aureo-marginatum'
5. One of the purple-leaved forms of *Cotinus coggygria*
6. *Physocarpus opulifolius* 'Luteus'
7. *Elaeagnus pungens* 'Maculata'
8. *Elaeagnus macrophylla*
9. *Philadelphus coronarius* 'Aureus' or 'Variegatus', or *Weigela japonica* 'Looymansii Aurea'
10. *Salvia officinalis* 'Purpurascens' or 'Purpurascens Variegata'
11. *Phormium tenax* 'Veitchii'
12. *Berberis thunbergii* 'Atropurpurea'
13. *Atriplex halimus*
14. *Cornus alba sibirica* 'Variegata' or 'Spaethii'
15. *Thuja occidentalis* 'Rheingold', or *Chamaecyparis pisifera* 'Plumosa' or 'Squarrosa'
16. *Weigela florida* 'Variegata'
17. *Atriplex halimus*
18. *Berberis thunbergii* 'Atropurpurea Superba'
19. *Eucalyptus gunnii,* std. or $\frac{1}{2}$ std. tree (providing shade for *Elaeagnus macrophylla* and philadelphus)
20. *Rosa rubrifolia*
21. *Symphoricarpus orbiculatus* 'Variegatus'
22. *Mahonia aquifolium* 'Atropurpurea'

200

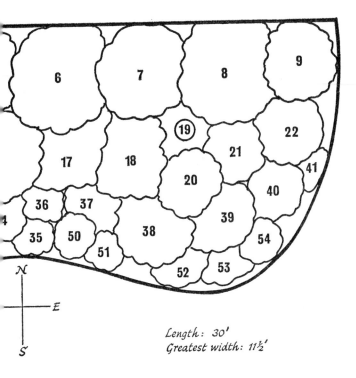

Length: 30'
Greatest width: 11½'

ᵏed Foliage Hues

23. *Senecio cineraria* 'Ramparts' or 'White Diamond'
24. *Ruta graveolens* 'Jackman's Blue'
25. *Cassinia fulvida*
26, 27, 28. *Phormium tenax* 'Variegatum'
29. *Lonicera nitida* 'Baggesen's Gold'
30. *Artemisia arborescens*, for warm gardens (elsewhere *Senecio laxifolius*)
31. *Phormium tenax* 'Purpureum', large-leaved form
32, 33. Smaller-leaved form of above, if possible
34, 35, 36. *Hebe armstrongii*
37. *Buddleia davidii* 'Harlequin'
38. *Cassinia fulvida*
39. *Senecio laxifolius*
40. *Hebe armstrongii* or *hectori*
41. *Hosta fortunei* 'Albopicta' (clump)'
42. *Sedum maximum* 'Atropurpureum (clump)
43. *Yucca filamentosa* 'Variegata'
44. *Ballota pseudo-dictamnus*
45. *Bergenia* 'Sunningdale' or *purpurascens* (clump)
46, 47. *Berberis thunbergii* 'Atropurpurea Nana'
48. *Hosta sieboldiana* (clump)
49. *Sedum albo-roseum* 'Variegatum' (clump)
50, 51. *Ruta graveolens* 'Jackman's Blue' or 'Variegata'
52. *Sedum albo-roseum* 'Variegatum' (clump)
53. *Sedum maximum* 'Atropurpureum' (clump)
54. *Bergenia* 'Sunningdale' (clump)

201

Plan 2: Green Borders

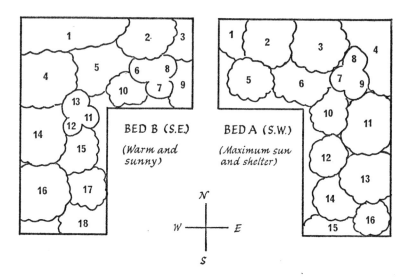

BED B (S.E.)

(Warm and sunny)

BED A (S.W.)

(Maximum sun and shelter)

N

W ——|—— E

S

Outside measurements: 14' x 17'
Inside   "   7' x 10'
Depth   "   7'

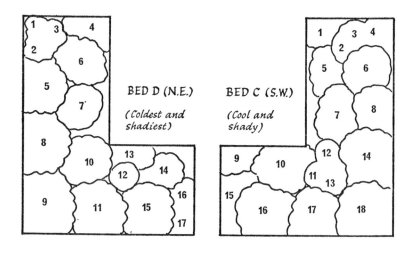

BED D (N.E.)

(Coldest and shadiest)

BED C (S.W.)

(Cool and shady)

202

Key to Plan 2: Green Borders

BED A (S.W.)
1. Clump of galax* (or hosta)
2. *Choisya ternata*
3. *Escallonia x iveyi*
4. *Magnolia grandiflora* 'Ferru-ginea' or 'Exmouth Variety'
5. *Euonymus* 'Silver Queen'
6. *Rhododendron amoenum* 'Coc-cineum'* (or *Daphne odora* 'Aureo-marginata')
7. ⎫
8. ⎬ Variegated phormium
9. ⎭
10. *Hebe hectori*
11. Variegated fatsia
12. *Yucca filamentosa*
13. *Euphorbia veneta* (*wulfenii*)
14. Clump of *Agapanthus campanu-latus* 'Albus'
15. Clump of *Bergenia cordifolia*
16. *Yucca filamentosa* 'Variegata'

BED B (S.E.)
1. *Magnolia grandiflora* 'Ferru-ginea' or 'Exmouth Variety'
2. Variegated form of *Viburnum tinus* or of griselinia
3. One or more *Sarcococca hook-eriana*
4. *Mahonia japonica* or *lomarii-folia*
5. *Hebe x andersonii* 'Variegata'
6. ⎫
7. ⎬ *Phormium tenax*
8. ⎭
9. Clump of bergenia
10. Clump of *Agapanthus campanu-latus* 'Albus'
11. ⎫
12. ⎬ Variegated phormium
13. ⎭
14. *Fatsia japonica*
15. *Hydrangea* 'Quadricolor'
16. *Skimmia japonica* 'Foremanii'
17. *Euphorbia characias* (compact form)
18. Clump of *Hosta* 'Yellow Edge'

BED C (N.W.)
1. Clump of *Iris foetidissima* 'Variegata'

2. ⎫
3. ⎬ *Danae racemosa*
4. ⎭
5. Clump of *Helleborus corsicus*
6. *Euphorbia characias*
7. *Viburnum davidii* (if berries wanted plant another in place of 8)
8. *Hydrangea* 'Quadricolor'
9. Clump of galax* (or of white-flowered forms of *Helleborus orientalis*)
10. *Euonymus fortunei* 'Silver Queen'
11. ⎫
12. ⎬ Variegated phormium
13. ⎭
14. *Choisya ternata*
15. Clump of *Leucothoë catesbaei** (or hardy fern or *Polygona-tum japonicum* 'Variegatum')
16. *Fatsia japonica*
17. *Mahonia lomariifolia*
18. *Camellia japonica* variety* (or *Viburnum rhytidophyllum*)

BED D (N.E.)
1. ⎫
2. ⎬ *Danae racemosa*
3. ⎭
4. Clump of bergenia or *Hosta* 'Thomas Hogg'
5. *Skimmia japonica* 'Foremanii'
6. *Rhododendron amoenum* 'Cocci-neum'* or 'Hinodegiri'* (ever-green azaleas) (or clump of *Helleborus foetidus*)
7. *Euonymus fortunei* 'Gracilis'
8. *Fatsia japonica*
9. *Rhododendron obovata** (or *Vi-burnum tinus* 'Variegatum' or one of the variegated laurels)
10. *Skimmia rubella*
11. *Mahonia japonica*
12. *Phormium tenax*
13. Clump of *Bergenia cordifolia*
14. Clump of *Helleborus corsicus*
15. *Choisya ternata*
16. ⎫
17. ⎬ *Sarcococca hookeriana* ⋅
⎭

203

camellias, evergreen azaleas, leucothoë and other lime-haters, but where any of these have been included in the plans I have suggested substitutes of similar proportions which are indifferent to the pH value of the soil.

It will be seen that the beds take the form of L shapes making four corners of a rectangle, thus offering a choice of aspects (from A, the sunniest and sheltered from the north and east, to D, the coolest and shadiest) and being suitable for use singly, in pairs or all together, as shown on the plan. The beds might equally well be backed by hedges, fencing or garden walls and the sharp angles of their inner sides could of course be rounded off to give a more curving contour to the front of each if preferred, without much affecting the planting plan. Though a little adjustment might make it possible to site these plantings to flank doors, french windows, etc., when considering them as house beds (and for this reason a fragrant subject such as choisya, daphne, or sarcococca, is usually placed alongside a possible entrance of suitable aspect), there seemed little point in making arbitrary allowance for the unpredictable position and size of windows. Climbers have been omitted for much the same reason and, as explained in connection with Plan 1, it is more practical to add most of the dwarf verge plants and carpeters wherever spaces occur on the perimeter as planting proceeds rather than to indicate their siting on the initial plan. The following lists therefore contain suggestions for:

1. Low-growing plants to be substituted for subjects likely to exceed 3 ft. in positions beneath windows.
2. Climbers suitable for walls backing house beds of green, cream or white foliage colour.
3. Carpeters, ground cover and other verge plants to be added as fillers, having regard to contrast of form with their neighbours.

1. Beneath Windows

Agapanthus campanulatus 'Albus'
Azaleas, dwarf evergreen*

Danae racemosa
Daphne odora 'Aureo-marginata'
Euonymus fortunei 'Silver Queen'
Euphorbia characias (compact form)
Ferns, hardy, various
Hebe x franciscana 'Variegata'
Hebe hectori
Hedera helix 'Congesta'
Hellebores, various
*Leucothoë catesbaei**
Lonicera pileata
Phlox paniculata 'Norah Leigh'
Phormium colensoi
Polygonatum multiflorum
Sarcococca hookeriana
Skimmia rubella
Smilacina racemosa
Viburnum davidii
Yucca filamentosa 'Variegata'

2. Climbers

Actinidia kolomikta (? see description)
Euonymus fortunei 'Gracilis'
x *Fatshedera lizei* and variegated form
Hederas, various
Hydrangea petiolaris
Jasmines, variegated or green
Lonicera japonica 'Aureo-reticulata'
Vitis coignetiae

3. Verge Plants and Ground Cover

Alchemilla mollis
Arum italicum 'Pictum'
Astrantia major 'Sunningdale Variegated'
Bergenias, various

Epimediums, various
Euphorbia robbiae
Ferns, various
Galax aphylla*
Hederas, various
Helleborus orientalis hybrids
Hostas, various
Mentha rotundifolia 'Variegata'
Pachysandra, plain and variegated*
Polygonatum, variegated
Vincas, various

Finally, for those who want the best of both worlds, I have compiled the following lists of good foliage plants which are also attractive in flower or in fruit. By making their own selection from the seasonal sections below, keeping as fair a balance as possible between each of these, they could plan mixed borders affording not only a variety of fine leaves but a succession of flowers, berries or seedheads from early spring to late autumn, with one or two winter flowers or fruits into the bargain. Full names and other details can be checked where necessary by reference to Chapter V, but I have again marked lime-haters with the cautionary asterisk to ensure that the earlier warning is not overlooked. (F) after a plant name indicates good fruits or seedheads rather than beauty of bloom and (FF) means that both flowers and fruits or seedheads are attractive.

(a) Trees, Shrubs and Climbers

EARLY SPRING

Amelanchier canadensis
Azaleas, evergreen*
Camellias*
Cornus mas (varieg. forms)
Erica arborea alpina*
Laurus nobilis
Mahonia aquifolium (FF)

Pieris, various*
Prunus x blireiana
Prunus x cistena
Rhododendron, species,* all in Chapter V except *cinna-barinum, concatenans* and *obovata*
Skimmias (FF)
Viburnums, various

LATE SPRING

Azaleas, evergreen*
Choisya ternata
Hebe 'Glauco-coerulea' and 'Pagei'
Mahonia repens rotundifolia
Paeonia delavayi (FF)
Paeonia lutea ludlowii (FF)
Rhododendron cinnabarinum and hybrids.*
*Rhododendron concatenans**
Weigela florida 'Foliis Purpureis' and 'Variegata'
Weigela japonica 'Looymansii Aurea'
Vitis vinifera 'Purpurea'

MIDSUMMER

Convolvulus cneorum
Cotinus coggygria
Cytisus battandieri
Eucalypts (FF)
Jasminum officinale, variegated cvs.
Philadelphus coronarius 'Aureus' and 'Variegatus'
Potentilla fruticosa 'Vilmoriniana'
Rhododendron 'Moser's Maroon'* and many other hardy hybrids
Santolina neapolitana

LATE SUMMER AND AUTUMN

Arbutus unedo and 'Rubra' (FF)
Ballota pseudo-dictamnus

207

Buddleia davidii, variegated cvs.
Callunas, foliage cvs.*
Escallonia x iveyi
Fatsia japonica and 'Variegata'
Fuchsias, variegated cvs.
Hebe 'Autumn Glory'
Humulus lupulus 'Aureus' (F)
Hydrangea macrophylla and variegated cvs.
Lonicera pileata (F)
Magnolia grandiflora and cvs. (FF)
Phormiums, various (FF)
Viburnum davidii, *V. rhytidophyllum* and its variegated form (FF)
Viburnum tinus 'Variegatum'
Yuccas, various

WINTER

Ilex aquifolium 'Pyramidalis Fructu-luteo' (F)
Mahonia x 'Charity', *M. japonica* and *M. lomariifolia*
Viburnum fragrans

(b) Non-Shrubby Hardy Plants

EARLY SPRING

Aquilegias, various
Bergenias, various
Cyclamen repandum
Epimediums, various
Erythroniums, various
Euphorbias, various
Hellebores, various
Peltiphyllum peltatum
Primula vulgaris
Vincas, variegated cvs.

LATE SPRING

Paeonia mlokosewitschii (FF)
Polygonatum multiflorum

27. Green foliage plants in a house bed, including (front row) bergenias, *Alchemilla mollis*, *Hedera helix* 'Congesta', *Hosta* 'Thomas Hogg'; (behind) phormiums, *Helleborus lividus* subsp. *corsicus*, *Camellia japonica* 'Mars'

28. A green and cream arrangement with foliage predominating, including leaves of *Mahonia japonica, Hosta* 'Yellow Edge' and *H.* 'Albopicta', *Bergenia cordifolia, Phormium tenax* 'Variegatum', *Curtonus paniculatus, Iris pseudacorus* 'Variegatus', *Hemerocallis fulva, Hydrangea macrophylla* 'Ami Pasquier', *Camellia japonica* 'Adolphe Audusson' and *Polygonatum multiflorum,* allied with the green seedheads of *Angelica archangelica*

Polygonatum japonicum 'Variegatum'
Rheum palmatum, 'Red-leaved Form' (FF)
Smilacina racemosa
Tellima grandiflora and 'Purpurea'

MIDSUMMER
Alchemilla mollis
Angelica archangelica (FF)
Aruncus sylvester
Astilbes
Astrantia major 'Sunningdale Variegated'
Crambe maritima
Cynara cardunculus
Elymus arenarius (FF)
Eomecon chionantha
Eryngium bourgatii
Eryngium variifolium
*Galax aphylla**
Galeobdolon luteum 'Variegatum'
Hostas, various
Onoclea sensibilis (F)
*Osmunda regalis** (F)
Paeonia, herbaceous varieties
Rodgersias, various (FF)
Thalictrum glaucum
Veratrums (FF)

LATE SUMMER AND AUTUMN
Acanthus spinosus
Agapanthus, various (FF)
Anaphalis yedoensis
Arum italicum 'Pictum' (F)
Colchicum autumnale
Curtonus paniculatus (FF)
Cyclamen neapolitanum
Euphorbia sikkimensis
Foeniculum, purple-leaved cvs.

O   209

Hemerocallis, various
Lobelia cardinalis 'Bee's Flame' and 'Queen Victoria'
Lobelia fulgens
Macleaya microcarpa 'Kelway's Coral Plume'
Miscanthus sinensis 'Zebrinus'
Onopordums, various
Sedums, various

CHAPTER VIII

How to Use It

When visiting the 'Flowers in Thanksgiving' Festival in Winchester Cathedral in 1966, a party of young Frenchwomen stood spellbound for a time on entering the vast nave, with its huge pedestal groups of flowers, its giant swags of greenery suspended from the pillars and its foliage arrangements at intervals between these. Their reaction, when it came, was something of a surprise. It was not the spectacular blooms, graduated from maroon and purple through reds to pinks and cream, but the '*verdure*' which was unanimously acclaimed as '*ravissante*'.

Happy as I was to find that the greenery could be such a show-stopper, I hope we are now agreed that foliage is not all '*verdure*', despite the large numbers who still appear to think so. One well-known demonstrator who makes a speciality of foliage arrangements mentioned recently that when she undertakes a demonstration on this subject she is almost certain to find herself billed to do 'all-green arrangements', as though the two were one and the same. Perhaps a look at Appendix B will serve to point the moral, proving that the range of colour, as well as of shape and texture, among foliage plants is almost as wide as among flowers, if somewhat more subdued.

The suggestions which follow for the use of foliage in floral decoration are purposely elementary, for the experienced will need no advice from me. But the novice may be glad of a few suggestions, perhaps being unaware of the many different functions of the versatile leaf, whether in a subsidiary role, sharing the lead, topping the bill or holding the stage on its own. Here are some examples of what I have in mind.

Subsidiary Role

Most commonly, I would say, leaves are used as a foil for the predominating flowers and/or fruits. (The term 'fruits' is of course used throughout in the sense of the N.A.F.A.S. Schedule Definitions, to cover all kinds of edible and inedible fruits, berries, seedheads and vegetables, from gooseberries to aubergines, holly berries, pea pods, mushrooms, nuts and dandelion "clocks".) In this case the motive may be partly one of economy, as a means of eking out flowers when these are scarce in the garden or dear in the shops. But even though an arrangement, however large, may cost less, it should also prove more effective, when bold leaf forms such as fatsia, hosta, bergenia or rheum are used for balance and weight and to provide restful areas for the eye, with the more finely drawn foliage sprays as a framework for the flowers. The outline foliage may be almost anything of suitable habit which can be spared from the garden or found in the wild, since it is not required to attract attention to itself at the expense of the dominating material. It should nevertheless be in good condition and free from blemishes.

Sharing the Lead

Giving it more of the importance it deserves, one may use foliage to partner flowers and/or fruits on an equal footing by making its own separate colour contribution to the scheme. In the examples which follow I would say that the honours were even between leaves and flowers. I remember once entering one of those now rather hackneyed Exhibition Classes depicting summer in some form or other, in which I combined dusky pinks and mauves with lime, with the addition of a large bronze bee nuzzling into a cluster of purple plums and grapes—not, you might think, brilliantly suggestive of 'High Summer' or such-like, and probably less so than the brighter, hotter hues of other entries. But the vitalizing colour contribution of yallery-greenery made by the foliage of *Physocarpus opulifolius* 'Luteus',

How to Use It

Philadelphus coronarius 'Aureus', *Hosta fortunei* 'Aurea' and *H.* 'Albopicta' prompted an eminent judge to see the whole as shot through with sunshine! I confess it was in reality little more than a *mariage de convenance* from what the garden happened to offer and devoid of the inspiration with which her imaginative eye endowed it.

In much the same way I have found that variegated foliage may be used to create an illusory colour effect in combination with certain flower hues. For instance, needing a pink and white arrangement for some special autumn occasion, I found that most of my garden flowers available at the time were more blue-pink than required, with a plethora of *Nerine bowdenii* in particular. But by including plenty of foliage from the variegated forms of *Weigela florida*, *Vinca major* and *Hedera canariensis*— all generously patterned with deep cream—the pinks of my nerines, lilies, roses and hydrangeas appeared appreciably warmer in tone than when isolated from the deep cream leaf colour, even the white flowers gaining in effectiveness by the admixture of pale yellow variegation.

Nor should we overlook the value of foliage in monochromatic arrangements—that is, in tints and shades of one basic hue. True monochromes are not easy to achieve and competition entries are often ruled out or down-pointed as not strictly according to schedule because some green leaves have been allowed to remain on the flower stems in an arrangement of some other one colour such as all-reds or all-yellows. In an all-green arrangement the usefulness of green leaves speaks for itself, though even in this comparatively easy version of the monochromatic it is possible to slip up by failing to distinguish between blue-, yellow- and grey-greens, which cannot be mixed within the definition of our colour term. Whereas the non-foliage-minded gardener may have to forgo the use of leaves altogether when attempting any other kind of monochromatic effect, the choice is greatly increased for those who grow a wide variety of foliage for cutting. There is, for instance, a splendid range of bronze leaves to assort with coffee-coloured roses, stocks and macleayas; beetroot-red foliage may complement flowers and

213

fruits ranging from crimson to pink; the infinite variety of silver, silver-white and silver-grey (but not silver-green) leaves may be combined with black and white; and lime-yellow or glaucous foliages make possible still further variations on the one-colour theme.

Star or Solo Performer

I believe that only the gardener can hope to achieve success with arrangements in which leaves predominate or are used entirely on their own, for in either one needs a wide variety of interesting shapes, sizes, colours and textures to draw upon. And yet there is something so subtly satisfying in the best of these arrangements that they win at least as much admiration from the discerning as the most expert assemblage of beautiful blooms.

My own feeling is that fruits lend themselves more readily than flowers to the first of these two kinds of arrangement. Generally speaking flower colours attract too much attention to themselves, in competition with foliage, to play second fiddle satisfactorily, even if the leaves preponderate in quantity or in visual weight: though green hellebores and euphorbias and other soft-toned bracted "flowers" are useful exceptions. It will, of course, be remembered that unopened flower buds (i.e. showing no petal colour) are permissible in foliage arrangement competition classes and since most of them are encased in calyces of copper, bronze, green or grey, they blend pleasingly with leaf colours, so long as they remain tight shut. But there is always a risk that silver sepals, for instance, may open upon bright yellow daisy-flowers or fat copper buds burst open to reveal petals of purest white, especially in the warm atmosphere of an exhibition hall.

In late summer and autumn in particular all kinds of garden and hedgerow berries, seedheads and other fruits are at hand to provide outline sprays or a 'centre of interest' in an arrangement of ornamental leaves. It is often something of a problem, even to the most experienced, to know what to do about the centre of an all-foliage arrangement, which should focus the beholder's attention and give some purpose, as it were, to the overall design. This problem ceases to exist when a few bronze-green "apples" of chaenomeles, sculptured magnolia seed pods, blue-green poppy-heads or berried clusters may be introduced into the heart of an arrangement of contrasting foliage shapes and textures. One such example is shown in the illustration facing p. 209, in which a few unripe seedheads of angelica are combined with the predominating assortment of green and variegated leaves. Although the green angelica heads are fairly large their delicate openwork construction prevents them from stealing the limelight as solid blooms of similar size and contrasting colour would have done. Despite the difficulty of deciding at what point one's foliage ceases to 'predominate', it seems to me easier for the novice to achieve a pleasing effect in the type of competition class entitled 'Accent on Foliage' than in one calling for a foliage arrangement *tout court*; but she will of course have to exercise restraint in the use of her berries, seedheads or whatever so that the predominance of the foliage is not in dispute.

For the beginner I think that the all-foliage arrangement is the most difficult of any, chiefly for the reason just expounded—and there is little help that one can give. It is possible and, I think, quite effective to assemble several leaves of one kind and of matching shape and size, such as *Stachys lanata* or *Hosta undulata*, round an unopened bud of similar colour on a straight stem, binding all the stalks together so that the leaves are arranged petal-wise to form a flower-shape, which helps to give importance to the centre of an arrangement (see illustration facing p. 224). The same thing is more commonly done with skeleton magnolia leaves in dried or Christmas arrangements. Then, again, there are plants of rosette-like leaf structure, e.g. pachysandra, *Verbascum bombicyferum* (seedling stage) and some euphorbias and rhododendrons, which offer a similar and more natural solution. But foliage arrangements would have a monotonous sameness if one were always to resort to the rosette shape to draw the eye. Variations on a foliage theme are endless, from contrasts of leaf design and texture in tints and shades of one colour to the intriguing gamut of blue-greens, scarlets, crimsons, purples, bronzes, coppers, browns, beiges, yellows and silvers, from which to devise any permutation or combination to suit one's fancy, not forgetting the additional wealth of variegated leaves in all manner of shapes and sizes to be found among garden foliage. But it remains to be said that only one's fancy, innate sense of fitness, or inspiration can be one's guide; for I doubt if those who lack a flair for foliage arrangement can acquire it from teachers and textbooks. They may, however, well do so by getting to know and love the leaves their garden grows.

Foliage in Christmas Decorations

Most of what I have said applies equally to foliage in Christmas decorations, whether these are to be of fresh material, or dried, painted or glittered. There is no need to stress the economy of combining evergreen leaves with fresh flowers at a time when the cost of the latter is highest, but the following example may show that even a large pedestal arrangement of flowers and foliage is not necessarily beyond one's means with a store of home-grown leaves to draw upon. Having bought no more than five miserly stems of pale yellow and three of apricot spray chrysanthemums for a large pedestal arrangement in a Christmas demonstration of fresh plant material, I supplemented these with branches of flowering hamamelis from the garden and the cream and green foliage of such evergreens as *Hedera canariensis* 'Variegata', *Phormium tenax* 'Variegatum', *Elaeagnus pungens* 'Maculata', the immensely valuable variegated Cherry Laurel (*Prunus laurocerasus* 'Variegata'), which is heavily splashed with cream to white and has a number of all-cream leaf shoots, and some large leaves of the variegated fatsia from a warmer Lymington garden (which I had kept with their stems in water in a cool, dark larder for over a month). Some glycerined leaves of *Curtonus paniculatus* and variegated aspidistra, both of which turn to a lovely copper, helped to accent the few apricot-coloured flowers, and large glass baubles lightly sprayed with copper

216

and a long-tailed ribbon bow of apricot shot with light green were added to give a more festive touch to the whole. But with or without these less expendable trimmings the cost was modest for so large and party-like a floral decoration in mid-winter.

Many evergreen foliages—and much coniferous material in particular—are extraordinarily long-lasting, both in and out of water. Indeed some pieces of blue-green chamaecyparis cut at the end of November for the same occasion and left lying, forgotten, on a moist bed of fallen leaves in almost total shade in my garden, were as fresh as ever and fit for use in late March. In this age of central heating conditions are of course much more trying for evergreens used for indoor decoration in winter, but they still stand remarkably well provided the water is kept topped up in the container. In a very dry atmosphere daily or even twice-daily spraying with water is also beneficial. Most evergreens also remain commendably fresh as material for garlands, swags, wreaths, conical arrangements and hanging decorations when embedded in damp moss, or water-retaining substances wrapped in polythene, or stuck into a large, raw potato or turnip.

For Christmas arrangements of painted natural plant material certain fresh evergreens such as laurel, rhododendron and magnolia may be satisfactorily painted or sprayed with colour, preferably after first sealing with some special preparation such as Unibond; but preserved leaves are especially adaptable and much more enduring. Some which have been naturally dried are suitable, but in my opinion those which have been treated by the glycerine method described in the next chapter usually give much better results. Not only is air-dried and other desiccated foliage extremely brittle, but the unavoidable shrivelling, however slight, often gives it a tatty look, even when camouflaged by paint or glitter. Not all foliages respond to glycerining, but most of those mentioned in the next chapter will be found suitable for spraying or painting and by experimenting you will no doubt discover many more. To get a good clean silver it is advisable to give one's leaves a white undercoat.

Containers

Finally, it may be helpful to add a few words of advice about suitable containers for foliage arrangements, though here again instinct is the surest guide to what is fitting and, even more important, what is not. As a rule glass, ornamented china or fine porcelain looks wrong. Plain, solid pottery in earthy tones of brown, rust, biscuit, dull grey or green is good, and so is bronze lustre. Most metals are better still, though silver, I think, is not —even silvery leaves being better set off by the more gunmetal-grey of pewter, lead or earthenware. Alabaster, though costly (and requiring a watertight lining) is magnificent for somewhat formal arrangements, and the coloured veining of marble is also attractive with suitably coloured leaves. Trugs, country-style baskets and mats or bases woven from natural plant material are especially appropriate. And wood in any form, from antique work-box or tea-caddy to bamboo cylinder, carved pedestal or flat wooden base, is ideal. It is not sheer brazen defiance of my own advice which has prompted me to illustrate an arrangement of foliage in a glass tazza (facing p. 224). My initial aim was to prove that it is possible to create from leaves alone an arrangement light and elegant enough to serve as a party piece for a silken drawing-room or formal dining-table, using cream, white and green variegation in leaves of contrasting size, shape and habit, with the introduction of one or two "foliage flowers "of *Hosta undulata*, as described on p. 215. The plain container of waffled glass, designed by or for Constance Spry, was chosen for this arrangement for no other reason than that of suitability. If you agree that it is appropriate in this instance its use may further serve to point the moral that advice is not necessarily binding nor rules unbreakable.

CHAPTER IX

How to Preserve It

There was a time when a dried arrangement could only mean one of two dreary alternatives—mustard yellow achillea and orange 'lanterns' of physalis teamed up with bulrushes, peeled honesty-discs and plumes of pampas grass; or a dumpy dusty posy of statice and crude-hued helichrysums. Today the use of borax, Silica Gel and similar substances has changed all that and the drying of all manner of unlikely blooms has become a specialized art. But no matter how skilfully contours and colours may be preserved by modern methods, to me a dewy freshness is the very essence of a flower petal and this one ineffable quality is necessarily destroyed in the process of preservation.

These colourful but mummified roses, zinnias, lilac, pansies and such-like may not be for me, but I make no such reservations about preserved leaves and seedheads. Foliage may be preserved by a number of different methods and of all these I consider that glycerining gives by far the best results for such subjects as will respond to this treatment, because not only the suppleness but so much of the original texture is retained. To me it is of the greatest importance that preserved leaves should retain most, if not all, of their original firmness of outline and substance and this they rarely do except when glycerined. I hope this quality is apparent in the arrangement of glycerined leaves shown in the illustration facing p. 225, which also brings out the contrast of textures between the glossy fatsia, galax and mahonia, the satiny aspidistra and the matt eucalyptus.

Glycerine Method

This consists of standing the stem-ends of foliage, or in some cases immersing whole leaves, in a glycerine solution for varying periods, usually until the leaves change colour. Opinions differ as to the proportion of glycerine to water, the most commonly practised recipe being one-third glycerine to two-thirds hot, or preferably boiling, water. Some like to make sure of a good 'take' by using a half-and-half mixture, but I have not detected much difference in the results, though the stronger mixture possibly works a little faster than the other. However certain largish leaves on single or very short stalks (the house plant, *Ficus elastica*, is a good example) should be totally submerged in a solution of equal parts of glycerine and cold water. Whichever method is used it is important to keep a check on the level of the solution, topping up if necessary to keep a depth of not less than 2 in. for standing stems and seeing that submerged leaves remain totally immersed. I have never had any success with items added later to a glycerine brew already in use, though it is often recommended that foliage should be added from day to day at will; but certain leaves succeed when preserved in a second-hand glycerine solution which has just been brought to the boil.

As for the timing, one can only play it by eye, since it may vary, with different foliages, from five to six days to as many weeks. It also depends to some extent on the effect required: for some leaves are also attractive when only partially preserved, the green of leucothoë or *Escallonia x iveyi*, for instance, becoming overlaid, but not entirely suffused, with bronze, and eucalyptus showing purple veining on a still more or less glaucous ground. Such half-treated material may shrivel after a time in a hot, dry atmosphere unless it has absorbed just enough glycerine to hold its shape without much altering its colour. In all cases one needs to keep a constant watch on the process, studying the undersides of the leaves, when in doubt, to determine the degree of absorption. If foliage is inordinately slow in taking up the solution through its entire surface it sometimes works to remove it and hang it head downwards so as to enable the preservative to percolate more readily to the extremities. Leaves left longer than necessary in glycerine are afterwards likely to sweat badly upon the faintest hint of moisture in the atmosphere and readily become mildewed, so it is unwise to try to play safe by overdoing the period of treatment. If this does happen, the best remedy is to swish the foliage gently to and fro in a bath of warm, soapy water and to dry fairly rapidly in a warm atmosphere. This kind of laundering is also effective for preserved leaves which have become dusty and begrimed.

Now for a few do's and dont's about the foliage itself. Everyone has probably tried to glycerine beech leaves, if nothing else, and perhaps not always with success, for it is a common mistake to leave the picking until too late. Generally speaking mid- to late summer is the best time for preserving deciduous leaves with glycerine. No matter what the deciduous foliage to be treated, it is no good waiting until it starts to change colour in the autumn. Nor is it advisable to attempt it before the leaves are fully mature, since the soft young tips of shoots invariably wilt. However, within these two seasonal extremes it is worth while experimenting with leaves at different stages of their development, because certain material preserved, say, at midsummer may well turn out a different colour from that of foliage picked from the identical plant and treated in September. Ultimate intensity of colour may also be affected by the amount of light received during the preserving process, treatment in a dark cupboard or shed often resulting in a darker hue than on a light window-sill.

Give your foliage a good look-over as you pick it, so that the glycerine is not wasted on nibbled, stained or otherwise disfigured leaves which will remain shabby-looking however skilfully preserved. Woody stems of foliage sprays should be split for several inches (the thicker the stem the more it needs splitting) and 2 or 3 in. of bark removed. It is usually unwise to be over-ambitious about the dimensions of a spray to be treated,

221

especially with such foliages as are slow in their reaction. A length of 18 in. is about the limit for safety as a general rule. I have had complete success with the small-leaved *Cotoneaster horizontalis*, which takes less than a week, using fully mature sprays over 3 ft. long and perhaps 2 ft. wide in parts, whereas in the course of several weeks the larger, leathery leaves of *Griselinia littoralis* refused to absorb the mixture beyond the lower half of a 2-ft. spray, dropping many of the topmost leaves, though quite short pieces from the same plant 'took' satisfactorily, if slowly.

Before passing on to the list of suitable subjects I should mention that automobile anti-freeze mixtures may be used instead of glycerine, but their artificial blue or pink colouring is apt to tinge the foliage to the point at which it may be classified as dyed material, which is anathema to me and usually prohibited by schedule-makers, and for this reason I cannot recommend it.

Finally, here are some suggestions as to suitable foliage for glycerine treatment, with brief notes on their reactions, though I would stress how much interest and excitement, as well as disappointment, is to be had from making one's own experiments. Some of the disappointment and much glycerine may be saved if it is remembered that leaves with smooth or shiny surfaces are on the whole a safer bet than those of rough texture. As already mentioned, the time required for absorbtion is too variable to allow of precise individual instructions on this point, so I have used the following code letters to indicate the rough average time likely in each case:

> (S) = Slow i.e. approximately six weeks.
> (M) = Medium, i.e. two or three weeks.
> (Q) = Quick, i.e. five to seven days.

Having done the bulk of my experimenting before the question of this book arose, in many cases I have no record of accurate timing, so these letters should only be regarded as a rough guide. Where no code letter is given I cannot remember how much time was required for absorbtion.

Foliage Suitable for Glycerining

Alchemilla mollis (M). Pleasing light brown, retaining its poise and velvety texture.

Aspidistra elatior (S). Pale straw colour, beautifully supple, silky texture.

— — 'Variegata' (S). Fine cinnamon, often with still visible lighter striping, but drier and more brittle than the type.

Atriplex halimus (Q). Retains grey hue for some weeks before fading to biscuit.

Aucuba japonica 'Variegata' (S) or (M). Result nearly black and variegation more or less disappears.

Bergenia cordifolia (S). Immerse totally and dry flat on absorbent material. Very nearly black, but some slight shrinkage and wrinkling unavoidable.

Buxus sempervirens (S). Clean biscuit hue combined with perfect neatness. Treat from late summer onwards.

Camellia japonica hybrids (S). Short lengths only, from which separate leaves can afterwards be mounted into sprays. Nigger-brown, glossy, solid.

Castanea sativa ("Sweet" or "Spanish Chestnut") (M). Short pieces only, picked late summer or early autumn. Light brown.

Choisya ternata (M) or (S). Short pieces of mature foliage. Biscuit to deeper beige, glossy. Very good when well preserved.

Convallaria majalis ("Lily-of-the-Valley") (M). Light brown, slightly flimsy.

Cotoneaster horizontalis (Q). *Mature* foliage up to 3-ft. lengths, remarkably good. Nigger-brown in a matter of days.

Curtonus paniculatus (S). Interminably slow if not fully mature. Lovely copper sword-blades, but less rigid than in life.

Danae racemosa (S). Long, arching wands, greenish brown for some weeks, finally light tan verging on copper. Perfectly preserved shape. First class.

Elaeagnus macrophylla (S). Short, mature pieces. Light silvery biscuit.

— *pungens* 'Maculata' (S). 18-in. lengths, quite a vivid yellow-brown edged darker tan. Excellent.

Epimedium (?). I understand mature shoots 'take' well, but have not tried this.

Escallonia x iveyi (Q). Dark bronze-green, retaining perfect shape. Also attractive when half-done, but will soon shrivel unless given just long enough in glycerine for this effect.

Eucalyptus, various (S). Varies from dark purplish-brown to grey-blue or purplish-grey, of supple texture. Half-preserved foliage remains glaucous with attractive purple veining, but is usually fairly brittle.

Fagus sylvatica ("Beech") (Q). A fairly impermanent darker green if half-preserved, or medium brown when finished; purple-leaved vars. darker. Treat in late summer or early autumn, but when still full of life.

Fatsia japonica (S). Support neck of leaf-stalk with thin props on either side of leaf and bind these together above leaf, immediately below it and at lower end of stalk. Thick, polished brown leather results, from light chestnut to dark blackish-brown according to age of leaf and time of picking. One of the best.

Ferns, various (Q). Young fiddleheads retain red-brown colour and coiled crozier tip. The more solid-leaved types glycerine well in mature leaf if immersed.

Galax aphylla (S). Mature leaves turn shiny light brown, of firmly rounded shape. They may also be immersed, which is quicker (M).

Gaultheria shallon (Q). Solid, semi-matt, leathery greenish-bronze. Very good.

Griselinia littoralis (S). Short lengths only. Very dark brown.

29. An arrangement of cream and white variegated foliage in a glass tazza on a pale green velvet base. Included are: Variegated forms of *Vinca major*, *Weigela florida*, *Aspidistra elatior*, *Yucca filamentosa*, *Miscanthus sinensis*, *Iris foetidissima*, *Hedera canariensis* and *Hosta undulata* 'Univittata', with central flower-shapes made from leaves of *Hosta undulata*

30. Glycerined foliage in biscuit, blue-green and various brown hues arranged in a bronze urn on a blue-green velvet base. Materials include *Eucalyptus gunnii, Cotoneaster horizontalis, Mahonia japonica, Danae racemosa, Curtonus paniculatus, Aspidistra elatior, Galax aphylla* and *Fatsia japonica*

Possibly better to immerse single leaves and mount them afterwards.

Hedera, various (?). Not very successful to date, and others' results often seem to me rather scruffy. I think only single leaves suitable and that they should be immersed. (Q) in this case.

Helleborus corsicus (S). Firm, sculptured shape and attractive hues from gunmetal to greyish-beige or light tan.

Ilex, green-leaved (Q). Darker green for a time, eventually turning dark brown.

Leucothoë catesbaei (Q) or (M). Green, subtly tinged bronze after about a week, or richer deeper brown if left longer. First class.

Lonicera pileata (M) or (S). Greenish at first, turning brown later.

Magnolia grandiflora vars. (S) or (M). Short pieces or single leaves turn glossy dark mahogany brown. Immerse single leaves if preferred.

Mahonia aquifolium (Q). Somewhat transparent light grey-brown. Longish sprays possible.

— *japonica* (S) or (M). Treat large pinnate leaves separately. Light to dark brown. Excellent shape and very enduring.

— *lomariifolia* (M). Pinnate leaves nearly 2 ft. long spectacularly successful. Firm fishbone pattern in dull brown with egg-shell finish.

Mahonia repens rotundifolia (Q). Treat individual leaves either standing or immersed. Light brown of good, strong shape and texture. Excellent.

Pachysandra terminalis (M) or (S). Mature rosettes only. Medium brown.

Phormium, various. These tall blades tend to roll longitudinally before they are ready, but by starting them in glycerine and finishing off under carpet they can be made to stay flat. Varying beiges.

P
225

Polygonatum multiflorum (S?). Difficult but worth any amount of trouble to achieve the lovely, silky light biscuit. Late summer foliage best. Avoid sprays of drooping habit; those from less densely shaded positions seem to have more stamina and are less likely to weaken half-way up stem, which may need supporting. Do not leave too long in glycerine even if apparently unfinished, but spread out to bleach in strong light.

Populus alba (M?). Leaves remain whitish beneath, turning blackish-brown on upper surface. Small lengths.

Prunus laurocerasus (S). Rich, glossy dark brown, but leaves sometimes need to be separately mounted.

—— 'Variegata' (S). Variegation results in light buff and bronze-brown. Shoots which are wholly cream when fresh turn light *café au lait* with darker veining.

Pteridium aquilinum—("Bracken") (Q?). Usually pressed; but beautifully supple when glycerined. Light reddish-brown. Nothing bigger than a side-shoot likely to succeed. Submerge.

Rhododendron, various (S) or (M). Short-stemmed leaf rosettes sometimes succeed, but single leaves easier, no matter how large. Good dark brown. For single leaves I prefer to stand tip of stem in glycerine rather than immerse leaf. Those with coloured indumentum, which should never be immersed, keep colour of underside remarkably well, with much more natural contours than when pressed. Also much less brittle. They occasionally need pressing to prevent curling even after glycerining.

Sarcococca hookeriana (M). Pleasing light brown sprays.

Viburnum rhytidophyllum (Q) or (M). Fine red-mahogany upper surface, remaining grey-white or pale beige on underside. Short shoots or single leaves.

— *tinus* (M). Dark greenish-bronze at first, later becoming rich medium brown.

226

How to Preserve It

Air Drying

This method of preservation is on the whole more suitable for certain flowers and seedheads than for leaves. Material must be thoroughly dry when picked and should then immediately be hung upside down in sparse bunches or stood upright in a dry, dark place, which must however be airy—that is, a curtained-off hanging area is suitable but a dark cupboard is not. Times required are unpredictable and the results necessarily desiccated in appearance and brittle to the touch. The latter fault can in some cases be partially remedied if one can remember to massage the leaves periodically during the drying process.

Suitable subjects are:

Araucaria araucana: dark brown and solid.

Artemisia, various: keep their grey hue, but look shrivelled unless massaged.

Aspidistras: intriguing convolutions but colour dull and texture brittle.

Curtonus paniculatus: dull green and light brown. Colour deader and texture more papery than when glycerined.

Cytisus scoparius vars.: almost black-green. Sprays can be tied or wired into desired shapes before drying.

Eucalyptus, various blue-leaved forms: pleasant light grey-blue or grey-green, but fragile. Stand upright, starting in shallow water.

Ferns: young fiddleheads retain their shape and much of their colour when hung upside down, but glycerining gives more body.

Helichrysum plicatum 'Elmstead': retains silver-grey hue.

Hostas, various: can be dried off with stem-ends in shallow water at maturity, becoming pale biscuit and paper-thin and taking on curious twists and convolutions which many admire, but they still look plain dead to me.

Magnolia grandiflora and cvs.: shiny, light to medium brown; brittle.

227

How to Preserve It

Populus alba: Grey-green above and silver beneath. Massage.
Viburnum rhytidophyllum: dark green with whitish reverse preserved by hanging upside down.

Pressing

This is a popular method of preserving autumn leaf colour in particular, but I so greatly prefer the suppleness and natural contours of glycerined foliage to the brittleness and unnatural flatness of leaves which have been pressed under weights that I only resort to this method for certain subjects which will not take up the glycerine solution, even though the natural colour is lost in the process. Bracken, picked just as it is about to turn colour in the autumn, beech and sweet chestnut picked at different stages to provide varied leaf colour, large-leaved rhododendrons, iris blades, many ferns, separate leaves of *Senecio laxifolius* (for subsequent mounting into sprays) and *Verbascum bombicyferum* are commonly preserved by pressing between newspaper or blotting paper under a carpet or heavy weight for long enough to expel all the moisture. Of these the only ones I have ever needed to preserve by pressing are bracken, before I discovered that it could be glycerined; the beautiful lacy fern, *Polystichum setiferum* 'Divisilobum'; and the grey-leaved senecio and verbascum. The latter is the one I find most useful, providing a good, large leaf which, though extremely fragile after pressing, can be partially strengthened by sellotaping a stub-wire up the back of the midrib.

I have also found it useful to follow up with a period of pressing after glycerining in the case of certain tough leaves which persist in curling even after absorbing the solution. This applies in particular to *Phormium tenax* which tends to roll its sword-blades into tight tubes. Neither method usually works in isolation, but the leaves can be permanently flattened by a combination of the two.

Ironing

Ironing may be used as a substitute for pressing under the

228

carpet, etc., and produces much quicker results, but is only successful with really flat leaves. Ideally a sheet of greaseproof paper covered by a sheet of newspaper should be placed over the leaves to be ironed and they should afterwards be kept flat beneath weights for a time. This, too, produces very brittle results. A few deft touches with a hot iron may also serve to restore the shape of old glycerined leaves which have become the worse for wear.

Borax, Silica Gel, Sand, etc.

It seems to me that there are so many ways of drying and preserving foliage as distinct from flowers that there is no necessity to adopt this rather exacting method, which is chiefly used to preserve flower colours and contours. Great care is needed in packing the material in the box of preservative and in dribbling such powdered or granulated substances into every crevice among leaves and petals; the timing has to be most precise and varies with each subject; and the resulting dehydrated material has afterwards to be carefully protected from atmospheric humidity. I have not tried drying foliage in this way, but I should expect it to be effective for large, woolly or furry leaves in particular. I intend to try the whole, large, silver leaf rosettes of *Verbascum bombicyferum* in the seedling stage, which are said to turn out well. *Hieracium waldsteinii* might also be suitable. (Untried.)

Skeletonizing

I would not discourage those with plenty of time on their hands from trying to skeletonize good strong evergreen leaves such as laurel, ivy, rhododendron or *Magnolia grandiflora* by the more or less natural process of soaking them for many weeks in dirty rain-water—the slimier the better. It should afterwards be possible to remove the green outer layers, leaving the network of veins intact; but this is not as easy as it sounds and calls for a great deal of patience. The resulting skeleton then needs treating with a household bleach, which works wonders and fills one with pride of achievement. Some magnolia leaves left, forgotten all through winter and spring, in a bucket of rain-water were easier to strip than any, the outer layers almost falling away as I washed them in warm water and gently stroked their surface. An earlier short cut, using a recipe in which, as far as I remember, lime and washing soda were boiled together with water, produced some splendid leaves but ruined my expensive preserving pan. On the whole it seems cheaper, if lazier, to buy one's skeletons from the florist.

CHAPTER X

How to Remember Names

Practical Reasons for the Use of Botanical Latin Names

It seems ridiculous to admit that one usually requires some moral courage to come out with any but the simplest of botanical Latin plant names, even when asked for them; but it is still not generally realized that the use of common names or nicknames makes for the utmost confusion in the nursery business and between gardeners and flower arrangers. "Ivy" is ivy and "Honeysuckle", I imagine, is honeysuckle anywhere in the British Isles: but what about "Ground Ivy" or "Swamp Honeysuckle", neither of which is what it pretends to be? I am in fact only playing for safety in refusing to adopt any but the most generally accepted and unequivocal English names on account of the sheer undependability of the majority, though I know full well that their international scientific names, usually called "Latin names", may evoke gasps, groans, giggles or guffaws.

And yet what a mistake it is to close one's mind to accurate botanical nomenclature if one is genuinely interested in growing plants, whether for flower arrangement or for garden adornment, for the pitfalls attendant upon the use of vernacular names are endless. My experience is that it is none too easy always to be certain that the nurseryman has supplied precisely what one asked for, but the odds against getting it are immeasurably increased if one is not willing to take the trouble to get the name right when ordering. And to take this a step further, I would say it is the duty of a demonstrator to be able to supply the correct names of the plant material she uses for the benefit of those of her audience who may wish to grow these things themselves.

231

How to Remember Names

Many vernacular names are probably of limited regional application and others are downright misleading. For instance, I am often asked if there is not an easier English name for *Cassinia fulvida* (unhelpful alias *Diplopappus chrysophyllus*) and indeed there is—"Golden Heather". But if this is what you order from the nurseryman you can hardly blame him if he sends you some yellow-leaved form of heather such as *Calluna vulgaris* 'Serlei Aurea', because the cassinia is in fact a member of the daisy family (*Compositae*) and not even remotely related to the callunas, or heathers (family *Ericaceae*), despite some similarity in the foliage. A nickname may sometimes apply to several different plants: thus "Dusty Miller" may suggest *Primula auricula* to me, but one of the artemisias or the centaureas to you, and possibly lychnis to your neighbour. Conversely a single genus may acquire a string of picturesque pseudonyms, offering a choice of "Bugbane", "Bugwort" or "Black Snake-root", for example, in place of the unambiguous cimicifuga.

Pronunciation

I hope these few examples will serve to persuade the more reluctant that the use of Latin names is not just a form of showing-off. They would probably be more readily accepted in everyday conversation if only we felt more sure of their pronunciation. Few of us have escaped the embarrassment of following up a diffident stab at an unfamiliar Latin name with a self-conscious ". . . or whatever it's called"; but when I went to work in the nursery business I soon discovered that customs in pronunciation were by no means hard and fast and that where one said "tomayto" the next man said "tomarto"—and not a blush between them. Classical scholars might wince at much of it but, generally speaking, accepted practice was very much simpler than I had imagined. When plant names are being continually bandied about between the master, the foreman and the nursery-hand in the course of their work these tend to boil down to whatever the foreman can take in his stride, or the nearest acceptable equivalent. If our foreman's "Op-it-ma" for 'Optima' was deemed to exceed the bounds of botanical licence it was nevertheless a relief to me to be able to jettison inadequate remnants of school Latin diction in favour of an earthy brand of simplification. I no longer mouthed out "Sparteeooom yoonkayoom" for *Spartium junceum* which, happily, had now become "Sparteeum junseeum" to one and all.

It is comforting to learn that in botany as in other professions (e.g. law, medicine, etc.) it is actually more correct to pronounce Latin like English, as was the habit of all Englishmen of education in the Middle Ages, and that the 'unreformed' pronunciation of botanical Latin has the blessing of the Kew authorities. So if, like me, you have little Latin and no Greek, you are not at such a disadvantage as you might suppose.

As for the seemingly formidable Japanese names attached to tree peonies, ornamental cherries, dwarf evergreen azaleas and such-like, your guess will surely be as good as the next man's, especially if you remember that in Japanese the vowels are pronounced approximately as in Italian and the consonants as in English, that there are no silent letters and that all syllables are equally stressed. Provided you roll Japanese names off the tongue with sufficient *panache* combined with observance of these details your personal renderings of "White Goddess", "Jewelled Lotus", "Dawn in Spring" or "Black Dragon Brocade" should raise no eyebrows.

Components of Botanical Latin Plant Names

In their efforts to record in an orderly fashion the astounding diversity of the plant kingdom, botanists have found it necessary to divide plants into a series of systematic groups. Of these the only ones which need our consideration are the family, the genus, the species, and the variety, form or cultivar.

(*a*) FAMILY—A good example of a botanical family is the *Compositae* or daisy family, within which are included dandelions, cardoons, chrysanthemums, artemisias, olearias, cassinias, sene-

cios and similar plants. Generally speaking neither the gardener
nor the flower arranger needs to know the family group to which
a plant belongs, but it is useful to remember, for instance, that
members of the *Ericaceae* or heath family (e.g. ericas and callunas, rhododendrons, leucothoë, pieris and many more) are
usually lime-haters. These are often referred to as 'ericaceous'
subjects and the term should serve as a warning, though some
of the winter-flowering heaths are familiar exceptions.

(*b*) GENUS—I know quite a few gifted demonstrators who are
content to master a plant's correct generic name—that is, its
first name—and let it go at that. And many of those they aim
to instruct will be just as easily satisfied. Of course this is one
step in the direction of botanical precision, but it will rarely
take us far enough of itself. For instance, we know that the
generic name of ivy is *Hedera*, but we will need to be more
specific if we wish to refer to a particular variegated kind. The
choice of the word 'specific' was coincidental, but it conveys precisely what I mean, since the species *H. canariensis* and *H. colchica*
both have a variegated form, let alone *H. helix*, which has several,
involving still further differentiation, as I shall explain when
dealing with cultivars (see (*d*) below).

(*c*) SPECIES—The second part of the name, the specific epithet,
will almost always be required in order to pinpoint the particular
member of the genus in question. There is no risk of misunder-
standing in referring to galax without a specific epithet because
Galax aphylla is the only member of the genus. But if we order,
say, actinidia from the nurseryman, how is he to know whether
we want the curiously variegated *Actinidia kolomikta*, or the
very dissimilar bold-leaved, plain green *A. chinensis*, to mention
only the two more commonly grown of the forty species of this
genus?

(*d*) VARIETY, or CULTIVAR—Just as a genus is divided into
species, so a species may be divided into varieties or cultivars,
or both. Hence a plant may need a third handle to its name in
order to distinguish it as a particular variant within the species.

How to Remember Names

(At this point I would suggest that if your concern with botanical nomenclature is practical rather than academic you may wish to skip the rest of (*d*), which explains how the last part of a plant name may serve to indicate whether it is a variant of the species occurring in the wild or one of garden origin. This is necessary to complete the story and certainly of interest to the horticulturally-minded, but those disinclined to pursue the matter further will manage well enough without a grasp of these distinctions.)

When a variant of a species occurring in the wild is considered by botanists as worthy of naming, usually because it forms a distinct population, the whole name will be of Latin form and italicized, e.g. *Erica arborea* var. *alpina*. The abbreviation is generally omitted, giving *E. arborea alpina*. A variant of garden origin or one taken into cultivation from the wild for its horticultural merit is now known as a cultivar, or cv. for short, standing for cultivated variety. Before the adoption of the International Code of Nomenclature for Cultivated Plants garden varieties (cultivars) were often given descriptive names in Latin or of Latin form, e.g. 'Maculata' in *Elaeagnus pungens* 'Maculata'; and to avoid inconvenient changes such established Latin nomenclature has been allowed to persist but, in general, cultivars are commonly given a fancy name in a modern language, e.g. *Camellia japonica* 'Gloire de Nantes' or *Senecio cineraria* 'White Diamond'. Such a cultivar name should always, repeat always, whether in Latin, English, Dutch, romanized Japanese or whatever, begin with a capital letter and be printed in roman type, e.g. 'Amanogawa', 'Gloria Mundi', 'Goldenheart', 'Il Tasso', 'Jackman's Blue', 'La Nuit', 'Miss Jekyll', 'Rheingold', 'Thomas Hogg', 'Zigeuner Knabe'. It is usual to enclose the cultivar epithet within single quotes, as above, which practice serves as a blessed light to lighten the Gentiles but is not, alas, compulsory.

Meaning of Botanical Latin Names

Before we go any further perhaps I should explain that the reason I have so frequently included the word "botanical" in writing of Latin plant names is that botanical Latin is in fact pretty different from the classical Latin of Virgil, Cicero and Caesar, and although the names take a Latin form, in which genders are respected and so on, they are not by any means always of Latin origin. An enormous number, for instance, are formed from Greek components (e.g. Lithos = stone, Sperma = seed, giving *Lithospermum*) and many more are derived from proper names, (e.g. *Cassinia*, after the French botanist, Henri de Cassini). Having made this point I shall feel at liberty to drop the "botanical" and refer to them simply as Latin names when it suits me.

SPECIFIC EPITHETS

To attempt to memorize some of the more formidable Latin names, complete in all their parts, may well daunt the faint-hearted, but if one is able to get at their meaning rather than tackle them parrot-fashion the job is greatly simplified. Whether as gardeners or as flower arrangers, most of us are resigned to mastering generic names; and cultivar names are unlikely to cause much trouble since the modern fancy kind are not in Latin anyway. And so it seems to me that it is with the specific epi-thets that help is chiefly needed.

Most of these are formed in one of three ways, each based on sound reason once we grasp their origin, and thus comparatively easy to remember.

1. *Person's Name*. One of the commonest forms of specific epithet is that which commemorates a human being. Famous plant-hunters, botanists, gardeners and others are immortalized many times over in specific adjectives such as *davidii, delavayi, farreri, forrestii, fortunei, henryi, lindleyi, sargentii, sieboldii, veitchii, wardii, willmottiae, wilsonii*, etc. And if you happen to know something of the hair-raising adventures of some of the early plant collectors in Asia, India, and the Americas you are unlikely to forget these heroes and their namesakes.

2. *Place of Origin*. Specific epithets based on a geographical

236

locality or more localized place of origin are also easy enough to identify and to memorize, especially when it is realized that the suffixes *-ensis* (*edinensis* = from Edinburgh, *nymansensis* = from the famous Nymans gardens in Sussex); *-anus* (*peruvianus* = from Peru, *africanus* = from Africa); and *-icus* (*japonicus* = from Japan, *libanoticus* = from the Lebanon) all indicate "pertaining to such and such a locality".

3. *Descriptive.* Perhaps our most valuable ally of all is the kind of specific adjective which describes some attribute of the plant itself, because once we are able to translate this often graphic epithet into English it begins to make visual sense. Fortunately it is, I think, one of the most usual forms of specific epithet, so that with the merest smattering of botanical Latin we may picture the plant it often so realistically depicts.

And so I have delved into the recent comprehensive work, *Botanical Latin*, by William T. Stearn (T. Nelson & Sons, London), in order to extract from it some of the specific adjectives most likely to apply to leaves or foliage plants, with the English translations, in the hope that this will bring the apparently dead and desiccated Latin to life and help to fix it in our minds by conjuring up a picture of some recognizable botanical trait of texture, shape or colour, or some other distinguishing feature, be it hairy or shiny, heart-shaped or egg-shaped, silver or purple, dwarf, stalkless or whatever. For the sake of brevity I have taken occasional slight liberties with the original definitions, but almost all those which follow are borrowed verbatim from the above-mentioned work.

Brief Latin/English Vocabulary of Specific Epithets including Sundry Prefixes and Suffixes

COLOURS

White: *albidus:* whitish
        albus: white, particularly a dull white
        candidus: pure glossy white

	lacteus: milky-white
	leuc-, leuco-: white-
Grey:	*argenteus:* silvery
	cinereus: ash-grey
	griseus: pearl-grey
	incanus: hoary, greyish-white
Black:	*niger:* black, especially glossy black
	nigrescens: becoming black
	nigricans: blackish
Brown:	*cupreus:* coppery
	ferrugineus: rusty, light brown with a little mixture of red
	hepaticus: liver-coloured, dark reddish-brown
Yellow:	*auratus:* flecked with gold
	aureo-, aureus: golden yellow
	chryseus, chryso-: golden yellow
	citrinus: lemon yellow
	flavescens, flavidus: yellowish, pale yellow
	flavus: yellow, paler than *luteus*
	fulvus: tawny
	lutescens: becoming yellow, yellowish
	luteus: deep yellow, buttercup yellow
	sulphureus: sulphur yellow
	xantho-: yellow-
Green:	*atrovirens:* dark green
	glauci-, glauco-: glaucous-
	glaucus: sea-green
	viridis: green
Purple:	*purpureus:* purple, colours between red and violet
	atropurpureus: dark purple
Red:	*carneus:* flesh-coloured
	cinnabarinus: vermilion
	coccineus: deep red from scarlet to carmine
	erythro-: red-
	rhodo-: rose-, rosy red
	roseus: rose
	ruber, rubr-, rubro-: red, red-

rubens: reddish
sanguineus: blood-red
Variegations:
  discolor: not of the same colour (as when two faces of
      a leaf are unlike in colour), variegated
  maculatus: spotted, blotched
  marmoratus: marbled
  pictus: coloured, painted
  variegatus: variegated

TEXTURES

  acanth-, acantho-: spiny, thorny
  bombycinus: silky
  bullatus: blistered, puckered
  carnosus: fleshy, succulent
  crassus: thick
  erio-: woolly-
  exasperatus: rough, harsh
  glaber, glabratus: smooth
  laevigatus: smooth and polished
  lanatus, lanuginosus: woolly
  lasi-, lasio-: hairy-, woolly-
  nitidus: shining, polished
  pilosus: hairy
  pubens, pubescens: downy
  pulverulentus: powdered, dusty
  reticulatus: marked with a network
  rhyti-, rhytido-: wrinkled
  rugosus: wrinkled
  spinosus: spiny
  splendens: shining, gleaming, brilliant
  squamatus, squamosus: scaly
  squarrosus: rough with outwardly projecting scales
  tomentosus: covered with dense short hairs
  trachy-: rough-
  villosus: shaggy

How to Remember Names

cordatus: cordate, i.e. with two equal rounded lobes at base

incisus: cut deeply and sharply

obovatus: reverse of *ovatus*; i.e. broadest at the top end

ovatus: egg-shaped, i.e. broadest at the lower end

palmatus: palmate, i.e. lobed or divided in the manner of an outspread hand with the sinuses between the lobes pointing to the place of attachment

rotundus: almost circular

sagittatus: shaped like an arrow-head

undulatus: wavy-edged

MISCELLANEOUS

a-, an-: lacking, im-

acaulis: stemless, or apparently so

acuminatus: tapering from inwardly curved sides into a narrow point

amoenus: beautiful

aphyllus: without leaves

aquaticus: growing in water

arboreus: tree-like

argutus: sharp, sharp-toothed

-ascens: becoming, i.e. not fully

brachy-: short-

calli-, calo-: beautiful

chamae-: low-growing

-chromus: -coloured

coronarius: coronary, of a wreath, suitable for garlands

crispus: kinky, curled, irregularly waved

decumbens: prostrate, with the tip rising upwards

dendr-, dendro-, -dendron: tree

dentatus: toothed

fastigiatus: with branches erect, clustered and parallel

fastuosus: proud, haughty

ferox: fierce (usually of spiny plants)

flaccidus: not able to hold up its own weight

foetidus: stinking

240

formosus: finely formed, beautiful (but *formosanus* = re-lating to Formosa, see *-anus*, p. 237)

fruticosus: shrubby, bushy

gracilis: thin, slender

grandi-: large-

graveolens: strong-smelling (i.e. *gravis* = heavy, *olens* = odorous)

helix: spiral

hetero-: different, uneven

hortensis: pertaining to gardens

integri-: entire-

lati-: broad-

lept-, lepto-: narrow-, slender-

littoralis, litoralis: pertaining to the seashore

lucidus: shining, clear, transparent

macr-, macro-: long-, large-

mas: male

maritimus: growing by the sea

micro-: small-

-morphus: -shaped

nanus: dwarf

nodosus: knotted, knobby

nudus: naked

nutans: nodding

odon-, odont-, etc.: toothed

-oides, -odes, -oideus: having the form or nature of

orth-, ortho-: straight-, erect-

pachys: thick, stout

parvus: small, puny

pauci-, paucus: few-, few

peregrinus: foreign

-philus: -loving

phyll-: relating to leaves; *-phyllus:* -leaved

pileatus: cap-shaped

plumosus: feathery

ponticus: pertaining to Pontus (a region of N.E. Asia Minor) *praecox:* precocious, developing early, bearing flowers before the leaves

pulcher: beautiful

pumilus: dwarf

pungens: piercing, terminating in a hard sharp point

radicans: rooting, putting forth aerial roots

repens, reptans: creeping, prostrate and rooting

rupestris: rocky, rock-dwelling

saxatilis: as *rupestris*

sempervirens: evergreen

sessilis: stalkless

speciosus: showy, splendid

spicatus: bearing a spike

stachy-, -stachys: relating to a spike

strictus: very upright

suffruticosus: somewhat woody, woody only at the base

tenui-: slender-, thin-

venustus: beautiful, graceful

virgatus: twiggy, long and slender

xero-: dry-

I hope I have said enough to convince those of you who have no time for botanical nomenclature that its use is in fact more practical than pretentious and that the greater the effort we make to master the Latin names of the plants which adorn our gardens and from which we cut for floral decoration the greater the interest we shall derive from what we learn. (I might add that the compiling of this chapter has greatly added to my own edification.) The process will be considerably speeded up if we take the trouble to attach a permanent label to every plant we grow, checking with a *reliable* reference book or catalogue to make sure that we have the name correct in every detail. If we are also wise enough to keep a garden notebook in which to record any useful information we happen on regarding the plants we grow or intend to grow, we will become familiar with their Latin names still more quickly and painlessly and will have them constantly at hand for reference or reminder. In my own earlier days as a shrub gardener I spent so much time browsing through plant catalogues and all manner of horticultural books and articles in my haste to learn as much as I could as fast as I could that I now find myself in the odd position of being more familiar with Latin plant names than with their English equivalents. But, apart from the fact that a number of quaint, poetic, picturesque or humorous horticultural nicknames have never come my way, it has been immensely useful to have learnt to run, however unsteadily, before I could walk.

I shall conclude this lengthy plea for the use of botanical Latin names with a final word or two of criticism of gardening programmes on television and, to a lesser extent, radio. In my opinion what appears to be the official policy of talking down to the public is the reverse of helpful and wastes a splendid opportunity for mass education. Certain speakers regarded as horticultural authorities seem to be as shy of Latin names as the merest tyro and their coy apologies whenever they bring themselves to utter one do nothing to dispel a general self-consciousness in this respect or to set a sensible example to the gardener who presumably switches on because he wants to learn. If they feel obliged to talk down to a part of their public there must, I contend, be a case for running alternative gardening series at A rather than O level. No good gardener ever believes he knows it all and many of those potential viewers and listeners who want to learn more are already comparatively well-informed and well-educated enthusiasts rather than kitchen-gardeners; but this section of the public is at present almost totally disregarded by television and wireless programme planners and trend-setters.

CHAPTER XI

The Three Fs

The pastime we call Flower Arrangement was once summed up in terms of The Three Fs—Flowers, Foliage and Fun—by a shrewd and gifted flower arranger, adding that one could get by without the first, but not without the other two. The third F is, I am sure, beyond dispute and I hope I have said enough about the beauty and versatility of leaves to prove the rest of her comment to be true as I believe it to be.

Hindhead
June 1967

Plants for Autumn Leaf Colour

The following list is not intended to be exhaustive, nor does it include subjects unlikely to provide useful cutting material (though none can be guaranteed as long-lasting). Many of the plants mentioned are not described in the text.

Hues range mainly from apricot, through flame, scarlet and crimson to maroon-purple, but various yellows are also included for contrast.

Calcifuge plants are asterisked.

Outstanding features other than autumn leaf colour are indicated in brackets, as follows:

(+ B) = having interesting bark.
(+ FL) = having attractive flowers.
(+ FR) = having attractive fruits.

Acer griseum, A. grosseri, A. pensylvanicum (+ B), and many others
—palmatum heptalobum 'Osakazuki' and other Japanese Maples
Amelanchier, various (+ FL)
Aralia, various (+ FL)
Aronia arbutifolia, A. melanocarpa 'Brilliant' (+ FR)
*Azalea, many deciduous species and hybrids and some dwarf evergreen
Berberis, many (+ FR)
Bergenia, various (+ FL)
Cercidiphyllum japonicum
Cornus florida, C. f. rubra, C. nuttallii (+ FL); *C. kousa chinensis* (+ FL + FR)
— kousa (+ FL +FR)

Plants for Autumn Leaf Colour

Cotinus americanus, C. coggygria (+ FL); and purple-leaved vars.

Cotoneaster, many (+ FR)

Crataegus coccinioides, C. prunifolia (+ FL + FR); and others

Cryptomeria japonica 'Elegans'

Curtonus paniculatus (+ FL + FR)

Diospyros kaki (+ FR)

*Disanthus cercidifolius

*Enkianthus, all (+ FL)

Epimedium, most (+ FL)

*Eucryphia glutinosa (+ FL)

Euonymus alatus

— *europaeus* 'Atropurpureus', *E. latifolius, E. yedoensis* (+ FR)

Fagus sylvatica, F.s. 'Cuprea', *F. s.* 'Purpurea'

*Fothergilla major, F. monticola (+ FL)

Geranium ibericum, G. macrorrhizum, G. pratense, G. psilostemon (armenum), G. sanguineum, and others (+ FL)

Ginkgo biloba

Hamamelis, most (+ FL)

Hydrangea macrophylla, many cvs., *H. quercifolia,* and others (+ FL)

Hypericum patulum henryi (forrestii) (+ FL + FR)

*Leucothoë catesbaei

*Liquidambar, various

Lysimachia clethroides (+ FL)

Macleaya microcarpa 'Kelway's Coral Plume' (+ FL)

Malus, various (+ FL +FR)

Nandina domestica, N. d. 'Purpurea' (+ FL)

*Nyssa sylvatica

Orixa japonica

*Oxydendrum arboreum

Paeonia, many herbaceous species and varieties (+ FL)—see those marked "ac" in Kelway's catalogue

Parrotia persica

Parthenocissus, all

Photinia, various (+ FR)

Prunus avium, P. x hillieri, P. x hillieri 'Spire', *P.* 'Pandora',

P. x sargentii, P. serrulata spontanea, and others (+ FL)

Quercus coccinea, Q. c. 'Splendens', and others

Rhus, all (+ FL)

Ribes americanum

Rodgersia, various (+ FL)

Rosa foliolosa (+ FL); *R. rugosa* (+ FL +FR); *R. r.* 'Blanc Double de Coubert'; *R. r.* 'Roseraie de l'Hay' (+ FL); *R. virginiana, R. virginiana* 'Plena' (+ FL + FR)

Sorbus, many (+ FR)

Spiraea japonica 'Macrophylla', *S. prunifolia* 'Plena' (+ FL)

Staphylea bumalda (+ FL +FR)

Stephanandra incisa, S. tanakae

Stranvaesia davidiana (+ FR)

*Stuartia koreana, S. pseudo-camellia, and others (+ FL + B)

Tellima grandiflora, T. g. 'Purpurea' (+ FL)

Thuja occidentalis 'Rheingold'

*Vaccinium arctostaphylos, V. corymbosum (+ FL + FR)

Viburnum, many (+ FL and, in some cases, + FR)

Vitis, most (+ FR in some cases)

Leaf Colour Categories

(as applied to plants described in Chapter V)

Yellow to Yellow-Green (excluding variegations)

Acer japonicum 'Aureum'
Angelica (at times)
Atriplex hortensis 'Cupreata'
Calluna vulgaris 'Beoley Gold'
—— 'Golden Feather'   } (early summer)
—— 'Joy Vanstone'
—— 'Gold Haze'
—— 'Serlei Aurea'
Cassinia fulvida
Chamaecyparis (some)
Cupressus macrocarpa 'Lutea'
Erica cinerea 'Ann Berry'
—— 'Golden Hue'
Hebe armstrongii
Hedera helix 'Buttercup'
Hemerocallis fulva (spring)
Hosta fortunei 'Aurea'
Humulus lupulus 'Aureus'
Laurus nobilis 'Aurea'
Lonicera nitida 'Baggesen's Gold'
Origanum vulgare 'Aureum'
Philadelphus coronarius 'Aureus'
Physocarpus opulifolius 'Luteus'

Leaf Colour Categories

Primula vulgaris (sometimes)
Sambucus nigra 'Aurea'
— *racemosa* 'Plumosa Aurea'
Thuja occidentalis 'Rheingold' (summer)
Weigela japonica 'Looymansii Aurea'

Apricot to Flame

Acer pseudo-platanus 'Brilliantissimum' (spring and early summer)
Alchemilla mollis (at times)
Bergenia (at times)
Calluna vulgaris 'Blazeaway' } (summer)
— — 'Robert Chapman'

— — 'Beoley Gold'
— — 'Golden Feather' } (winter)
— — 'Joy Vanstone'
Mahonia japonica (in parts)
Thuja occidentalis 'Rheingold' (autumn and winter)

Scarlet

Azalea, Dwarf Evergreen (some in winter)
Bergenia (at times)
Calluna vulgaris 'Blazeaway' } (winter)
— — 'Robert Chapman'

Erica cinerea 'Golden Drop' } (winter)
— — 'Golden Hue'
Euphorbia sikkimensis (spring)
Mahonia japonica (in parts)
Pieris formosa forrestii and cvs. (spring and early summer, sometimes again in autumn)
Rheum palmatum, Red-leaved Forms (spring)

Leaf Colour Categories

Red-Purple

Atriplex hortensis 'Rubra'
Cotinus coggyria 'Kromhout'
—— 'Notcutt's Variety'
—— 'Royal Purple'
Lobelia cardinalis 'Bee's Flame'
—— 'Queen Victoria'
—*fulgens*
Orach, Giant Red
Plantago major 'Rubrifolia'
Vitis vinifera 'Purpurea' (young leaves)

Purple

Salvia officinalis 'Purpurascens'

Bronze-Purple to Copper

Acer palmatum 'Atropurpureum'
—— 'Dissectum Atropurpureum'
Azalea, deciduous (many)
Berberis thunbergii 'Atropurpurea'
—— 'Atropurpurea Nana'
—— 'Atropurpurea Superba'
Chamaecyparis (some)
Chard, Ruby (with scarlet stems)
Cotinus coggygria 'Foliis Purpureis'
Cryptomeria japonica 'Elegans' (winter)
Epimedium (spring, autumn and winter)
Erica cinerea 'Golden Drop' (summer)
Fagus sylvatica 'Cuprea'
—— 'Purpurea'
Foeniculum vulgare (some)
Hebe 'Autumn Glory' (tipped)
Hydrangea macrophylla cvs. (some in late summer)
Leucothoë catesbaei (spring and winter)
Ligularia dentata 'Desdemona'
Mahonia aquifolium (winter)

Leaf Colour Categories

— — 'Atropurpurea'
— *japonica* (in parts)
Myrtus bullata
Paeonia suffruticosa varieties (some, tinged)
— herbaceous varieties (early spring, many also autumn)
Peltiphyllum peltatum (spring and autumn)
Pieris taiwanensis (spring and early summer)
Prunus x blireiana
— *cerasifera* 'Atropurpurea'
— *x cistena*
Rhododendron 'Moser's Maroon' (young shoots)
Rodgersia (spring and autumn)
Sedum maximum 'Atropurpureum'
Stephanandra incisa ⎱ (spring and autumn)
— *tanakae* ⎰
Tellima grandiflora 'Purpurea' (late summer to spring)
Vitis vinifera 'Purpurea' (mature leaves)

Bronze-Brown

Amelanchier canadensis (spring)
Astilbe, many
Azalea, deciduous (some)
Foeniculum vulgare (some)
Hedera canariensis (winter)
Phormium tenax 'Purpureum'
Pittosporum tenuifolium 'Atropurpureum'
Tellima grandiflora (late summer to spring)
Weigela florida 'Foliis Purpureis'

Blue-Green

Aquilegia alpina
Cedrus atlantica 'Glauca'
Chamaecyparis (some)
Crambe maritima

Elymus arenarius
Eomecon chionantha
Eucalyptus gunnii
— *perriniana*
Euphorbia myrsinites
Hebe pimeleoides 'Glauco-coerulea'
— *pinguifolia* 'Pagei'
Hosta fortunei 'Hyacintha'
— *sieboldiana*
Rhododendron cinnabarinum
— 'Lady Chamberlain'
— 'Lady Rosebery'
— *concatenans*
Ruta graveolens 'Jackman's Blue'
Sedum 'Autumn Joy' (tinged red)
Thalictrum glaucum

Silver to Grey

Anaphalis triplinervis
— *yedoensis*
Artemisia, many
Atriplex halimus
Calluna vulgaris 'Hirsuta Typica'
— — 'Silver Queen'
Centaurea gymnocarpa
Convolvulus cneorum
Helichrysum petiolatum
— *plicatum* 'Elmstead'
Hieracium waldsteinii
Onopordum
Salvia argentea
Santolina chamaecyparissus
Senecio cineraria 'Ramparts'
— — 'White Diamond'
Senecio leucostachys
Teucrium fruticans

Leaf Colour Categories

Verbascum bombicyferum

Grey-Green and Silver-Green

Alchemilla mollis
Aquilegia vulgaris nivea
Ballota pseudo-dictamnus
Chamaecyparis (some)
Cynara cardunculus
— *scolymus*
Cytisus battandieri
Elaeagnus macrophylla
Helleborus lividus subsp. *corsicus*
Macleaya microcarpa 'Kelway's Coral Plume'
Paeonia mlokosewitschii (smoky pink in youth)
Pittosporum tenuifolium
Populus alba
Potentilla fruticosa 'Vilmoriniana'
Pyrus salicifolia 'Pendula'
Rosa rubrifolia (shot plum-purple)
Santolina neapolitana
Sedum x 'Ruby Glow' (shot smoky red-purple)
Senecio laxifolius
Sorbus aria
— — 'Lutescens'
Stachys lanata
— — 'Silver Carpet'

Green

Acanthus
Agapanthus
Angelica
Araucaria
Arbutus
Aruncus sylvester
Aspidistra

253

Astrantia major
Bergenia
Buxus sempervirens
Camellia japonica cvs.
Chamaecyparis (some)
Choisya ternata
Colchicum autumnale
Cotinus americanus
— *coggygria*
Cotoneaster horizontalis
Crambe cordifolia
Curtonus paniculatus
Cytisus, most
Danae racemosa
Epimedium (summer)
Erica arborea alpina
Escallonia x iveyi
Euphorbia, most
x Fatshedera lizei
Fatsia japonica
Ferns, hardy
Galax aphylla
Gaultheria shallon
Ginkgo biloba
Griselinia littoralis
Hebe hectori
Hedera canariensis
— *helix* 'Congesta'
— — 'Sagittaefolia'
Helleborus foetidus
— *orientalis* hybrids
Hemerocallis (summer)
Hosta fortunei
— *lancifolia*
Ilex x altaclarensis 'Camelliaefolia'
— *aquifolium* 'Pyramidalis Fructu-luteo'
— — 'Scotica'

Leaf Colour Categories

Laurus nobilis
Leucothoë catesbaei (summer)
Ligularia dentata 'Othello'
Lonicera pileata
Magnolia grandiflora and cvs.
Mahonia, various
Pachysandra terminalis
Paeonia delavayi
— *lutea ludlowii*
— *suffruticosa* varieties
— herbaceous varieties
Peltiphyllum peltatum
Phormium tenax
— *colensoi*
Polygonatum multiflorum
Primula vulgaris
Prunus laurocerasus
Rhododendron, various
Sarcococca
Skimmia
Smilacina racemosa
Tellima grandiflora (summer)
Veratrum nigrum
Viburnum davidii
— *rhytidophyllum*
— *tinus*
Vitis coignetiae
Yucca, various

Variegated—White, Cream or Yellow

Acer negundo 'Variegatum'
Acorus calamus 'Variegatus'
Actinidia kolomikta (also pink)
Ajuga reptans 'Variegata'
Aspidistra elatior 'Variegata'
Astrantia major 'Sunningdale Variegated'

Leaf Colour Categories

Aucuba japonica 'Variegata'
— — 'Goldenheart'
Buxus sempervirens 'Aurea Maculata'
— — 'Aurea Marginata'
— — 'Elegantissima'
— — 'Latifolia Maculata'
Buddleia davidii 'Harlequin'
— — 'Royal Red Variegated'
Cabbage, Ornamental (some)
Chamaecyparis (some)
Cornus alba sibirica 'Variegata'
— — 'Spaethii'
— *mas* 'Elegantissima' (also pink)
— — 'Variegata'
Cotoneaster horizontalis 'Variegatus'
Daphne odora 'Aureo-marginata'
Elaeagnus pungens 'Dicksonii'
— — 'Maculata'
— — 'Variegata'
Euonymus fortunei 'Gracilis'
— — 'Silver Queen'
— *japonicus* 'Albo-marginatus
— — 'Aureo-pictus'
— — 'Macrophyllus Albus'
— — 'Ovatus Aureus'
Euphorbia marginata
x *Fatshedera lizei* 'Variegata'
Fatsia japonica 'Variegata'
Fuchsia gracilis 'Variegata' (also coral-pink)
Galeobdolon luteum 'Aureo-variegatum'
— — 'Variegatum'
Glyceria maxima 'Variegata' (also some purplish-pink)
Griselinia littoralis 'Variegata'
— *lucida* 'Variegata'
Hebe x andersonii 'Variegata'
— *x franciscana* 'Variegata'
— 'Snow Wreath'

256

Leaf Colour Categories

Hedera canariensis 'Variegata'
— *colchica dentata* 'Variegata'
— *helix* 'Glacier'
— — 'Jubilee'
— — 'Marginata'
— — 'Sagittaefolia Variegata'
— — 'Tricolor' (also purplish-pink or red-tinged in winter)
Hosta crispula 'Aurea Maculata'
— *fortunei* 'Albopicta'
— — 'Yellow Edge'
— 'Thomas Hogg'
— *undulata*
— — 'Univittata'
Hydrangea macrophylla 'Quadricolor'
— — 'Tricolor'
Ilex aquifolium 'Golden King'
— — 'Lawsoniana'
— — 'Silver Queen'
Iris foetidissima 'Variegata'
— *japonica* 'Variegata'
— *kaempferi* 'Variegata'
— *laevigata* 'Variegata'
— *pseudacorus* 'Variegatus'
Jasminum officinale, variegated forms
Kale, Ornamental (some)
Kerria japonica 'Picta'
Lamium maculatum
— — 'Album'
— — 'Roseum'
Ligustrum lucidum 'Tricolor' (also some pink in youth)
— *ovalifolium* 'Aureo-marginatum'
— *sinense* 'Variegatum'
Mentha x gentilis 'Variegata'
— *rotundifolia* 'Variegata'
Miscanthus sinensis 'Variegatus'
— — 'Zebrinus'
Pachysandra terminalis 'Variegata'

R

Leaf Colour Categories

Phalaris arundinacea 'Picta'
Philadelphus coronarius 'Innocence'
— — 'Variegatus'
Phlox paniculata 'Norah Leigh'
Phormium tenax 'Variegatum'
— — 'Veitchii'
Pieris japonica 'Variegata'
Pittosporum x 'Garnettii'
— *tenuifolium* 'Golden King'
— — 'Silver Queen'
Polygonatum japonicum 'Variegatum'
Prunus laurocerasus 'Variegata'
— *lusitanica* 'Variegata'
Rhododendron obovata (? *ponticum* 'Variegatum'?)
Ruta graveolens 'Variegata'
Salvia officinalis 'Icterina'
Scrophularia aquatica 'Variegata'
Sedum albo-roseum 'Variegatum'
Symphoricarpus orbiculatus 'Variegatus'
Viburnum tinus 'Lucidum Variegatum'
— — 'Variegatum'
Vinca major 'Variegata'
— *minor* 'Aureo-variegata'
— — 'Variegata'
Weigela florida 'Variegata' (two forms, one cream/white, one much yellower)
Yucca filamentosa 'Variegata'
Zea mays 'Gracillima Variegata'
— — *japonica*
— — — 'Gigantea Quadricolor' (also pink, red-brown or reddish-purple)

Variegated—Purple to Pink

Cabbage, Ornamental (some)
Fuchsia magellanica, variegated forms
Kale, Ornamental (some)

Leaf Colour Categories

Salvia officinalis 'Purpurascens Variegata'
— — 'Tricolor' (also cream-white, red and grey-green)

Variegated Copper-Bronze

Ajuga reptans 'Multicolor' (also cream and apricot)
Berberis thunbergii 'Atropurpurea Rose Glow' (also pale pink)
Fagus sylvatica 'Tricolor' (also some white)
Leucothoë catesbaei 'Rainbow' (also yellow, green and white)

Veining or Marbling of Contrasting Colour

Arum italicum 'Pictum'
Chard, Ruby
Cyclamen neapolitanum
— *repandum*
Eryngium bourgatii
— *variifolium*
Erythronium dens-canis
— *revolutum* 'White Beauty'
Lonicera japonica 'Aureo-reticulata'
Silybum marianum
Tellima grandiflora
— — 'Purpurea'

Leaves Backed with Contrasting Colour

Cassinia fulvida
Elaeagnus macrophylla
— *x ebbingei*
Ferns, hardy, many
Hedera canariensis
Ligularia dentata 'Othello'
Magnolia grandiflora 'Exmouth Variety'
— — 'Ferruginea'
Populus alba

Leaf Colour Categories

Rheum palmatum, Red-leaved Form
Rhododendron argyrophyllum
— *arizelum*
— *bureavii*
— *campanulatum*
— *falconeri*
— *fictolacteum*
— *fulvum*
— *macabeanum*
— *mallotum*
— *niveum*
Senecio greyi
— *laxifolius*
Sorbus aria
— — 'Lutescens'
Viburnum rhytidophyllum
Vitis coignetiae

Index According to Plant Categories

Index According to Plant Categories

264

Index According to Plant Categories

266

Index According to Plant Categories

Index According to Plant Categories

Hardy Perennials

269

Index According to Plant Categories

Index According to Plant Categories

S

273

Index According to Plant Categories

274

Index According to Plant Categories

278

Index According to Plant Categories

General Index

280